Shireen Morris is a lawyer, postdoctoral fellow at the University of Melbourne Law School, and a senior adviser on constitutional reform to Cape York Institute. She is the co-editor of *The Forgotten People: Liberal and Conservative Approaches to Recognising Indigenous Peoples* with Damien Freeman (MUP, 2016) and the editor of *A Rightful Place: A Roadmap to Recognition* (Black Inc, 2017). Shireen is a regular commentator on TV, radio and print media.

'This unique memoir is the story of an individual pilgrimage by a non-Aboriginal Australian into the heart of Aboriginal hope. It might even be capable of reversing the government's glib and hurried rejection of the Uluru Statement from the Heart.'

Thomas Keneally

'For seven years, Shireen Morris has been one of the most passionate and courageous advocates for Indigenous people and their overdue recognition in the Australian Constitution. Anyone who has followed the debate will know of Shireen's articulate and persuasive advocacy. This book, for the first time, gives expression to her own story—not the experience of blackfellas or whitefellas, but the unique perspective of an Australian who is the daughter of Fijian-Indian immigrants. This story provides a crucial new frame for contemporary reconciliation that incorporates the Indigenous, the British, and the multicultural. Her book shows that reconciliation is not just about black and white. It's the responsibility of all Australians.'

Noel Pearson

RADICAL HEART

THREE STORIES MAKE US ONE

SHIREEN MORRIS

MELBOURNE
UNIVERSITY
PRESS

MELBOURNE UNIVERSITY PRESS
An imprint of Melbourne University Publishing Limited
Level 1, 715 Swanston Street, Carlton, Victoria 3053, Australia
mup-contact@unimelb.edu.au
www.mup.com.au

First published 2018
Text © Shireen Morris, 2018
Design and typography © Melbourne University Publishing Limited, 2018

This book is copyright. Apart from any use permitted under the *Copyright Act 1968* and subsequent amendments, no part may be reproduced, stored in a retrieval system or transmitted by any means or process whatsoever without the prior written permission of the publishers.

Every attempt has been made to locate the copyright holders for material quoted in this book. Any person or organisation that may have been overlooked or misattributed may contact the publisher.

Text design and typesetting by Cannon Typesetting
Cover design by Design by Committee
Printed in Australia by McPherson's Printing Group

 A catalogue record for this book is available from the National Library of Australia

9780522873573 (paperback)
9780522873580 (ebook)

Contents

Introduction: Seven Years	vii
1 Where I Come From	1
2 Discovering Cape York	22
3 The Expert Panel	39
4 The 'One-Clause Bill of Rights'	61
5 To the Right and Up	71
6 In Search of the Radical Centre	86
7 Forging the 'Con Con' Alliance	101
8 Low Expectations	126
9 Black Robe	139
10 The Art of Persuasion	155
11 A Snowflake's Chance in Hell	177
12 The Uluru Statement from the Heart	192
13 The Rejection	209
Conclusion: Towards a Fairer Australia	224
Acknowledgements	231
Notes	233
Index	239

Introduction: Seven Years

THIS FEELS LIKE a seven-year itch, needing expression. An itchy brain callus, or unresolved intellectual irritation. The kind that develops from consistently butting one's head against brick walls.

We try a multiplicity of tactics: digging under, going around, climbing over. We try using cooperation, compromise, military-like manoeuvres and alliances. But there are more brick walls and ever higher hurdles.

It's not the people blocking progress. The people want change.

Working on Indigenous constitutional recognition for the past seven years has demonstrated to me that most Australians harbour a deep desire to resolve the fundamental torment of our nation—the nagging moral question that has troubled our country since 1788. The majority of Australians want to address the injustice that has for too long characterised this nation's dealings in Indigenous affairs. They want to see the First Peoples finally ensured a fair go in our nation's Constitution.

The political action, however, is yet to meet the people's intent. The politics is the problem, and the lack of morally courageous leadership. Changing the Constitution requires a 'double majority' referendum. But getting the support of a majority of voters in a majority of states is not unachievable—if only there were leaders willing to champion the cause.

It makes you want to shake them. Tug their smug neckties. Yell obscenities to wake them from their cosy cocoons of power and galvanise them to action. But they are so busy clinging: clinging to power, and wielding it for little.

In September 2017, it made my brain callus itch.

I took myself off to the tropical island of Gili Air, near the coast of Lombok. As far from Australia as my frequent flyer points booked two days prior would take me. I tried not to think about the Constitution or the politics for one whole week. It was partially successful. But in between novels, swimming and bouts of intestinal trouble (it was the ice cubes, insidiously hidden in cocktails), I reflected on the past seven years.

Seven years thinking about how Australia's Constitution might be reformed to provide a fairer place for Aboriginal and Torres Strait Islander peoples. Seven years working with Indigenous leaders, constitutional lawyers, thought leaders and politicians, trying to find the common ground. Seven incredible years, where ingenuity, creativity and teamwork led to many triumphs; and too many defeats. A frustrating story, itching to be told.

I've set out the intellectual case before, through legal articles, opinion pieces and TV arguments. A thesis. Now I want to tell the story of hunting the radical centre on Indigenous constitutional recognition.

I tell it not as an Indigenous Australian. Though I was born in Melbourne, I don't subscribe to Andrew Bolt's strained and superficial definition of Indigeneity as meaning simply being born in a place.

As a non-Indigenous advocate for Indigenous constitutional recognition, some would say I occupy a strange position. I am descended neither from First Nation, nor from British coloniser. I am descended from those who came after. My parents, like so many immigrants, came here in search of opportunity. But I have no dual citizenship (as far as I know). I am just Australian.

As an Australian, I was filled with hope witnessing the unprecedented achievement of the First Nations' Uluru Statement from the Heart, endorsed by a standing ovation of the Indigenous delegates at Uluru in May 2017. I saw how far we'd come in the political debate. I knew this was the best chance Australia had ever had, and perhaps will ever have, of meaningfully addressing the legacy of our colonial past.

Then in October, in a statement full of lies and fearmongering, Prime Minister Malcolm Turnbull dismissed the Uluru Statement, and hopes were dashed. It was a callous display of unilateral exercise of government power over the powerless. The historic First Nations consensus was rejected by yet another government that assumed it knows better what is good for Indigenous people, than Indigenous people themselves.

Turnbull said the Australian people would not support a First Nations voice to Parliament—a constitutionally guaranteed Indigenous advisory body, to provide Indigenous input on laws and policies with respect to Indigenous affairs. I believe he is wrong. Omnipoll and now Newspoll research have proved him wrong: around 60 per cent of Australians support an Indigenous constitutional voice—and that is in the face of sustained government opposition.[1]

I hold on to hope, because something extraordinary and historic was achieved at Uluru, creating a unique opportunity and momentum that will not easily be beaten. This moment is historically unprecedented. Indigenous Australians formed a national consensus on the reforms they want. This has never happened before. Key conservative supporters of the proposed reforms are lined up and growing in number. Those constitutional conservatives (commentators, lawyers and politicians), who would usually argue 'No' to constitutional reform, on this issue are now saying 'Yes'—to the same reform Indigenous people have asked for. This has never happened before either. Labor and the Greens support the proposals, and public advocacy for the Uluru Statement is growing ever louder. The nation seems poised on the verge of breakthrough progress in Indigenous affairs—in spite of the lack of political leadership.

Just imagine if there was some.

This book is not the full story of this achievement: the full story is decades of Indigenous advocacy for serious constitutional reform.

This is only my story of seven years' hard slog and teamwork, a mere snippet in the 200-plus years of our country's search for reconciliation.

It's a story of politics, law and strategy. Of failed solutions and breakthrough ideas. Of bridging divides and forging unexpected alliances. Of changing our minds to adopt better solutions, and watching so many others slowly change theirs too. Of building empathy and seeing things from others' points of view. Of searching for the elusive 'radical centre' and finding it exists—only to watch it undermined. Of standing up to power, despite the fear.

This story is told drawing on my personal recollections, notes, emails and letters, as well as research material publicly available. My intent here is not to objectively recount the long history of this struggle, but to tell how it felt to be a part of the action: watching history being made by the reformers, revolutionaries and geniuses with whom I have been privileged to work—the leaders who try so hard to change Australia for the better, and may yet succeed.

In many ways, I tell it as an outsider. It sometimes feels like you need to be either blackfella or whitefella—not immigrant descendant—to have a legitimate point of view about the past and future of our nation. In other ways, I tell it as an insider, observing from within the unfolding action in my work as constitutional reform adviser to Noel Pearson, one of the main drivers of the constitutional recognition movement.

Yet this world and work are more than a job. I, like so many others, want to see a better and fairer nation, for all Australians. Primarily, therefore, I tell this story as a hopeful citizen. As an Australian who wants to see change in my lifetime.

1
Where I Come From

WHITE AUSTRALIANS TEND to ask me where I'm from. 'I'm from Richmond' or 'I'm from Melbourne' isn't usually the answer they're looking for. What they're really asking, politely and often out of genuine curiosity, is 'How come you aren't white?'

It's an understandable question. The common assumption that the typical Australian is of the pale-skinned European variety still prevails, despite our rich diversity. As if being white is self-explanatory, but being dark-skinned requires further justification—which seems odd, given the First Peoples of this land were black.

Perhaps this fact has been successfully scrubbed out of our national memory and so our contemporary national identity? Witness the mainstream reaction to the performance of a traditional Aboriginal war dance on our Aussie Rules football field: the outrage suggested such cultural expression was somehow offensively un-Australian. Yet is there anything more Australian?

I don't mind explaining how I turned out to be Australian. It's why I'm here, and why I have a stake in the Indigenous constitutional recognition debate. Perhaps my background is the reason I care.

I'm Australian, yet not white, because the British—the former rulers of my ancestors' subcontinent—took colonised peoples all around the world. My people were cheap labour. This brought hardship and injustice to my forebears. But it also, eventually, brought the opportunities and privilege of the West. My family story is shaped by the exploits of Empire. The shaping was both bad and good.

In the land of my forebears, British rule exacerbated division. It pitted Hindu against Muslim and exploited schisms of caste and class. It gutted the Indian economy to feed British wealth and plundered Indian jewels to adorn British museums. White men with monocles called the shots over skinny brown bodies, sending reluctant Indian sepoys to fight for Crown and Commonwealth in return for the promise of independence. That independence came too late, and came with bloody fragmentation of the nation.

The English word for the spoils of conquest or thievery, loot, is derived from a Hindi word, *lut*. As Indian politician Shashi Tharoor demonstrates in *Inglorious Empire*, the British relentlessly looted India and transformed the once prosperous—though far from perfect—nation into one of the poorest. Indians starved so their conquerors could prosper.

The exploitation was also exported. The British took industrious Indians across the seas to the colonies, to flee the slums and see the world, and to pay their debts. Debts owed to their white landlords under crooked taxes, exacted through force and paid off through hard labour.

My people were indentured servants sent via British ships to the Caribbean, Mauritius, Ceylon, Kenya, and to South Africa—where Mahatma Gandhi fought apartheid in relation to his own people but as a young advocate, it seems, not the blacks.

It is confronting to read Gandhi's descriptions of the Indigenous Africans as 'savages', differentiating his subcontinental crew of darkies as somehow superior to the African variety. As if there was a hierarchy: with whites at the top and Indians understandably below, but not as low down as the local blacks, whom he referred to with the derogatory term adopted by the ruling Afrikaners: 'kaffirs'. How is it that even the Great Soul, the intelligent lawyer, bought into the colonial rhetoric?

Colonialism is clever, its neat categories seductive. They become accepted, even by the oppressed, even as they try to resist. Even today.

Even as we fight back, we fight among ourselves. This is how it clings to power.

Gandhi was an inspiration to my family and me, so accounts of his early racism are dispiriting. His views about Africans seemed to broaden as he aged, however. Gandhi went on to lead India's nonviolent resistance to British rule. Perhaps he was just a lawyer, working each legal and political system as best he could given the circumstances and politics. Perhaps he just had to worry about his own people first and foremost. History is never just one thing. In colonial stories, heroism and villainy coalesce and combine.

Here in Australia, some call for removal of statues of white colonialists—Arthur Phillip, Governor Macquarie, Captain James Cook. Others defend their colonial legacies. Maybe both are right. In 2016, some Ghanaians protested about Gandhi's alleged racist attitudes and called for a statue to be toppled.[1] But in South Africa, the heroic Nelson Mandela said the Mahatma's teachings helped topple apartheid.

Colonialism may be clever, but its heroes and villains are never clear-cut.

My mother's family went from Andhra Pradesh in South India to the Pacific islands of Fiji. They were *girmitiyas*, contracted under indentured-service agreements to grow sugarcane for the British. After serving out their indenture many settled in Fiji. They stayed for generations, and called themselves Fijian-Indians.

Mum is one of seven Fijian-Indian siblings who were born and grew up on a sugarcane farm in Lovu, near Lautoka in the west of the island of Viti Levu. Her mother's mother was known as a holy woman in a village further inland, deep in the hills. It was either holiness, or hallucinations. My grandmother told me the stories: the old woman would disappear into the jungle to chant and pray, then return dishevelled, her hair matted. She was a spiritual teacher, privy to the ways of ghosts and gods. My grandmother Nani learned from her.

Nani now lives between Fiji and Australia, moving between adult daughters. She is tiny and buoyant and prays daily to Krishna, and to the famous Indian guru Sai Baba—the fraud reports on *60 Minutes* held no sway against her convictions. Though dead, Baba still visits her personally from time to time, his afro haloed in godly light.

Her praying weaves its miracles. At ninety-two, she remains a nimble soul who finds hilarity in small things despite having lived a hard life. Hers was a 'love marriage', ironically. Mum's father was a vivacious headmaster at the Lovu school, a champion of his children's education, and an alcoholic.

Things in Fiji were tough and simple. Mum and her siblings walked barefoot to school, studied, worked in the sugarcane, and hid under the house when necessary. The house was raised to accommodate floods, and children scared of thumps and screams. They didn't have much, but they had each other and their education.

Mum was a smart, studious and quiet girl. She prayed daily to Saraswati, the Hindu goddess of knowledge, wisdom and learning, and sought solace in nature, the moon and stars. She wanted to be an astronaut, to travel to space, and kept a textbook under her pillow, open on the key page so its lessons could seep into her brain. I tried this once with maths and saw numbers in my sleep.

Education was the family's passion. Mum recounted once being sent home from school because fees hadn't been paid. She sobs like a child recalling how she had to leave class, when she was so eager to learn. Each of the siblings remains scarred in their own way—the brother perhaps most of all, for he was a boy and couldn't protect them. Today the children are grown up: doctors, teachers and a nurse. Education bred gumption.

Once, on a visit home during her uni holidays in Australia, Mum poured a full bottle of her dad's whiskey down the sink. He ceased yelling, perhaps in awe. He had insisted on university education, and now the balance of power was shifting. Soon the women would rule the roost.

Our family culture is determined by the feisty Fijian-Indian females from that sugarcane farm in Lovu. They grew up full of sass and sex appeal, with skinny Third World legs adorned in seventies flares and miniskirts, eventually sporting kick-arse curves fed by Western junk from uni cafeterias. They were quick to attract husbands; some attracted two. They became six matriarchs, presiding over their raucous brown progeny, creating their own educated empire that extends now from Fiji to Australia, New Zealand and the UK, yet remaining tied to each other and to Nani, their long-suffering mother, under whose distant guidance you could say they attempted to colonise the West right back. My cousins and I were forged by these fire-tongued women. They raised children who could think and talk. Women ready to battle. The powerful conquerors of our own destinies.

Mum didn't stay the quiet child. She became a dynamic GP, renowned for thoughtful patient care and for calling 'bullshit!'—it's her favourite word, especially in conversations with my dad.

Her father died relatively young of a stroke. In slow and mangled words, he apologised to Nani on his deathbed. He should have apologised to his children too.

Nani now roams the Pacific, with on-hand medical care from her daughters at every location: Sydney, Melbourne, Nadi. 'I'm ready to die now,' she says with a contented smile. She's written specific instructions: cremation, simple sari, particular prayers. Probably Sai Baba presiding. No one wants to think about it.

I remember holidays at the sugarcane farm. We grandchildren would sit on the porch while our mothers peeled mangoes from trees in the yard. I'd speak my mother tongue, badly, and they'd laugh at my Aussie accent. We ate Nani's lamb curry and spicy fried fish on the floor in the prickly heat.

I remember the Indigenous Fijian women selling mud crabs house-to-house to Indian families. The holy Hindu man would come, beating his drum and offering blessings and ash for our foreheads. A tropical downpour might prompt us to rain-dance in the street, the fat drops pounding the potholes like happy crabs jumping. Fiji was paradise, even in storms. The hurricanes were bad, but people were resilient.

It was my family's home, but the Indians of course were not Indigenous. When my ancestors were brought to Fiji, generations before, it had ongoing ramifications. Divisions bubbled.

While Fijian-Indian families like my own lived side-by-side with Indigenous Fijians as friends, colleagues and neighbours, there was resentment too. The population was about fifty-fifty, but the two cultures remained largely separate. The Indians ran businesses and prospered economically, probably better overall than the Indigenous Fijians. The result of the migrant work ethic, perhaps; the sugarcane labouring bred tough stock.

Under British rule, Fijian-Indians struggled to achieve fair political representation. When independence was achieved in 1970, political power was transferred mostly to select Indigenous Fijian chiefs, who had a constitutional veto over important matters. Political power remained largely with the Indigenous Fijians until 1987, when the multicultural Fiji Labour Party led by Dr Timoci Bavadra came to power by forming a coalition with the Fijian-Indian–dominated National Federation Party.

The constitutional order proved unstable. In May 1987 there was a military coup, led by Indigenous nationalist Lieutenant Colonel Sitiveni Rabuka, which overthrew the Bavadra government. A second coup rejected Queen Elizabeth II as Fiji's head of state and Fiji was effectively expelled from the Commonwealth. A new Constitution entrenching Fijian-Indian exclusion was enacted in 1990 and many Fijian-Indians were fleeing the discrimination.

In 1997, another new Constitution sought to balance ethnic representation, while still maintaining Indigenous Fijian dominance. It led to Fijian-Indian trade unionist Mahendra Chaudhry becoming Fiji's first and only Fijian-Indian prime minister in 1999. But discontent among nationalist Indigenous sectors spewed into another coup in 2000, led by George Speight. Chaudhry lasted only one year in office before he was thrown out.

Chaudhry is a distant relative, something like my mum's sister's husband's cousin. I remember my parents telling me about him being stuck in jail.

Through the instability, Fijian-Indians were encouraged to leave for their own safety. My own relatives, mostly educated and mobile, were luckier than others. Some stayed, many fled. The Fijian-Indian population dwindled and the economy declined. There were struggles over land, and the lease renewal on our Lovu farm was mishandled. An Indigenous Fijian family moved in. There are no more holidays back there.

In 2000, Indigenous Fijian military commander Frank Bainimarama overthrew the Speight regime in a counter-coup. In 2007, Bainimarama became prime minister. Described ironically in one headline as a 'despot for diversity',[2] he fought to dismantle policies that discriminated against Fijian-Indians and promoted 'multiracial meritocracy'. That same year, Bainimarama explained the political unrest of the previous years to the UN General Assembly:

> Of the two major communities, indigenous Fijians were instilled with fear of dominance and dispossession by Indo-Fijians, and they desired protection of their status as the indigenous people. Indo-Fijians, on the other hand, felt alienated and marginalised, as second-class citizens in their own country, the country of their birth, Fiji.[3]

Fear drove division. It was ironic: fear of dispossession by the Fijian-Indians, when it was the British who had done the colonising—of both Fiji and India. Some would describe it as lateral violence: two sets of victims lashing out at each other when the real oppressor is too all-powerful and all-pervasive, and so becomes invisible. Then different brands of brown people are left to squabble among themselves.

I remember watching on TV a British-Indian journalist who dared to ask British officials, 'What will Britain do to help Fijian-Indians being told to leave Fiji? The Crown was responsible for taking them there—shouldn't they take responsibility now?' From memory, there was no good answer.

In a statement broadcast on the BBC back in 1987, Queen Elizabeth II condemned 'the illegal action' and 'use of force' by Colonel Rabuka. I was seven years old, and watched the coup unfold from the comfort of Melbourne's eastern suburbs. It was only later I was struck by the oddity of the Crown's morally superior position, condemning the forceful usurpation of a nation's political power. It seemed rich, coming from the world's most successful conqueror.

While Fiji had become a nation at war with itself, the former colonial power stayed prosperous and powerful in the distance, already enriched by its successful exploits in conquered lands the world over.

The Queen's condemnation of the coups, though hypocritical, was correct. Discrimination, violence and force cannot be justified just because someone else did it before. In any case, it's never possible to turn back time and start again as if colonisation never happened. The challenge is to find a peaceful solution that unifies rather than divides, which is just and inclusive of all parties, which addresses legitimate grievances and concerns and sets in place the fairest and most stable arrangements, given the history, politics and circumstances. Sometimes that must mean reconciliation over repudiation of colonising forces. Togetherness over separateness. Inclusive settlement over division.

Many in Fiji felt affinity with the monarchy, despite the history. 'I'm still loyal to the Queen,' Bainimarama reflected in 2009. 'One of the things I'd like to do is see her restored as our monarch, to be Queen of Fiji again.'[4] He got his wish in 2014, when Fiji fully re-entered the Commonwealth. A new, non-discriminatory Constitution had finally been implemented in 2013, establishing equal voting rights and non-discriminatory political representation. Though Fiji remains a republic, the Queen is still decreed Fiji's 'paramount chief', though with no constitutional powers. There is love, where one might expect there to be hate.

It was hard for me to make sense of it all, growing up. It would be easier to understand if things were black and white. They never are.

In Australia, the Indigenous peoples are the historically oppressed and dispossessed. In Fiji, while the Indigenous Fijians were colonised themselves by the British, they were also later the oppressors and displacers of the Fijian-Indians. Any group can be oppressed; any group can be oppressors. It depends on circumstances: environment, numbers, power, inclination. Citizens of goodwill need to look out for those excluded and unjustly disempowered, whatever their colour or creed.

Looking back on Fiji's fraught constitutional history affirms the comparative success and stability of Australia's Constitution, and highlights the intricate complexity of the challenge of Indigenous constitutional recognition. The appropriate solution will be balanced. The challenge for Australia is to provide recognition of Indigenous peoples in a way that unites and reconciles, that rights past wrongs and strengthens relationships—but does not divide or fracture. Australia must find its own solution that works for us. No democracy addresses its colonial history or resolves its constitutional relationship with Indigenous peoples in the same way. As Indigenous lawyer and activist Noel Pearson observes, there is no cookie-cutter democracy. The right solution for Australia will appropriately ensure past injustices are not repeated, while retaining and indeed strengthening our robust and stable democracy and citizenship. I believe achieving such reform is possible.

Fiji initially tried to guarantee its Indigenous chiefs political dominance, including through veto powers. But attempted segregation, as is often the case, ultimately led to instability and unrest. New Zealand found more moderate ways to empower Maori people with a representative voice, creating a culture that inclusively celebrates Maori heritage as New Zealand's heritage, while maintaining remarkable constitutional stability. Canada has instituted recognition and protection of Aboriginal rights in its constitutional system, which includes a duty to consult Aboriginal people in matters affecting their rights. And the Scandinavian countries—Norway, Sweden and Finland—are prosperous democracies that give a voice, representation and cultural recognition to Sami peoples.

Australia's Constitution, despite its stability and success, still perpetuates a great wrong with respect to our most disadvantaged and disempowered minority—Indigenous Australians. It has not dealt with the fundamental fact of Indigenous peoples, their dispossession and prolonged discrimination against them. The Constitution imposes an unjust silence with respect to our country's original owners. While we must be vigilant in upholding our successful constitutional system, our aim now must be to find appropriate mechanisms to embrace and include the First Peoples, and to allow the silence to be broken. The Uluru Statement from the Heart provides the way: it modestly calls for a First Nations constitutional voice in their affairs, and a Makarrata Commission to facilitate agreement-making.

The Uluru Statement is a peace offering the nation is yet to accept.

My father's family bequeathed the name Morris. They are from Navsari, Gujarat, in north-west India. The original surname was Morriswala. Perhaps it was shortened to sound more Anglo, or perhaps there are some unknown Anglo roots (though Gujaratis are often light-skinned).

Gujaratis are renowned businesspeople, yet Dad's beginnings in India were poor, like Mum's. As Hindu kids he and his siblings were sent to train in anti-Muslim camps and learn the ways of hate. Indoctrination began young. Before Dad was born, his father spent a few days in jail when the organisation Rashtriya Swayamsevak Sangh (RSS) was suspected of being part of the assassination of Gandhi. Their father later moved to Fiji for work, and was joined by Dad's eldest brother. The family remaining in India, including my dad, were often wanting for food and basic supplies. Absent his father's discipline, Dad lived a wild child's life in the filthy Navsari streets. He skipped school, played cricket in the dirt and tried to piss into bus windows. His cousin had the better aim.

The rest of his family migrated to Fiji, not as indentured servants but as free migrants in search of a more successful life. They all settled in Suva, in the south-east of Viti Levu, and ran a printing business. His parents grew older. His mum chewed *paan*. She developed toothless red gums and secretly drank brandy, despite her husband's disapproval. The Morris family, like my mum's side, were obsessed with study—an Indian trait, evidently. Dad worked hard in high school and got good marks.

Mum and Dad grew up on opposite ends of the main island, and had no idea each other existed. They each left Fiji in the early 1970s, before things began to change dramatically for Fijian-Indians. After high school, both won scholarships to study medicine in Melbourne. This was to Mum's disappointment, at first—she still wanted to become an astronaut. But Fiji didn't need astronauts, the scholarship people said. They needed doctors. She accepted the opportunity, at just seventeen years old.

They arrived in Australia towards the end of the White Australia policy, and met each other at Monash University. Both were part of the Indian student crowd that naturally hung out together.

Theirs too was a 'love marriage', ironically, which they pursued against Dad's parents' wishes. He was supposed to have an arranged match with an unspecified Gujarati girl of the same caste. Mum was Indian, and Hindu, but she wasn't the right *type* of Indian or Hindu. She didn't speak Gujarati. She wasn't fair-skinned: as a South Indian, her skin was darker. More squabbling between different shades of brown, leading to forbidden love across cultural divides. Dad's family disowned him for a time. Neither his parents nor his siblings came to their wedding, held outside under a tin roof at the Lovu farm with the blessing of Mum's more progressive family.

The initial drama of Dad's parents' rejection kicked off what would for decades be a tumultuous marriage. His parents wrote nasty letters disavowing the relationship for years. We lost my baby brothers after Mum's problematic pregnancies. At six weeks old, my little brother Neeraj died in hospital, in Dad's arms. Later, our twins were miscarried late term. Dad's parents wrote letters, proclaiming the tragedies divine retribution for my parents' original sin.

I was in Prep when Neeraj died. I so much wanted a little sibling and told them to keep trying. My brother Nishant was finally born when I was eleven, in Grade 5. I remember being told the news in class. He was a healthy boy, though six weeks premature, like me. To this day Nishi is the most precious thing in each of our lives: smart, kind, sensitive, concerned with refugees and Indigenous rights in Australia. Like me. Like Mum and Dad.

It is a family obsession we each come at in different ways.

Step back to view the big picture and it seems like never-ending dominoes. The British oppressed those of dark skin, utilising racism to subjugate, divide and conquer new lands. The Indigenous Fijians, already subjugated by the British, eventually deployed similar tactics against their fellow Fijian-Indians. In turn, and clearly without any thought for a strategy of solidarity, those Fijian-Indians, while being discriminated against first by the British and then by the Indigenous Fijians, also spent time and energy deploying racism among themselves: Gujaratis versus South Indians.

You can't blame everything on the British—much is Indian bad behaviour and archaism. But if the structures of Empire shaped the societies, laws and politics of the countries they conquered, they also shaped the psychology of citizens. Indians buy 'fairness cream' and search for fair-skinned marriage partners for their sons and daughters. If you traverse shaadi.com, the Indian marriage website, you are asked to specify whether the candidate's complexion is 'dark', 'wheatish' or 'fair'. If you subscribe to such standards, there are pros to being a fair-skinned Gujarati (I'm only half one). The trade-off for Gujaratis, though, is increased body hair. South Indians are darker-skinned but comparatively hairless—such are the boring beauty dilemmas with which South Asian women, if they buy in, are faced.

My dad's fair skin means he is semi-regularly mistaken for Greek or Italian by his patients in Melbourne. He's been privy to some racist remarks to which he might have otherwise remained ignorant: a fair-skinned imposter in the world of white Australians. One patient complained about Indian and Asian students, suggesting they should be marked on a separate scale to the white kids. 'All they do is study! They work so hard, it just doesn't give the white kids a chance!' I laughed when Dad told me, then went back to my books.

For all the sustained conflict of Mum and Dad's relationship, theirs is a battling, enduring love. I sometimes wished they would just divorce and spare us the continual drama. But what unites them is their love for my brother and me. They dote on us. They spoil us, push us and prod us. Sometimes too hard, invoking our fury. They demand we excel and then brag about us. We are their life and pride.

I grew up in the eastern suburbs of Melbourne and lived a privileged life, the daughter of doctors. My middle-class day-to-day was a long way from the Fiji farm or the streets of India.

I was free to study and daydream. I read *Sweet Valley Twins* and wished I was blonde. And a twin. At fourteen, in search of a more befitting identity, I cultivated an interest in American hip-hop. I did my hair in braids and, as an idiotic teenager, went to the Salt-N-Pepa concert with my mum.

I was sent to a fancy Baptist high school in Kew—the school of William Carey, a Christian missionary to India who translated the Bible into Indian languages and campaigned against *sati* (widows burning on their husband's funeral pyres)—even though we were technically an unreligious kind of cultural Hindu. I didn't convert: I found the story of a virgin pregnancy too hilarious.

My parents were rebellious to a degree. Their marriage went against the strictures of tradition, and so my upbringing was progressive for an Indian family. The social ethos was largely Western. Though we lit candles and sparklers for Diwali, the Hindu festival of light, Christmas was the bigger deal, with a tree and presents. Our food and work ethic remained largely Eastern. I studied and worked the way migrants study and work. But I also had freedom.

Returning home drunk after a party at a friend's house one night, I went to sleep with some dry hay in my hair, and woke up to Mum handing me anti-marijuana pamphlets from the surgery, convinced the hay was weed. She was smart—just not street smart. As a lively primary schooler, Nishi started learning from me the swear words of the day, which were beyond what Mum could comprehend. 'What's a wanker?' she asked me one day, full of academic curiosity. I can't recall how I explained that one.

Despite eleven years between us, Nishi and I were close. I'd drive him around, the two of us singing along to pop tunes. He'd swing his legs in the back seat and shout out raunchy lyrics. He'd camp out in my room and I'd light candles and do magic tricks, his eyes shining with wonder.

In Year 12 I got an ENTER of 98.85—I think the highest possible score was 99.95, so I figured it was a decent outcome. Dad's reaction didn't suggest so. 'You would have done better if you'd worked harder,' he said. Can't argue with the logic. His comment was unfair, however, and I've never let him forget it. Turns out I can hold a grudge like my mother. Or perhaps not quite that well.

Australia gave me all the opportunity of a rich Western nation, above and beyond the three Rs of my parents' time and place. I learned to play piano (badly), struggled with ballet (my legs can go in at 90 degrees, but barely turn out). I learned to sing jazz, pop and opera in European languages. I did plays and performed in bands and, after completing an Arts English major at Melbourne Uni, went to acting school in London then spent the decade of my twenties traversing the stage—all with my parents' support.

I spent three years in the UK's thriving theatre scene. I was Princess Jasmine in *Aladdin* and the Bharatanatyam-dancing, classical-singing ayah in the British classic *The Secret Garden* in Scotland. I sang and rapped and acted in children's shows across England. After my London stint, Shakespeare in Melbourne's Botanic Gardens became my theatre staple: I was Titania, Queen of the Fairies, in *A Midsummer Night's Dream*; Olivia in the mistaken-identity cross-dressing love triangle of *Twelfth Night*, and a blue-haired, bow-legged courtesan in *A Comedy of Errors* at the Athenaeum. I acted in an original zombie version of *Macbeth* called *Macbeth Re-Arisen*, and revelled in the luscious rhythms of Elizabethan iambic pentameter and the vivid physical expression that only the stage allows.

Performing Shakespeare's poetry was like connecting with the 'mother tongue of mankind', as German philosopher Johann Herder described it. It provided an interface with a universal, higher humanity; a classical culture too often forgotten in the expediency of modern life, which leaves little room for art and memory. Herder, writing exultantly in 1773, said Shakespeare spoke 'the language of all ages, peoples, and races of men'. Fearing the loss of this ancient high culture, Herder ruminated that 'even this great creator of history and the world soul grows older every day': the 'words and customs and categories of the age wither and fall like autumnal leaves' and 'we are already so far removed from these great ruins of the age of chivalry' that 'soon perhaps, as everything becomes effaced and tends in different directions, even his drama will become quite incapable of living performance, will become the dilapidated remains of a colossus, of a pyramid, which all gaze upon with wonder and none understands'.[5]

Herder on Shakespeare gave voice to an existential anxiety: the fear of forgetting our ancient culture and wisdom, and losing our civilisation's greatest achievements. As Noel Pearson would in later years convey to me, Indigenous Australians carry this same existential anxiety—but so should all Australians. For Australia's ancient songlines, art, stories and philosophy are this continent's equivalent of Homer, the Mahabharata of my own Hindu culture or, indeed, Shakespeare. Forgetting our Indigenous Australian culture, like forgetting Shakespeare, would be a loss not just for Australia, but for the world.

In my twenties, however, I was simply enjoying the language and limelight.

My best friend since we were ten, Arash, a geeky Iranian boy who shared both my academic nerdiness and my flamboyant creativity, was my artistic partner-in-crime. We had graduated from poems in primary school to pop songs in our youth. Inspired by Michael Jackson and to a lesser extent Janet, we harboured dreams of pop superstardom and chased a record deal for our original works, recorded in his parents' Doncaster basement and, later, his living room. The closest we got was deploying an inappropriately raunchy album cover: me in a blue bikini top sporting bindi, bangles and big eyes. Arash, who by this stage had come out of the closet, was the photographer, and had glittered me up to the campest possible degree with body shimmer from his parents' salon. The image got the attention of a bigwig Aussie music manager who invited me to Sydney for a meeting, commented approvingly on my 'provocative' ethnic look, then suggested I might do better in India before sending me on my way.

I did two small guest roles on *Neighbours*, the iconic Australian TV series. Three lines as Martha Jones, the *Erinsborough News* receptionist. Slightly more dialogue as Carli Chan, in a cafe conversation with the delightful Brett Tucker, playing Dan. It didn't seem to matter that the actor playing Ms Chan was clearly Indian, not East Asian. I generally only got TV auditions when a specifically non-white character was written into the script, which was rarely. When *Neighbours* finally got a full Indian family on Ramsay Street many years later, the show copped racist abuse online for being un-Australian, and they didn't last long, so Carli Chan's one-episode debut might have been progressive for the time. *Neighbours* now is more multicultural than it was back then.

I played a Muslim woman in a hijab on Channel 10's short-lived comedy show *The Wedge*—in a skit about Islamophobia, bogans and a bomb scare, which I don't know ever made it to air. My white co-actress assumed I was authentically Muslim and had been discovered in some hidden traditional enclave; she seemed baffled to learn it was just a convincing costume and that I'd been found through my agent, just like her. Perhaps the cultural appropriation wouldn't be acceptable today (far-right politician Pauline Hanson's 2017 appearance in a burqa in Parliament garnered more airtime and outrage than my portrayal). But back then, only SBS and the ABC seemed to insist on ethnic authenticity—and only from their non-white performers. One time, Arash taught me Iranian phrases to use at an audition. I rocked up and spoke gibberish with conviction, the white producers nodding enthusiastically: *Baccchhkatarre naamasccch! Beroooooonesch merkonnen!* Didn't get the job.

White was the unchallenged neutral in the entertainment industry, too. Brown actors were either tokenistically interchangeable in the commercial scene, or we had to be demonstrably authentic in the artsy scene, because that was more politically correct—as if brown people could only play ourselves, because being dark is a mask you can't take off, but white skin is an artist's blank canvas. I don't know which approach pissed me off more.

I loved working as a performer, though. Traipsing the stage, acting the fool for others' entertainment. Using my voice and face and body and brain to tell a story. Moving an audience. Communicating a character.

Things change, however. Over time, I got bored. The hours were tough. The money was bad. And, having nourished my inner artist for a decade, I was craving the intellectual. I went back to university, this time Monash, to study law. I opted for the Juris Doctor degree, which, with fewer contact hours, meant I could still work in shows.

I'd always been interested in power and justice. In the years to come, though I could never have predicted it, I became a scholar of Australia's Constitution: the Constitution imposed by Australia's colonial founding fathers on ancient Aboriginal land.

I was born in Melbourne, but there are times I have felt not completely at home. Perhaps that explains my interest in social justice and constitutional reform.

I first felt it when a room full of cross-legged four-year-olds chanted, 'Black Shireen, black Shireen!' at me in kindergarten. The teacher stayed silent. Even at four, I gathered that 'black' had derogatory connotations.

Once, a white boy approached me and demanded to know whether I spoke 'Australian'. I only thought of the appropriate comeback—'It's English, dickhead'—when he'd gone. Bested by a cocky ten-year-old, at twenty-four. Pathetic.

My un-Australianness arose at a birthday party. A white family friend observed the Indian caterers adding to my throng of brown-skinned family members. 'I feel like a stranger in my own country!' he joked. I wondered then, as I have since, why Australia was more his country than mine?

Sometimes it's less polite. A drunk outside a nightclub in Cairns yelled out late one night to call me an attractive 'monkey', or a similarly perverse insult. My comeback was again too late, and went unspoken. In those moments I could almost feel the colonialist prodding my skin with his cane, holding up his magnifying glass to check me for fleas before declaring me a good specimen.

In such moments, I feel for other Australians, who have likely experienced similar things and much worse. For if our white family friend felt estranged in his own country after spending a few hours eating curry in a house full of Indians, how estranged might the

Indigenous minority feel in the position of poverty and powerlessness that has, since 1788, been their lot?

Australia has a black history, and a multicultural present and future. That reality is too often denied. Though we are now, by and large, a tolerant and peaceful country, I'm convinced we can do better.

Law seemed like a good way to argue for change.

Dad told me in Year 12 that I should take up the law because he reckoned he could never win an argument with me. It's true that I enjoy a feisty debate. In the thick of an argument is probably my favourite place.

I was in two minds about law at first, however. Lawyers are so often seen as vultures, preying on the weak. In discussions about constitutional reform, they talk about 'lawyers' picnics'. I imagine bloodthirsty barristers dipping crackers into the wounds of ruptured nations.

There may be lawyers who salivate over division and feed on human conflict. But lawyers are also mediators and peacemakers. If law is a tool of war and oppression, it is also a tool of reconciliation and justice. Gandhi said, 'The true function of a lawyer is to unite parties riven asunder.' In the end, I agreed.

I am also conscious of my privileged position as the descendant of immigrants to Australia, and aware of the opportunity and prosperity to which I've had access. That same opportunity has not been shared justly with the original owners of this land. It's fair to say that immigrants have been given more of a fair go in this country than Indigenous people. How can that be a dignified state of affairs?

Take Australia's history of voting rights. The *Commonwealth Franchise Act 1902* in section 4 stated: 'No aboriginal native of Australia Asia Africa or the Islands of the Pacific except New Zealand shall be entitled to have his name placed on an Electoral Roll unless so entitled under section forty-one of the Constitution.'

I discovered the case of a Victorian Indian man, Mitta Bullosh, who challenged his exclusion from Commonwealth voting in 1924. The Commonwealth subsequently altered the Act to allow Indian people the vote—but not Indigenous people, who didn't get equal voting rights across the board until some four decades later. *Indians got the vote before Indigenous people, in my home state of Victoria.*

If only Mr Bullosh had advocated for the rights of his Indigenous compatriots along with his own.

It made me realise: immigrant Australians, and their descendants, need to get behind Indigenous struggles for recognition and equality in this nation in which our families, by and large, have enjoyed much opportunity and success, yet in which we too have known discrimination and exclusion. Hindus might call it a karma argument: treat others fairly, lest you are one day reborn in their shoes. Christians would say you should do unto others as you would have them do unto you. In other words: have empathy. We non-white Australians must be bolder in backing up our Indigenous compatriots. They need our support.

Noel Pearson—lawyer, orator and author, founder of the Cape York Institute and eventually my boss—says an individual, like a society, is made up of layers of identity and affiliation. I'm no different. As the ogre says in *Shrek* in rather less elegant language, ogres are like onions. They have layers.

For seven years I worked for an Indigenous Australian leader at an Indigenous Australian organisation, as an advocate for Indigenous rights. I survive on daily cups of English Breakfast and Earl Grey tea, but am also addicted to chilli. I still get a kick out of Shakespeare: English is my language, my Fijian-Hindi is poor. I'm sometimes too obsessed with success, as if I have something to prove—I blame my immigrant parents, and the fact that brown people in this country need to be twice, three times as good as others to have impact.

I hate colonialism, but figure maybe the pomp and procedure of the monarchy has its place in our national life. Perhaps I've been swayed by *The Crown* on Netflix. I accept that Australia's British heritage should be duly recognised. But Australia should cherish our First Nations heritage too, and equally.

I'm inspired in this regard by Pearson's characterisation of Australia as a triune nation. He is correct: our national story is in three parts. These three stories, brought together, make us one: Australians.

There is our ancient Indigenous heritage, which is etched into our landscapes and runs in the veins of our rivers and seas. This heritage is the rightful inheritance of all Australians.

We are irrevocably shaped by our inherited British institutions: the structures of democracy and law that are fixed forever upon this land through the Australian Constitution, and commemorated in street names and structures like Melbourne's Queen Victoria's hospital and market, the Windsor Hotel on Spring Street, where the founders met in 1898 to finalise their draft of the Constitution, and by Federation Square. This British inheritance also endures for the benefit of all Australians: it has created our stable and prosperous democracy.

And we have been enriched by our multicultural achievement: the gifts of peoples and cultures from around the world, in which we now all share. Australians benefit from the achievements of immigrants and their descendants in the fields of medicine, science, business and the arts.

We are lucky to enjoy the fruits of multiculturalism in all corners of our continent. Australians can get dumplings in the Chinatowns of our major cities, pho in the Vietnamese precinct of Victoria Street in my local Richmond, and pizza that rivals what you get in Italy. We can traverse the colonial architecture, street names and statues that celebrate Britain. But the most ancient part of our national trilogy is still largely invisible and out of reach to most Australians. The First Nations still lack their rightful place in our contemporary life.

I remember bristling when fellow Aussie travellers in London marvelled at the ancient majesty of British historical achievements but belittled our own. 'England has so much history!' they proclaimed. 'Australia is so young, we don't have history like this.' They were talking about castles and buildings and books. I sent urgent lyrics back to Arash in Melbourne so he could compose a piano track appropriately reflecting the melancholy of the mother country's grey monuments, and the sadness of my country's strange forgetting of its own ancient story. *Two hundred years is far too long, to realise that we've all been counting wrong*, I sang into the microphone back in Melbourne.

Today I wonder why there are so few statues of Indigenous warriors and leaders erected next to Macquarie and Phillip and Cook.

Why do no black faces stare them down with pride and as equals, symbolising the ongoing dialogue that began with first contact and that should now be formalised through a First Nations constitutional voice? We should be building new monuments, not talking about tearing down old ones. Our national symbols should tell the full and true story of our shared country, in all its complexity—with all its bloodshed and victories, its heartbreak and success.

Australia's best architects should be busy designing the constitutionally enshrined First Nations body, as called for by the Uluru Statement from the Heart, to be a permanent institutional embodiment of this country's First Nations heritage in Canberra. It should stand proudly in the parliamentary triangle: a permanent Indigenous voice in our Australian democracy. As Pearson observed, the tents became demountables. The demountables should now become sandstone: a building to pay tribute to the Tent Embassy occupants and other Indigenous activists who for so long have fought for their right to be heard.

The Constitution is about power, and national monuments are expressions of state power. Rather than tear down statues, institutions and constitutions, we should adapt and expand them so they include and empower the First Nations. Reconciliation over repudiation. Unity over division. We should imagine Australia anew, without forgetting the old. We should articulate a fuller expression of who we are.

This is the moral challenge of Indigenous constitutional recognition, the cause I came to take on, and that we all face.

2

Discovering Cape York

I DISCOVERED CAPE YORK in late 2010. By plane. Jetstar, Melbourne to Cairns. The heat outside envelops you when you step out on the tarmac, like a heavy blanket on air-conditioned skin. Exotic and stirring. Like discovering new land.

Cook did it in 1770, by ship, after months on the high seas. His discovery was the more impressive and historic, without air conditioning or flight attendants. Without the half-sized Jetstar toasted sandwiches. But it was no less subjective than mine.

When he made his treacherous voyage south, Cook carried with him secret instructions from the British king authorising him to 'take possession of convenient situations in the country in the name of the King of Great Britain' but to do so 'with the consent of the natives'. They knew people were already there.

On 22 August 1770, Cook declared possession of the east coast of Australia. He did so at Possession Island, which already bore its ancient name, Bedanug or Bedhan Lag, bestowed by the Kaurareg people who had lived there for thousands of years.

Cook wrote in his journal about the black figures he saw walking on the shore. Yet, contrary to royal instructions, there was no agreement. No negotiation was entered into; there was no treaty. There was no consent.

For Cook and the British Empire he represented, Australia was a new land that he discovered. The true first discoverers, however, the original owners, had arrived on the continent thousands of years prior. To them Cook was a foreign invader. As Torres Strait Islanders Kenny Bedford and Josephine Bourne commented in *The Australian* after the May 2017 regional dialogue on Indigenous constitutional recognition at Thursday Island:

> Cook did not 'discover' the Torres Strait Islands. Our ancestors were already here. Our people have been living here for thousands of years, hunting dugongs, fishing and trading. We are a seafaring people. When we saw the foreign ship approaching, we used smoke signals to warn each other.[1]

My brother once took a selfie in front of Captain Cook's Cottage in Melbourne. He posted it with the caption: 'Discovered this cottage!' I wondered if any other brown people possessed the cultural self-centredness (or military power) to assert 'discovery' of land that was already home to white people. Perhaps only on social media.

In the documentary of his book *Guns, Germs, and Steel*, anthropologist and geographer Jared Diamond provides plausible theories for the success of European societies as conquerors and the failure of others to achieve the same expansion. Environmental circumstances enabled Europeans to successfully pursue agriculture to such an advanced degree that they could cease hunting and gathering and feed themselves with surplus food. These populations could then use their time and energy to develop technology and superior weapons—the means to protect their own lands and conquer others.

Diamond's explanation demonstrates that Indigenous Australians developed differently to Europeans not because they were innately or genetically inferior, but because they had different natural resources at their disposal. Where the Europeans had access to a variety of plant materials and animals suitable for domestication, which enabled the pursuit of extensive agriculture, the Indigenous peoples of Australia had less manageable species—kangaroos, koalas and possums. So, while Indigenous peoples excelled at adapting to and surviving in their environment, they didn't become conquerors of inhabited foreign lands.

Conquerors, wielding their power, created rules to govern their own conquering. The discriminatory doctrine of discovery was expediently Eurocentric in its logic, because just as history (it is said) is written by the winners, so too are the laws enshrining their victories. Under international law of the colonial era, usurpation of foreign nations was allowed where those nations were not ruled by a Christian sovereign monarch. Convenient.

As I would discover in Far North Queensland, the difficulty in achieving law reform (and, more so, constitutional reform) to empower those who have been disempowered is convincing those in power to share some with peoples they've historically held down. Such reform is contingent on those in power having empathy and rising above pure self-interest. Only an empathetic, moral conqueror would willingly share any power with their conquered—and it's something of a contradiction in terms. It requires a self-conscious act of reconciliation, against type and training. Other countries have managed to achieve structural change that empowers their First Peoples. Australia has yet to find its way.

I carried no secret instructions when I left cold Melbourne to discover Cape York (albeit through the safe portal of the Cape York Institute, based in Cairns), nor directions to navigate my course. Just my internship handbook and a suitcase full of summer clothes, an inherited moral compass and a curiosity to know better this unexplored corner of my continent.

My perspective was so far narrowly southern and sheltered. I was about to discover Australia's northern, other side. Its underprivileged side. It would be a discovery, too, of the unexplored in me: the non-actor, the advocate, the lawyer. The who-knows-what. I'd just turned thirty and had almost finished law. Looking back, Cape York was the turning point. The beginning of the discovery of my true nature.

I'd expected more of a corporate environment. Bustling and youthful, with (I'd hoped) handsome lawyers in trendy suits. It wasn't like that.

The office was cramped and dark. Cape York Institute in 2010 operated out of dingy rooms on Cairns' Sheridan Street, with chunky old-school computers, broken chairs and fluoro lights that prompted my migraines. The air conditioning was always too cold. I was a nervous intern, goose-pimpled and perpetually popping Nurofen.

Outside the office, Cairns was distantly familiar: it felt like Fiji. All vivid green, with a heavy damp at that time of year, approaching holidays and wet season. Daytimes were sticky with low grey clouds or searing sun, and heat that blackened my face so I had to buy a hat.

I'd pant alongside the other interns, who were slim vegetarian types. We'd drag our thonged toes from our share house through the dew, arriving at the office with dirty feet and filmed in sweat. There were no trams, no traffic, no suits. Rather, shorts and singlets. Cairns was walkable and whimsical, tropical and a bit wild, with an earthy hum and buzz different to the temperate urbanity of Melbourne.

In Cairns, there are lush green hills on one side and sea on another. You see pelicans at the Esplanade or a stingray in the shallows on a lucky day. Signs warn of saltwater crocodiles; I imagined them making bubbles in the brown water. No beach swimming: an artificial lagoon and, further north, beaches netted due to stingers.

Cairns has aggressive willie wagtails and green ants that sting (with honey-flavoured bums you can lick, if you're game, with a small tongue-zap—an ancient Aboriginal discovery, one of the intern girls told me). There are screeching bats that migrate in the early evenings to find their roosts above stinky, shit-stained pavements. I wondered how they pooed while hanging upside down—still a mystery. I learned the word for accumulated bat crap: guano.

The Far North Queensland coastline is bedecked with forest and mangrove against secluded beach, with boardwalks to explore the underworld of roots and crabs and sludge, and boats out to the reef and its islands. We interns would spend weekends seeking out crystal waterfalls and freshwater creeks, venturing inland where the crocs were friendlier. We'd swim in the ice-cold Mossman Gorge and explore further north where the Daintree sprawled, where tree frogs croaked on ferns and palms and massive cassowaries roamed the bush.

Cairns itself was a party town of dazed travellers and transient professionals, where relaxers lazed and barbecues buzzed and black kids leaped into water, screaming and glistening. I'd never seen so many Indigenous Australians.

In my theatre days I'd worked with some Aboriginal actors—Kylie Farmer, a gorgeous Juliet, and Kamahi Djordon King (aka the fabulous drag queen Constantina Bush) who played Tybalt to my Lady Capulet—but that was mostly it. Up north, non-white faces seemed in greater abundance. And not just Indigenous people. There were Papua New Guineans, Islanders, Japanese, Koreans. This Far North felt further from Australia's hub but closer, somehow, to the rest of the world.

I moved into a share house of foreigners and the intern girls who arrived one-by-one: Raquel, the kooky Mexican; Alice, the nature-loving hippie from the Hawkesbury; Jess, the delicate, pale-faced Tasmanian. All in their early twenties, enthusiastic greenies and lefties, from anthropology or social science faculties. Me the only lawyer, and older. And a meat-eater. More academic. Less inclined to hug trees (Raquel and Alice would occasionally embrace an attractive trunk, pausing to absorb its spirit, as Jess and I looked on, giggling).

I was also more single—the only one without a boyfriend, having left my latest romantic disaster behind down south. Cairns was an emotional escape, perhaps, as much as the start of an intellectual exploration. A sea change from theatre, study and disappointing men.

The last failed relationship had been a few years prior: a would-be musician who had fashioned himself as a kind of middle-aged Australian Kurt Cobain, complete with acoustic guitar and tremulous vocals. He had the tortured artist's alluring vulnerability—but turned out more jealous tyrant. He joined me on my first and only trip to India, a holiday punctuated by his tantrums, inflicted with dramatic, red-faced flair on me and passers-by each time an Indian man looked my way, which was relatively often. 'These people are animals!' he seethed on a train full of brown faces, all marvelling at the Western/Indian woman with the furious white guy on her arm. He couldn't stand their curious eyes. I prayed my countrymen didn't understand English.

Patience was my great strength and weakness. A terminal geek, I probably harboured a high-school fantasy of being accepted by the cool kid—a fantasy that adulthood was yet to expunge—and so adopted a Zen-like tolerance of male bad behaviour. Perhaps I feared their idiocy was actually my fault: my imagined unfaithfulness was a recurring theme with these guys. Whether it was the wannabe muso with his hissy fits, or the insecure Indian in Sydney whose sobbing (complete with dripping snot) made me wonder if I had actually cheated, or the gorgeous-but-utterly-insane illegal immigrant from Albania (my first ill-chosen boyfriend in London), each of them obsessed about my (allegedly deliberate) courting of the male gaze, and made me pay for it. Each was an unmitigated disaster.

What the fuck is wrong with me? I inevitably wondered. I was still wondering when I arrived in Cairns. I felt rather foolish next to the self-assured, comfortably partnered twenty-something interns who never put up with idiot boyfriends, knew what they were looking for, and seemed more certain of their place in the world than me.

Alcohol flowed more freely in Cairns, in the holiday spirit. The revelry helped. Backpackers danced drunk on nightclub tables and occasionally we interns would join in. On these nights out, or in the early mornings after, I'd see glimpses of Cairns' dark side. I could party then go home to a nice bed, but others less lucky would retire drunk to the grass. The black drunkenness on display in the street or the town square seemed less revelry and more despair. Prolonged intoxication mixed with hopeless poverty, which is misery.

I saw Aboriginal people swigging bottles in brown paper bags in the town centre, or in the park during the day with kids playing beside them. They seemed angry, not happy. A skinny black man would come past the office, swaying weakly, to ask for change or a bottle of water. His ankles were so thin I thought they might snap. A Cairns Base Hospital doctor told me of the disorientated Aboriginal woman who'd woken up, naked, on the pavement near the Esplanade. 'Who been in me …?' she growled sullenly, touching her crotch while tourists out to breakfast averted their eyes. Mike Winer, our internship supervisor, described an Aboriginal man unconscious on the concrete outside the hospital, with people stepping over him. As though he was 'part of the furniture'.

On my first night in Cairns, I remember listening to the noises of nature. Crickets and rain. The bats with their primordial screaming. Two Aborigines, fighting on the footpath downstairs. 'You fucking cunt! I hate you, you black cunt …' Their voices seemed to elicit a roll of thunder in the distant hills, like the country moaning in the night. I sweated under the fan.

Beneath Cairns' tropical gleam and shine, I caught glimpses of unlucky Australia. I never saw it growing up in Melbourne's leafy outer-eastern suburbs of Park Orchards and North Ringwood, and it was rare around my inner-city Richmond flat. Up here, however, parts of it were uncovered: the ancient, unhealed wound. Black, left-behind Australia. The human despair upon which this nation's great prosperity is founded. Which persists and worsens, while Australians avert our eyes.

I'd signed up for six weeks of voluntary policy work at Cape York Institute (CYI). My constitutional law lecturer, Melissa Castan, daughter of the late Ron Castan QC (counsel for Eddie Mabo in the historic *Mabo* decision) and a human rights guru at Monash, taught me Indigenous rights and encouraged me to apply for an Aurora internship. The first time I applied I didn't get it. Second time, I did.

I opted for CYI because I found Noel Pearson's writing on the Indigenous 'right to take responsibility' challenging and instinctively correct. I'd read the *Little Children Are Sacred* report on sexual abuse in the Northern Territory for a uni project and shed unexpected tears at the harrowing stories of child suffering, outraged at my own ignorance of the problem. How could this happen in Australia, the lucky country?

My research led me to Pearson, then to anthropologist Peter Sutton's *The Politics of Suffering*. Their analysis was enlightening. I saw how a purely leftist rights-based approach, unbalanced by the importance of the responsibilities usually championed by conservatives, might risk the wellbeing of children and other vulnerable people in Indigenous communities—though, properly understood, a right or freedom entails a responsibility to respect others' rights and freedoms, particularly the rights of the vulnerable. Problem was, in Indigenous affairs it seemed the responsibilities inherent in rights had sometimes been underemphasised.

I could also see, however, that the Northern Territory Intervention of 2007 didn't get it right. It sought to curtail child abuse and neglect by applying welfare quarantining and restrictions on alcohol and pornography, but with its imposed and hasty implementation and suspension of the *Racial Discrimination Act*, it was missing key ingredients: Indigenous empowerment and equality before the law.

A passion for equality became my first intellectual obsession.

Mike Winer was one of the CYI stalwarts, an ally since the land rights struggles of the 1990s. A tall hippie and environmentalist, Mike was excitable and a bit frazzled, with an eager laugh and a larrikin's manner. After initially working as an advocate for the Wilderness Society and setting up a branch in Cairns, he forged an alliance with the Cape York Land Council and later began working for CYI. Mike's perspective was shifted when a little Aboriginal kid covered in scabies sat on his knee, he told us once. He witnessed the child's excruciating disadvantage and realised that black lives in Cape York were in more urgent need of assistance than the environment. Trees were important, but human beings were more important. And with the right approach, both should prosper. I agreed.

Mike had us investigating environmental and economic development opportunities in Cape York. Because I was the soon-to-be lawyer, I worked on the Wild Rivers controversy. Cape York Institute, led by Pearson, had been battling the Queensland Labor government, which had teamed up with the Greens to push through legislation that would subject Cape York land to strict environmental protections, particularly around the Cape's pristine rivers. The legislation diminished the already-scarce economic development opportunities for impoverished black communities. Aboriginal people had won back much of their land, but now government was burdening it with layers of unwieldy regulation, making economic development almost impossible.

It seemed distinctly unfair. Non-Indigenous Australians had developed much of Australia's landmass to build their prosperity, leaving only its furthest reaches untouched. Previously without land rights, restricted through discrimination and disadvantage, and naturally protective of their country in any case, the Indigenous people up north had not developed their land, and had missed out on the progress boom that other Australians had enjoyed. While Indigenous people were stuck in poverty, the unspoiled beauty of Cape York gave the greenies, ravenous for their Kyoto targets, hope. Cape York Indigenous people were expected to pay for white people's damage to Australia's environment. After decades of white colonisation and dispossession, this was the green version.

One week we explored the Cape with Mike. We went to Kowanyama, Coen and Starcke, where traditional owners took us around their country. We saw vast green lagoons, hectares of ghostly tea-tree, and hills covered in unspoilt forest. We had picnics by secluded creeks, and breathed the air that Indigenous people had kept clean for thousands of years without rigid environmental restrictions.

Within a few weeks I produced a research paper setting out arguments against the imposition of Wild Rivers. The paper identified that the root cause of the vulnerability of Aboriginal property rights was the legal logic underpinning them. The *Native Title Act* and *Aboriginal Land Act* set Indigenous people up with weaker forms of property rights than non-Indigenous Australians. I struggled to understand why. The arguments about a *sui generis* right didn't seem convincing. Why weren't they equal?

I was naive and inexperienced in native title law but this, in retrospect, allowed me to look at the issue with fresh and idealistic eyes. To go back to first principles and ask why. Mike let me run with it.

I produced a second paper analysing the *Mabo* decision. I read the High Court judgements and constructed an offbeat, slightly audacious argument. The judges had got it wrong, I suggested. Not that they were wrong to recognise Indigenous rights in land—this was correct and just. They were wrong to accord an inferior form of title. It shouldn't have been rights under 'traditional laws and customs'. This, I argued, imposed a culturally relativist and limited conception of Indigenous property rights, which was discriminatory in effect and unhelpfully restrictive on Indigenous peoples' freedom of choice and control over their land. Culture and tradition, while important, should have been legally irrelevant. My argument revolved around the idea that possession and inherited ownership were the true sources of Indigenous rights to land. The judges should have accorded full fee-simple ownership to Aboriginal people, where possession and inherited ownership had not been displaced by the Crown. As Pearson has asked: why has the English law of possession been upheld for 'the Crown's subjects generally' but not for the 'benefit of native citizens'?[2] There was much on which he and I seemed to agree.

I'll never forget the first day I met Noel Pearson. Mike took us into his office at the end of volunteering to present our work. The other women went first, while I sat, scared. Pearson was a domineering presence, silent and glowering.

When it was my turn, I took him through my argument about the *Mabo* case. An exchange ensued. Noel had some contrary points. As the conversation progressed, I grew less scared. 'You can't say the High Court in *Mabo* got it wrong,' Noel said. 'But they did get it wrong,' I countered. 'They perpetuated discrimination. They should have given full ownership.' It was a robust discussion, and though Noel's knowledge exposed the vastness of my ignorance and idealism, there were also moments where I felt my logic had him. Mike told me he'd never seen Noel so stuck for a response. Ever the diligent student, I was pleased I'd done a good job. The internship came to an end.

I headed straight off to another one, at the NSW Law Reform Commission in Sydney. After the vibrancy of Cape York Institute, it was tedious. At CYI I had been able to pursue intellectual questions and think creatively about solutions. I could write and argue with personality and express original ideas. The Law Reform Commission had me doing data entry from other people's submissions. On fines or something. It didn't light my fire.

A few weeks in, Mike called. 'Noel wants to offer you a job,' he said.

Noel called some days later. I could barely hear his grumbly voice down the line, but was too timid to say so. From the snippets I gathered, he wanted me to move to Cairns to work on constitutional reform. I didn't know what it was all about and was wary of being sucked in as some kind of boring secretary. Just to be clear, I said, 'I'm not interested in being a PA and doing admin. I want to do something challenging and interesting.' I don't know where my impudence came from.

'Yeah,' Noel rumbled distantly. 'No, I think it'll be really good.' I decided to believe him.

I gave immediate notice to the Law Reform Commission and escaped home for Christmas. By February, I'd moved up to Cairns. Two law subjects still to go.

I was an outsider to the struggles of Cape York people, but began to learn of the challenges they faced.

I travelled to the four Cape York Welfare Reform communities: Mossman Gorge, near the resort town of Port Douglas; the former Lutheran mission of Hopevale, where Noel Pearson grew up; the mixed town of Coen; and the former mission of Aurukun on western Cape York. I'd fly over in tiny light aircrafts, gazing down at the Australian landscape as the plane bumped and ducked over puffs of wind. A new life, suddenly.

The foreignness of these communities was startling at first. The barbed-wire shopfronts and dilapidated houses were often strewn with junk and had broken or taped-up windows. Some seemed like a scene from a dated communist movie, more like my visits to torn-up Albania or Fiji than life in Australia. I visited Yarrabah, another former mission hidden away outside Cairns, by the sea where the skeleton of an old ship was lodged in the mud (from colonial times, I imagined). I marvelled at the secluded nature of these communities. Out of sight, out of mind.

I also saw germinating change. The Welfare Reform programs championed by CYI were having some good impact. There were houses with burgeoning gardens and some industry. Hopevale would get a banana farm. Parents could save money for their children's education through programs encouraging financial planning. Alcohol Management Plans (AMPs) had increased community stability. The local Family Responsibilities Commissioners were instilling a sense of local leadership and decision-making to address social problems, and the community-led quarantining of welfare was, for some, a welcome restriction to cease the flow of cash to booze, gambling and drugs. Distinct from the Northern Territory Intervention, community decision-making power was key. Later, I saw the impressive Direct Instruction schools championed by Pearson—Aboriginal kids chanting words in both English and their traditional languages, faces alight and attentive, were uplifting to behold.

But I also got a sense of the Indigenous position of powerlessness in government decisions made about them. It hit home with Aurukun. If you understand the tragedy of Aurukun, you understand the tragedy of Indigenous affairs in Australia.

Aurukun remained the most unstable Welfare Reform community. It was still afflicted with violence and volatility. Here the hopelessness, despite best efforts at reform, remained palpable. It felt similar to Hopevale, but with deeper scars. Deeper welts in women's faces. Deeper distress in some of the children's eyes.

As I furthered my learning, it became clear that the imposed and discriminatory decisions of successive governments had led to the Aurukun community's current dysfunction and disadvantage. My comprehension of the challenge of Indigenous constitutional recognition was informed by my growing understanding of the history of Cape York communities, and especially the plight of the Wik and Wik Way peoples of Aurukun.

That history is long and sad. State violence against Indigenous people in the colonisation of Queensland has been well documented. It included state-authorised killing of Indigenous people aided by the Queensland Native Police. There was prolonged discrimination in voting laws. Queensland was the last state to confer equal voting rights on Indigenous people, in 1965.

The remedy for the bloodshed was imposed 'protection'. The Wik and Wik Way peoples were forcibly removed from their traditional lands and brought to the Aurukun mission in chains. They were put under the protection of the Presbyterian Church, which had been ruled since 1925 by the formidable and often cruel missionary Bill MacKenzie. Mission life was harsh but the community was stable—no murders, which was a change from the massacres of the frontier that had decimated the Queensland tribes.

Protection entailed severe discrimination, however. The Protection Acts empowered appointed protectors to control many day-to-day aspects of Indigenous people's lives. These laws and policies included unequal and stolen wages, forcible removal of children, and controls on where people could live and who they could marry. The protection era in Queensland lasted until the 1970s—around the time my parents came to Australia to attend university. After that, mission control of Indigenous lives was replaced by government control. The church was moved out, but state-sanctioned discrimination against Indigenous people continued.

Rich bauxite deposits in the land propelled continued subordination and economic exclusion. In 1975, the government seized control of Aurukun's extensive bauxite reserves and gave it to a French multinational, Pechiney, without consulting with or obtaining consent from the Aurukun community.[3] Aurukun people challenged the decision. The case went all the way to the Privy Council,[4] and the mine was never developed. Poverty continued.

In the same era, while my parents were full swing into their medical degrees at Monash, the people of Aurukun tried to purchase the Archer River cattle station, which was on their traditional lands. Queensland premier Joh Bjelke-Petersen tried to stop them through a policy to prevent Indigenous people from purchasing large tracts of land. The policy was discriminatory, and Wik leader John Koowarta challenged it under the 1975 *Racial Discrimination Act* (RDA).

In 1982, the High Court held in favour of Koowarta and found the policy in breach of the RDA. It was a great victory for the Wik people. But the Queensland Parliament swiftly dodged the court's decision: it declared the Archer River station a national park, which meant it couldn't be purchased. Years of legal battling proved ultimately ineffective in curtailing the abusive intent of the Queensland government.

The Wik people couldn't buy land on their own country—the country they had lived on for thousands of years. While my parents, immigrants to Australia, could go househunting in leafy Park Orchards and purchase their very own little piece of Australia on which to start their new life, the original Australians up at Aurukun could not.

In 1985 I turned five years old, and was probably getting called 'black Shireen' in kindergarten. But I went home every day to a safe home, in a safe suburb, with plenty of food, to a house my parents owned.

In that same year, the former mission of Aurukun was changed forever by booze: the government introduced a grog canteen though the local people, especially the women, opposed it. The government did it anyway because it needed the revenue. It began a decades-long alcohol binge and led to community breakdown for generations to come. Alcohol-fuelled violence became prolific. At one stage, Aurukun became notorious for having one of the highest murder rates in the world.

Kids growing up in Aurukun got nothing like the life chances I got.

In the 1990s, Aurukun people fought to close the canteen. Community leaders asked for AMPs to curb the debilitating flow of alcohol. When the plans were finally introduced, there was a significant reduction in violence across Cape York. Things improved but sly grog, drugs and violence, compounded and perpetuated by inherited psychological trauma, fetal alcohol syndrome and mental illness, plus a lack of jobs and education, remained an ongoing problem.

In 2006, there was a gang rape of an Aurukun child.[5] Nine Aboriginal perpetrators pleaded guilty to raping a ten-year-old girl. Despite the accused having lengthy criminal histories, they were initially sentenced leniently and the juveniles' convictions weren't recorded.[6] Disturbingly the judge, Sarah Bradley, implied during proceedings that the girl had consented—a legal impossibility for a ten-year-old. Professor Marcia Langton, writing in the *Griffith Review*, put words to the fury I felt reading the judgement: it 'expressed utter contempt for the girl and basic norms of humanity'.[7] Bradley's judgement was later overturned.

Langton is a respected anthropologist, geographer and Indigenous advocate, and the Foundation Chair of Australian Indigenous Studies at Melbourne University. I first met her at Pearson's bidding in 2011, before moving to Cairns to start work. With her luminescent silver hair and pale blue-grey eyes, Langton was a striking and powerful presence, about as scary as Noel—perhaps scarier—but with a screen star's beauty. Our chat began well. Then I inadvertently said something she didn't like about the concept of race. She transformed in an instant and slammed the desk. 'There's no such thing as race!' she snapped. 'Don't you get it?!' I jumped, but instinctively adopted my Zen-like calm. 'I think you misunderstood me,' I said. 'I agree with you about race.' Her fury abated like a hurricane subsiding. Meeting Marcia Langton was like coming face-to-face with a force of nature.

I want to be a woman like her when I get older, I thought. Powerful. Feminist. Ferocious.

Langton's commentary was an authoritative indictment on the injustice of that Aurukun rape sentencing, and highlighted the ways in which unwarranted leniency towards Indigenous perpetrators can result in discriminatory disrespect for the Aboriginal victims of crime.[8] Pearson reiterated the analysis, explaining to the ABC how well-meaning judicial leniency, accounting for cultural, historical and social factors underpinning Indigenous disadvantage and offending, could in fact compound the problem. 'In my view, the best service that the judicial system can do to help Aboriginal society is to make sure that high standards and low tolerance of abuse [are] maintained,' he said.[9] Reading their commentary, I felt intense solidarity with Pearson and Langton. They were undoubtedly correct.

It was largely from Pearson and Langton that my appreciation of both left- and right-wing racism was gleaned. To me, discriminatory double standards in the form of leniency seemed as unjust as its opposite. Initially it was discriminatory oppression by government: the hard bigotry of racist control. This had morphed into discriminatory leniency and non-intervention, driven by white guilt—often well intentioned but equally damaging. The soft bigotry of low expectations, to borrow the phrase coined by George W. Bush and given new life by Pearson. Both approaches were unjust.

Aurukun was still troubled when I got to CYI in 2011. Sly grog was still a scourge. The situation was not helped by the Liberal-National Queensland premier, Campbell Newman, who in 2013 irresponsibly tried to make the Aboriginal equal 'right to drink' an ideological issue.[10] I thought of the right to drink as against the right of children to be safe. Under what warped logic could an imagined right to consume alcohol be considered worth a mention?

In 2016, the Direct Instruction school in Aurukun got temporarily closed down after youths outside it rampaged, threatening a teacher and community safety. That school had been a glimmer of hope for the scarred community, and the Aurukun women for months had been pleading with police to crack down on the violence perpetrated by disengaged Aboriginal youths. Their pleas were ignored.

Reports of horrific police reticence emerged. Police stood around overseeing so-called 'fair fights' between community members, it was reported. They handed out lollies to bystanders watching the violence, with children looking on, it was alleged. The community had asked for zero tolerance on violence and grog, but the police preferred 'cultural appropriateness' and 'cultural sensitivity'—a light touch.[11] In other words, letting the people of Aurukun break the law and beat each other to a pulp.

Is the state now so desensitised to tales of Indigenous suffering that it knows not how to intervene, I wondered? Has the violence become acceptable, so now we in the broader community avert our eyes and do nothing? I haven't figured out whether it is deliberate racism, a calculated effort to keep people down, or just bad policy- and decision-making, coming from a good place but resulting in perpetuated misery nonetheless. Maybe it's both.

But the facts tell the story. Aurukun people wanted to own their land—government stopped them. They asked for economic development rights—government prevented them. They said no to the grog canteen—government imposed it, then later, when AMPs were in place, politicians promoted the right to drink. Aurukun people asked for strict enforcement of laws and a crackdown on violence—police handed out lollies.

It never seemed to matter which side. Left or right. Whether soft or hard touch. The people of Aurukun were powerless. They'd been treated like dirt by everyone.

3

The Expert Panel

MY JOB AT Cape York Institute was to come up with CYI's constitutional reform policy. The intellectual challenge was like spark plugs for my brain.

When I began in 2011, Noel Pearson was a member of the Expert Panel on Constitutional Recognition of Indigenous Australians. The panel had been put together by Prime Minister Julia Gillard's Labor government in December 2010, and was tasked with reporting to government on options for constitutional change, including advice on levels of support for the options among Indigenous people and the broader community. The panel was to report by December 2011.

In that first year, Noel and I had to not only to come up with the reforms CYI would advocate: we had to figure out how to positively influence the panel, and therefore the national debate.

My understanding of the Constitution had, until then, been just theoretical. I'd enjoyed the theory—I got my two highest marks in constitutional law and administrative law. There was something about the neat and logical workings of public law—subordinate rules made under higher rules, higher laws that cancelled out lower laws—that tickled my sense of order and justice. I liked the idea that laws needed the appropriate constitutional authority to be legitimate. Plus, public law cases were most interesting. They involved the struggles of usually vulnerable and powerless individuals and groups against the might of the state.

Cape York Institute was my introduction to the practical, on-the-ground workings of the Australian Constitution. It was my first experience of the Constitution's adverse human impact. In my first year, I learned four crucial things about the Constitution and what it meant for Indigenous people and their place in Australia.

First, the Constitution created Australia. I'd never thought deeply about the significance of this legal and political fact before. When I did, it was perspective-shifting.

Australia was born when the Constitution of our Commonwealth, part of a UK Act of Parliament, came into force on 1 January 1901. It was an odd revelation. For my first thirty years, I'd attended barbecues in Melbourne and enjoyed the holiday on 26 January feeling vaguely patriotic, while also understanding the complexity of the date that had heralded dispossession for Indigenous peoples. But the historical and moral incongruence didn't fully dawn on me until I looked at the Constitution from a different perspective—from way up north in Cairns—and heard firsthand the concerns of Indigenous people about the date of our national day.

I realised then the illogicality of it, too. *There was no Australia on 26 January 1788.*

Australia didn't yet exist when Arthur Phillip stuck his flag in the sand at Sydney Cove in 1788 and declared British sovereignty. That moment created the colony of New South Wales. It did not create Australia. No wonder Australia Day evolved to be more divisive than unifying: the date we commemorate presents an incomplete founding reality. As a date to celebrate Australia, 26 January is logically wrong as well as morally wanting.

In years to come I would witness with broadened perspective our annual Australia Day furore, the cyclical history war of a nation spiritually and psychologically uneasy with itself, and begin to see more clearly the reasons behind our unresolved torment. We Australians gather at barbecues to count down our anthems and revel half drunk in the half-told story of our land—never quite knowing whether to celebrate or grieve. We rally in turns proclaiming our patriotism or mourning our loss, sorting ourselves into Invasion, Survival or Australia Day parades. On 26 January, the nation gazes at its own reflection and asks: who are we? What does it mean to be this thing called Australian? We don't yet have a full answer.

I later came to the view that Australia Day tensions will persist until our nation comes to terms with the wrongs of the past and resolves them through formal reconciliation. I came to believe that Australia Day should be held on the date we finally bring together our Indigenous heritage, our British inheritance and our multicultural triumph. It should be the date the nation votes for Indigenous constitutional recognition, to belatedly include Indigenous people in the Constitution and ensure the injustices of the past cannot happen again. In 2016, I wrote an opinion piece in *The Age* making the case for a shift in thinking along these lines.[1] A comment from a member of the public suggested a brilliantly efficient solution: why not hold the referendum on 26 January, then? Rather than changing the date—plenty of Australians are attached to 26 January in any case—could we transform and redeem it? Could we do that which should have been done in 1788 and in 1901? Sign the treaty. Reform the Constitution. Unify the country.

That idea surfaced in 2016. In 2011, I merely grasped more fully the moral, philosophical and political implications of the fact that the Constitution of 1901 created Australia.

The second thing I learned was crucial in understanding the challenge of Indigenous constitutional recognition: the Constitution is all about power.

The Constitution is a power-sharing compact by which the disparate colonies agreed to unite as a single federation. It is a unity pact, or treaty, containing the rules and processes by which the parties agreed to coexist and work together productively and peacefully in the new nation. This compact recognises the pre-existing political communities—the colonies, now the states—and guarantees them appropriate representation and rights in the system. All except one pre-existing community, however: the Indigenous original owners of the land were left out of the deal.

In the 1800s, when the colonial founding fathers negotiated how power was to be distributed in the new nation, Indigenous peoples were not included in discussions. There were no First Nations representatives at the constitutional conventions, and the Constitution produced contained clauses explicitly excluding them.

Power was shared out, and Indigenous people got none. The Constitution, for Indigenous peoples, creates a position of perpetual powerlessness.

Anthropologist W.E. Stanner wrote about the 'torment of powerlessness' that besets Indigenous peoples in all their dealings with government. The source of that powerlessness in the most fundamental sense is the Australian Constitution. It has presided over laws denying Indigenous property rights, denying equal wages, denying equal voting rights, controlling who they could marry and where they could live—and it denied them a fair say in all these policy decisions. These laws were all possible because the Constitution allowed them. How might the Constitution empower Indigenous peoples in such decisions? This is the fundamental problem Indigenous constitutional recognition seeks to fix.

The third thing I learned, which follows on from the second, was that Australia's Constitution does not treat everyone equally.

Where most Western liberal democracies have a bill of rights, including some kind of equality before the law or non-discrimination guarantee, Australia's Constitution has the opposite: racially discriminatory clauses. The 'race power' enables Parliament to enact discriminatory race-based laws (ours is the only Constitution in the world, as far as I'm aware, that gives Parliament such a power). Section 25 contemplates the states banning races from voting. As perusal of the constitutional convention debates reveals, these clauses were inserted by the colonial drafters with the intent of controlling and excluding the 'inferior' and 'coloured' peoples.

How was it I'd never realised our Constitution conferred upon Parliament the theoretical power to stop Aborigines from voting, prevent Asian people from buying houses, or disallow Africans from living in certain areas? I went through the discriminatory possibilities, some of which, I discovered, had in fact been past policy.

While the days of the White Australia policy were behind us and the 'two Wongs don't make a white'–style racist political rhetoric was (mostly, thankfully) a thing of the past, it seemed extraordinary that the Constitution had not caught up with the nation's embrace of multiculturalism, or the fact that 'race' was now acknowledged as an outdated, pseudo-scientific concept.

I learned that the 1967 referendum only fixed part of the problem. In that referendum, Indigenous Australians were finally counted in the census, and the Commonwealth Parliament obtained its power to legislate for Indigenous affairs (the exclusion of Indigenous people from the race power was removed, and this power became exclusively used for Indigenous affairs legislation—prior to 1967 it was never used). But that referendum did not implement any constitutional rules to ensure Indigenous people would be treated more fairly than in the past. It gave Parliament the power to make laws about Indigenous people, but didn't guarantee Indigenous people a fair say in those laws. And it did not ensure equality before the law for all Australians. Indigenous people suffered as a result.

The fourth thing I learned, which is obvious given insights about Indigenous constitutional powerlessness and inequality, is that Indigenous Australians have always sought practical and substantive constitutional reform and recognition to empower them in their relationship with government. Constitutional reform to ensure fairer treatment. It has never been just about symbolism for Indigenous people.

From William Cooper's 1937 letter to King George VI, which asked for Aboriginal representation in Parliament, to the Yolngu bark petitions in 1963 asking for a fairer hearing in decisions made about them and their land, to the 1988 Barunga Statement, which asked for an Indigenous representative body and a treaty, Indigenous advocates had never asked for a mere symbolic statement or preamble. As Yolngu elder Galarrwuy Yunupingu put it, Indigenous advocates were seeking 'serious constitutional reform'.[2]

In 1999, then Liberal prime minister John Howard, evidently oblivious to this history of Indigenous advocacy for substantive constitutional recognition, ran a referendum to insert a new symbolic preamble merely mentioning Indigenous peoples, together with a question on the republic. The symbolic mention was opposed by many Indigenous groups, but Howard went ahead anyway. Both referendum propositions failed abysmally, leaving the question of Indigenous recognition open for future agitation.

Constitutional recognition was put on the agenda again by Howard in 2007, then by Kevin Rudd, then by Gillard with the formation of the Expert Panel. It would be kept on the agenda by future Liberal prime ministers Tony Abbott and Malcolm Turnbull. Australia has been trying to answer this question for a long time.

But to find the right solution, you first need to correctly characterise the problem. That's what I tried to do at the start of 2011. I looked at the problem from all angles, seeking to understand every contour. Hoping to crack the right answer.

Do you ever get that feeling of brain salivation? That achy feeling in the frontal lobes when confronted with the juiciest of problems? Problems deliciously complex and ripe for solving. The feeling of neurons firing and new connections forming, brain cells pulsating with fresh blood and new facts. Your mind widening to see the world anew.

I remembered that feeling from some twelve years prior, studying university-level philosophy as an extension subject in my final year of high school. I hadn't felt it in my years as an actor.

But I felt it again when confronted with the challenge of constitutional reform at Cape York Institute. The problem went to the core of our nation. When I saw its enormity, I couldn't look away.

It wasn't all excitement and mental stimulation. I was also having a crisis of confidence. I had a growing appreciation of the problem, but was totally unsure about the appropriate solution.

Each day I'd lope up Sheridan Street in my floppy sandals, arriving with frizzed hair and sweat droplets hanging off my nose. I'd dive in: reading, taking notes, writing. I started churning out research and ideas.

I had to make it up as I went. There was little guidance on how to proceed, and the role hadn't existed before I arrived. Plus I'd never worked in policy before, let alone in law. I'd temped as a receptionist and data entry clerk to supplement my acting income. I'd been a check-out chick at BI-LO in Ringwood, and did a short stint as a waitress at an Indian restaurant before quitting due to harassment from the all-male staff. But this was my first 'proper' job. I could draw only on my skills as a student. I thought of the people of Aurukun and their structural disempowerment, and felt totally inept.

Noel had given me his PowerPoint slide deck from several years prior. It contained ideas about cultural rights, structural reform and an equality guarantee. I also had his extraordinary letters to John Howard urging substantive constitutional recognition. In a letter dated 10 October 2007, Noel argued for a set of structural reforms, including a Rights and Responsibilities Commission and an Indigenous representative body to interface with the Australian Parliament.

I was desperate for feedback, but Noel was so busy with other work that whatever I was producing he usually wasn't reading. When he did, the ideas were summarily dismissed as 'incoherent'. And sometimes, even without his reading them: 'Shireen's first cut of the argument is not compelling (I have yet to read it, but this is my guess)', one email stated confidently. These dismissals would often come in front of staff and heads of policy, to my repeated mortification. It helped that I was used to rejection and criticism from my acting days, but as a former top student it was still a shock. Suddenly I didn't have all the answers.

I was excruciatingly nervous in Noel's silent presence. I'd babble uncontrollably and he'd press one eye, as if in intellectual agony, or close them both in long-suffering meditation. I was impatient and worried I was terrible at my job. Noel began to bring in fellow CYI staff member John, a philosopher and Aboriginal language expert, to join in on the awkwardness with us. We became a trio in silence. Interminable pauses. Sustained eye-poking. Heartfelt sighs. I'd stare at my blank notepaper attentively, waiting, wanting to stab myself in the head with my pen to make it stop.

Then occasionally the silence would be broken by intense philosophical conversations. Conversations about nomenclature and first principles: nation-states, nations, peoples, and the differences between them. John was passionate about Aboriginal language and culture. I'd argue the case for an equality guarantee in the Constitution—this, I'd decided, was the most important reform. John would argue for cultural and language recognition and retention.

Our 'dialectical tension', as Noel described it, was crucial in hammering out our eventual policy position. There were many emails exchanged, as well as face-to-face conversations. (John's and Noel's emails would open with a Guugu Yimithirr greeting, *Yubalay* or *Wanhdharra*. Eventually I retaliated with a *Namaste* and a quip in Hindi, but this only further excited John, who promptly tried to translate it.)

Noel would sit as a kind of umpire overseeing our debate, keeping a watchful eye on the synthesis emerging out of the creative tension between our competing viewpoints. John and I would thrash it out, and Noel would intervene to give direction. He liked this dynamic, I came to learn: the three-way intellectual exchange. The robust push-and-pull that could give rise to exciting ideas. That might uncover the 'radical centre'.

Eventually we settled on what was, in a sense, our first attempt at a 'radical centre' position on constitutional recognition—an amalgamation of the dual important principles of equality and cultural recognition: removal of the race clauses, appropriate replacement of the race power, a languages recognition clause, and an equality guarantee in the Constitution.

An equality guarantee—or racial non-discrimination clause—would be the key substantive reform. This guarantee would empower Indigenous peoples to challenge Parliament through the courts when it imposed discriminatory top-down policies and laws. It was the game-changer, the power-shifter. I felt it was right and just. And equality was a principle you could sell.

Having agreed on a robust and balanced package of constitutional reforms, we then divvied up the writing of the policy paper among the three of us.

While these ideas were being nutted out, I travelled around with Noel to the Expert Panel meetings, which were long and bureaucratic.

Mark Leibler, the successful Jewish-Australian lawyer and founding partner of Arnold Bloch Leibler, and Patrick Dodson, former Catholic priest, Indigenous activist and the well-known 'father of reconciliation', were the co-chairs of the panel. Around the table sat the formidable Professor Marcia Langton, the up-and-coming constitutional law expert and human rights guru Professor Megan Davis, and a host of other players—Mick Gooda, then Aboriginal and Torres Strait Islander Social Justice Commissioner; Fred Chaney, former Aboriginal affairs minister for the Liberal Party; Henry Burmester, former chief general counsel in the Australian Government Solicitor; and other influential individuals. Burmester represented the government in the seminal Hindmarsh Island bridge case, which highlighted the constitutional vulnerability of Indigenous rights.

Then there was Noel, who would often arrive late, like a grumpy rock star. I'd trundle awkwardly behind him, not knowing where to stand or sit. Officious discussion would ensue. Noel would press his eye, as if hoping to poke it out (I was pleased I wasn't the only one who prompted the eye-poking). Occasionally he'd sigh noisily.

For the first few meetings, it was all process. The players scoped each other out. No one spoke up about what they thought the constitutional reforms should be. As the months progressed there was more substantive discussion. Davis shyly offered well-attuned academic insights from an international human rights law perspective, drawing on her extensive scholarship. I could see she was an intelligent and impressive Indigenous woman with a huge future. Langton raised her concerns regarding the race clauses in the Constitution and persuaded the room that they must be removed. She also kept watchful eye on the men, lest they become too cocky in their pronouncements. If a man repeated an idea first raised by a woman who might have been ignored (as is often the way in such meetings), Langton would call it out. I'd watch her twitch and shift in her chair, trying to contain her feminist rage. Then occasionally she would breathe fire and, like a dragon descending on a lamb, tear apart the unsuspecting man's words for their hidden sexism as if extracting gizzards. I'd cheer silently from my spot up the back. Langton added necessary heat to the panel.

Pearson's performances, by comparison, were usually understated (he too could breathe fire, but he saved it up for special occasions). Longstanding allies, he and Langton were steadfast in their friendship, sharing obvious respect and love.

When Pearson talked, the room fell silent. The panel members strained to hear him, but his words were original and insightful and always elegantly delivered. Even Leibler—who generally bossed everyone around, who barked orders at the bureaucrats and who, many years prior, was mentor and teacher to the young Pearson, who had done his legal articles at ABL—deferred to Pearson's superior intellect. Pearson was the natural leader of the group, an astute lawyer and the most formidable brain in the room. His was a charisma and power I'd never seen.

The actor in me noted the dramatic techniques that enhanced his presence: quiet and stillness, the intense slowness of his voice, gargantuan pauses building suspense, the late entrances and slow, statesmanlike walk. When you want to capture people, you don't shout—you whisper. You use a deep resonance to convey authority. You don't rush—you slow down. You pull back and make the audience come to you. Pearson was a master at it. He had his audience enthralled, me included. I felt intensely proud to be his lackey.

On our travels we developed a more comfortable rapport and he became more of a mentor.

Noel summoned me to his office in Cairns one day to provide some tips on writing. I'd fancied myself a poet and author when I was little, before becoming distracted by the performing arts. Writing was the main part of my job and I was enjoying it. Noel must have noticed.

'You need to write more like Lord Denning on the English Court of Appeal,' he said. 'Use shorter sentences. Tell a story, with simple language. Like this.' He pulled up the lyrical opening of Lord Denning's 1977 dissenting judgement in *Miller v Jackson* on his mobile phone. In resonant tones, he read:

> In summertime village cricket is the delight of everyone. Nearly every village has its own cricket field where the young men play and the old men watch ... They tend it well. The wicket area is well rolled and mown. The outfield is kept short. It has a good club house for the players and seats for the onlookers ... Yet now after these 70 years a judge of the High Court has ordered that they must not play there any more. He has issued an injunction to stop them. He has done it at the instance of a newcomer who is no lover of cricket. This newcomer has built, or has had built for him, a house on the edge of the cricket ground which four years ago was a field where cattle grazed. The animals did not mind the cricket ... Now he complains that when a batsman hits a six the ball has been known to land in his garden or on or near his house ... So they asked the judge to stop the cricket being played. And the judge, much against his will, has felt that he must order the cricket to be stopped: with the consequence, I suppose, that the Lintz Cricket Club will disappear. The cricket ground will be turned to some other use ... The young men will turn to *other things* [my italics] instead of cricket.[3]

Here Noel paused dramatically, channelling the English lord's fusty morality. A twinkle in his eye and an imperious raised eyebrow implied that these *other things* would beget society's ruin. 'Other things' were sex and drugs and punk music. And illegitimate pregnancy, inevitably. 'The whole village will be much the poorer,' Noel concluded, 'and all this because of a newcomer who has just bought a house there next to the cricket ground.'

I laughed, delighted at Noel's theatrics. He was a performer, like me, and his delivery reminded me of my dad reading me stories. I thought then that I might come to like this bloke. I took his advice and strove to write simple, articulate policy papers.

Under Noel's leadership, we conducted legal consultations and workshops with lawyers such as Gilbert and Tobin corporate law partner Danny Gilbert, University of NSW constitutional law professor and human rights expert George Williams, Professor Sean

Brennan, barrister David Yarrow and my former constitutional law lecturer, Melissa Castan, plus other members of the panel, including Langton, Davis and Gooda. I went through public submissions and the panel's consultations with Indigenous Australians and the wider public, pulling out quotes to incorporate in our developing document. I also included suggested constitutional amendments, drafted with the assistance of the lawyers.

In the end John didn't deliver his language recognition section—ever the perfectionist, he got too caught up with preliminary philosophical conundrums. So I wrote it. And Noel didn't deliver his introduction section, either—he got too caught up with all the other more urgent policy and political matters he was also trying to manage: education, welfare reform, alcohol management and land rights. So I wrote the introduction too. And I wrote my equality argument bit, of course. So, as it turned out, I wrote the whole thing.

Noel was always too pressed for time, overworked and distracted. He was so spread thin across so many areas that I couldn't get him to read the draft in development. Not for the entire first ten months.

The panel members reacted to me with caution. I was an observer at their meetings, instructed to attend by Noel, but was kicked out more than once by motion or vote. This would be a recurring theme in my job—getting evicted from meetings by blackfellas and whitefellas alike, sometimes both together in a united approach. It felt how I imagined getting kicked out of *Big Brother* or *Australian Idol* must feel. The public walk of shame, as if I'd been caught sneaking in and butting into their business. My dark skin was handy in this role: no one could ever see me blushing.

The deadline for submissions came and went. I was still struggling for feedback on my written work from Noel. CYI asked for an extension.

But Noel still hadn't read the draft policy paper. Eventually, our CEO, a tall and jovial Icelandic man called Gummi, told me to put the submission in to the panel anyway. Noel grudgingly gave his blessing,

I submitted it (from memory at one of those public computers at the airport, on the way to a panel meeting—I had no smartphone back then) and it was distributed to the panel members, who were to read it overnight. Noel was to discuss it the next morning. At 11 p.m. I took him through the document he still hadn't read and he asked me to prepare slides for him to present to the panel the next day. I did them, exhausted and a bundle of nerves, fearful of humiliation the next day.

At breakfast, however, Noel was perky. 'I sat in the bath this morning and read your submission, Shireen,' he said. Weird, but okay. 'I knew if I left you to your own devices you'd do a good job! It's excellent. And well written.'

Noel didn't use the slides. He spoke off the cuff to the panel on the proposed reforms. In his arresting, solemn way, he urged them to raise their ambitions. Do not settle for a mere preamble, he urged, putting to bed any previous suggestion that minimalism may be the best option because it was what government wanted.

From memory, no one else on the panel actively argued for an equality guarantee in the Constitution. Though an equality guarantee was called for in several submissions, it was Noel's advocacy and CYI's submission that put a racial non-discrimination clause firmly on the Expert Panel's agenda, where it was accepted and embraced, then collectively advocated.

The reforms proposed were ambitious, but ambition was Noel's natural position. He would only aim high, never low. Constitutional reform was no different, despite the onerous test of a double majority referendum.

Noel knew the political difficulty. He believed real change was necessary and, with the right political strategy, possible. His words inspired everyone.

It was an exciting time, and we were full of hope. CYI's submission was significantly influential on the panel's work.

Crucially, Dodson responded positively. He referred to Noel affectionately as 'Noely' that day, and commended our work with a tear sinking down into his beard. Though he disliked some of the CYI rhetoric, he said, the submission inspired him.

Dodson's support was important. It was the first step to a united Indigenous position. Indigenous solidarity on the desired reform proposals would make negotiation with government more effective, and would likely lead to a better outcome for Indigenous people. The Expert Panel report needed to be unanimous, but more importantly, the Indigenous leaders on the panel needed to be unanimous.

The three most politically crucial leaders in this regard were Noel Pearson, Patrick Dodson and Marcia Langton.

Dodson carried power as the Indigenous elder co-chair and the father of reconciliation. Where Noel was the intellectual bright spark, Dodson was the moral patriarch—just as Langton was the moral matriarch, with a fierce intellectualism all her own.

The three together were a kind of holy trinity of Indigenous politics. Dodson was on the left, preaching rights, and Marcia was further to the right, championing responsibility (Noel explained that she began further left, but was pushed to the right largely by the failure of the left to properly grapple with Indigenous social disadvantage). Noel, being slightly younger, was like their talented love child, drawing from divergent political parentage to pursue the radical centre—the 'right to take responsibility'.

Noel would remind me that it would take a smart political strategy for the 3 per cent Indigenous minority to round up the support of the 97 per cent non-Indigenous majority. Working together, however, the three leaders could span almost the entire political spectrum, rounding up left, right and in between. Together, they could muster the 97 per cent of non-Indigenous Australians who would need to vote yes at a referendum for the reforms to succeed. Noel and Marcia were already a team. Working constructively with Dodson too would forge a formidable—and cross-partisan—alliance, if they could manage it.

Langton seemed critically wary of the 'black men in the black hats', however: the brand of Indigenous male leadership that wore a black akubra. Dodson sported one with a hatband in iconic Aboriginal colours, and in later years Noel would don a black hat too. But back then, for Langton, the black hat seemed to represent everything repugnant about the 'boys' club' style of black politics that for too long had dominated Aboriginal leadership—the style that too often denigrates women and empowers the 'big men'. As I came to understand, Langton's critique of this sexist leadership culture was frequently warranted.

I'll never forget the sumptuous dinner party hosted by mining magnate Andrew 'Twiggy' Forrest at a Sydney restaurant. I have no idea why I was there, mingling with the high-flyers like an imposter. Langton gave an impromptu speech and riffed about the black men in their black hats, rolling her eyes exaggeratedly at the 'noble savage' nostalgia propagated by those sporting the outdated outback costume. All image, no substance, seemed the message. Fluff and nonsense. Boomerangs and bullshit. 'Brolgas in the wetlands … blah, blah, BLAH!' Langton drawled in her throaty twang, the world-weary dismissal of a woman who'd seen it all and wasn't impressed. Noel and I roared. There was so much diversity of thought and opinion among the Indigenous leadership. A united position would be hard to achieve.

Twiggy Forrest was at my table that night, and for some reason I decided to test out on him my equal Indigenous property rights argument, which he didn't seem to like. I don't know why, but I pressed the point—perhaps feeling cheeky. Forrest, having heard my job description, took the opportunity to let me know that constitutional reform was not the answer. Aboriginal disadvantage will be solved by jobs and education, he advised sternly but kindly across the table of miners and businessmen. It won't be solved by 'constitutional land rights lawyers', he said—which is what he thought I was. I imagined Twiggy's ancestor Sir John Forrest, the first premier of Western Australia, who, according to the constitutional convention debates, urged the inclusion of racist clauses because he was concerned to exclude 'Asiatic or African alien[s]' from the goldfields. His descendant seated at dinner didn't seem like a bad guy. He seemed good-willed and I noted his genuine respect for Noel and Marcia. Twiggy would come around on constitutional reform. Just not yet.

Noel and I left that dinner in mirthful spirits. Not only because of the brolgas, but also because of Twiggy. 'Did you know who that was?' Noel asked, as we walked down the steep hill from Rockpool. 'Yes!' I said. Noel didn't tell me off. He seemed pleased I'd given Twiggy a gentle prod.

If Noel had an ambitious reform vision, he wasn't the only one. Ambition was catching.

Liberal pollster Mark Textor's comments at another panel dinner also encouraged ambition. Make a big target rather than a small one, he advised. Be bold. The panel seemed buoyed. An equality guarantee was the way to go.

Another pollster drifted in and out during those weeks: Tim Gartrell, a campaign expert on the Labor side. He got hold of the CYI submission and made a point of congratulating me. 'This is a real feather in your cap,' Gartrell said, echoing the sentiments of some panel members, including Gooda and Chaney. The mood was optimistic.

Many were still cautious of me, however. Noel wanted me to work on refining the drafting of the constitutional amendments, and this annoyed some people. One of the most senior male lawyers on the panel grumbled: 'Shireen is not a real lawyer.' It was true: I wasn't. I was still a law student. I'd flown to Melbourne twice from Cairns to sit exams for my last two subjects—copyright and equity—having missed every class. I was yet to graduate.

Back in Cairns, I was called to a Saturday-night dinner with Alan Tudge, a member of parliament from the Liberal Party with a seat in Melbourne, together with Gummi and others from the staff. Tudge was a former deputy director of CYI. Gummi asked me to print the CYI submission for Tudge, who was to be on a plane to Cape York with Tony Abbott, then Opposition leader, the next day. Tudge said he'd talk to Abbott about the submission and wanted Abbott to read it on the plane.

When I gave him the submission, Tudge responded with barely concealed disdain. He said he'd wanted it earlier, and barked reprimands at me across the restaurant table. I was baffled. I barely knew him and tried not to react. Gummi dropped me home afterwards and apologised on Tudge's behalf. The next day in the office I was told the problem was probably my gender. It wouldn't be our last tense interaction.

I told Noel about Tudge's unexpected venom, as I did after any odd exchange. Such intel on the quirks of a politician's mind was useful, and we'd add it to our accumulating bank of knowledge on the political landscape and its players. Noel was alive to the subtlest of personal power plays, and strategy considerations infused the most mundane of his decisions.

For example, he didn't want CYI to do a boring submission to the panel. 'We don't submit,' he'd said, pointedly. 'We develop a policy. A full policy argument.' I understood the point. This was all about power, after all. Obtaining and using it. Practically speaking, however, we had to submit to get our ideas considered. Contrary to popular belief, Noel became practised in strategic submission. So did I.

We'd tell ourselves it was for the end goal, for it's not the bully who truly holds power: the bully betrays his own insecurity. The Zen-like submitter, compliant and calm, grasps her power and calculates her moves, aware of the brute force of those above. She bides her time, a patient persuader, knowing she can outsmart, or hopefully convert, the bullies in the long run. Or maybe, more simply, win their love and friendship. Their empathy.

But I thought of Langton, and the fire and fightback I so admired, and wondered about my mild-mannered patience in the face of unwarranted male aggression. When Noel couldn't attend a panel meeting one day, he instructed me to present to them our constitutional drafting in development. Some of the men were grumpy about it and delivered a barrage of interruptions and interjections. 'Let her speak, will you!' Langton demanded, and they piped down. I was grateful.

A few years later, a well-known Aboriginal man occupying a position of public prominence lost his temper at me for simply asking a question in a group discussion. A switch seemed to flip and his calm demeanour turned instantly to rage: he stood and stepped forward, raising his voice. Noel was not there, but Langton immediately stood in between us, her hands raised, keeping him at bay. She told me later the man was known for domestic violence, and she'd been worried he might punch me. I went to the toilets and cried: I'd given up my weekend to fly to Sydney, on the invitation of Indigenous leaders. I wished I hadn't bothered. (That same weekend I ended up debating constitutional lawyer Frank Brennan, however, so it turned out to be worthwhile.)

I'll never forget Marcia's protective intervention. It was far from the last time I was yelled at by powerful men, whether black or white. But of the many who would put me in my place in years to come, Noel was never among them. He'd criticise my work if he didn't like it, or chastise a bad decision. But there was no sexism, nor a hint of racism. It didn't matter that I was an Indian-Australian, non-Indigenous and a woman. It didn't matter that I was relatively young. Noel encouraged me to rise up and grasp my power. To reach higher and not submit. He was the only one, aside from my family, who did this.

Yet submit we did. We had to. Submitting was part of persuasion.

Noel argued that for constitutional reform to happen, Nixon needed to go to China—a political metaphor referring to President Richard Nixon's 1972 visit to the People's Republic, conveying the idea that you need a reputable, hardline conservative leader to undertake ambitious reform or progressive diplomacy. We needed right-wing leaders to champion recognition and reconciliation in Australia. We needed to plant a stake in the ground at 5 p.m. on the right end of the political clock-face spectrum. Everyone to the left would be easier.

Constitutional reform, Noel explained, is a 90 per cent game. It wasn't enough just to have progressives on board. We needed both sides. Substantive change had to be championed by a conservative leader, to get both left and right. It needed a right-winger with genuine goodwill towards Indigenous people.

Noel was hoping it would be Tony Abbott, then Opposition leader.

Accordingly, Noel nurtured a 'bromance' with Abbott, the 'Mad Monk'. It was a sustained wooing. Dates to his traditional country up on the Cape. Coffees and lunches. Well-timed texts. Building the relationship. Doing the groundwork and preparing to persuade. Watching on, I couldn't figure out if it was genuine friendship or pure strategy. 'Are you actually friends?' I asked Noel one day.

'Don't be silly. He's a redneck,' Noel replied, as if that fact should be obvious. 'But,' he added after a moment, 'he's got this Catholic, paternalistic compassion for blackfellas. There is goodwill, as condescending as it tends to be. He supports recognition. So we gotta persuade him.'

When Noel recollects the relationship now, he describes it differently. They were real friends, he says. There was mutual respect. And it seemed that Abbott was genuinely concerned about Indigenous peoples. That was a good thing.

Back in 2011, after reading the CYI submission on that plane ride to Cape York, Abbott emailed Lew Griffiths, Noel's dedicated and passionate media adviser. Abbott told Lew he wasn't supportive of a racial non-discrimination clause, our key proposed reform. He just wanted to remove references to 'race' from the Constitution and replace the race power, and he supported a symbolic mention in a new preamble. A minimalist model. 'There's goodwill in the Coalition party room, but no one should underestimate the potential for resistance to extensive change,' Abbott warned.

Noel was not about to give up. We gotta get the drafting of the amendments right, he instructed. Then we gotta persuade these bastards.

In refining the draft amendments, I took advice mainly from Professor George Williams, the prominent constitutional and human rights lawyer. Noel wanted the racial non-discrimination clause to be framed more like equality before the law—he thought this might work better for the conservative right. I was too naive to question the wisdom of receiving advice only from left-leaning human rights lawyers, but these were the experts we knew, and to whom we had access. George emailed helpful feedback and I forwarded his positive comments to Noel.

'But you're not a real lawyer,' was Noel's one-line reply.

I grinned idiotically at my desk. Noel had taken to offering positive reinforcement, and it was working. 'Almost there!' he'd email in response to another drafting version, then 'Very close!' to the next. He had evidently figured out that 'close to perfect'–type encouragement would elicit the best efforts from this Indian nerd. He was right. (I'd been trained well—one time when I got 99 per cent on a maths test, Mum sat me down to discuss where the 1 per cent had gone.) I duly became like Pavlov's dog, hungry for praise. Eventually Noel was happy, and we submitted our updated draft clauses to the panel.

Late in 2011, Expert Panel polling confirmed that a racial non-discrimination guarantee was the most popular amendment among Australians from across the political spectrum.[4] Left and right. I was sitting up the back of the meeting, as usual. Noel turned and raised his eyebrows at me. Support from 80–90 per cent of the public! Across the spectrum! That was a referendum winner. It made sense: who could argue with the idea that all Australians should be equal before the law? The poll bolstered our efforts. Our instincts were right. Equality was the answer.

In the end, the panel largely adopted the reforms CYI advocated. Megan Davis and Henry Burmester were in charge of the panel's constitutional drafting, with the advice of external lawyers. The panel's proposed reforms were:

- Remove section 25 (a dead-letter constitutional provision contemplating barring races from voting)
- Remove the race power (a power supporting laws for Indigenous affairs but also enabling discrimination)
- Replace the race power with the new section 51A (power to make laws for Indigenous people, incorporating a built-in preamble with statements of recognition)
- Adopt a racial non-discrimination clause (prohibiting racially discriminatory laws and policies)

- Adopt a languages recognition clause (recognising Indigenous languages as the original Australian languages, and recognising English as a national language).

The details of the drafting differed from CYI's approach, however, and I harboured some concerns.

The panel adopted the section 51A power with an Indigenous-specific symbolic preamble built in, rather than the general preamble CYI advocated, which recognised the three parts of Australia: the Indigenous, the British and the multicultural. The proposed section 51A incorporated recognition of Indigenous peoples' 'traditional lands and waters' and their 'culture and heritage', and talked about the need to 'secure the advancement' of Indigenous peoples. Given my concerns with the limitations of native title, I was worried the use of the word 'traditional' might be confining on future legislative change to strengthen Indigenous property rights. I was also unsure about use of the term 'advancement', which I felt might be problematic politically. I didn't succeed in getting my worries heard, however, despite efforts to raise them with Noel and, to a limited extent, Marcia.

The panel also ultimately recommended the kind of languages clause that CYI proposed, but not without drama. Noel was champion of the clause, but at the last minute I realised the panel were about to ditch it without him realising. I whispered to him towards the end of the last meeting, urging him to advocate in defence of the clause if he wanted it in the report. He did. Forcefully.

There was scrambling and excuses as everyone reacted to Noel's chastisement. When the meeting was over, I in turn was chastised by those who felt the kerfuffle was my fault for not briefing Noel sooner, or properly. I was realising that part of my job was to take the brunt of people's redirected and repressed annoyance at Noel. Most were too intimidated to tell off the great Noel Pearson, so they told me off instead. I submitted (they weren't listening to my protestations anyway).

The panel included the languages clause in their recommendations. They were good proposals. Thoroughly researched and consulted, carefully drafted, and supported by robust legal advice. It was a unanimous report. It felt like a win.

We'd been naive, however. I hadn't understood the politics. Though we'd been aware of the need to pursue a 90 per cent strategy, the proposals were ambitiously progressive. In the limited sphere of our interaction and legal advice, our approach had unwittingly come too much from the left.

The wake-up call from the right was just around the corner.

4

The 'One-Clause Bill of Rights'

THE EXPERT PANEL report was delivered to government in January 2012. But objections to the main reform—a racial non-discrimination clause—erupted before the report was even public, via leaks. The criticism poured forth like hot bile from the demon-possessed girl in *The Exorcist* after her head spins round. Political prophets marched out, delivering one by one their grim indictments with the arrogant certainty of holy writ.

The reforms seemed doomed before they'd even got going.

Australian Catholic University vice-chancellor Greg Craven let rip in early December. Any racial non-discrimination clause was basically a 'one-clause bill of rights', he said in the papers. 'It will start a mini bill of rights debate, which is a debate that has never been won.'[1] Craven coined the phrase that would stick, summoning to arms Australia's prolific anti–bill of rights brigade.

Craven was right, I grudgingly realised later. Australia hadn't even succeeded in implementing a legislated federal bill of rights, let alone any new constitutional rights clause. Every previous attempt at inserting new rights clauses into the Constitution had failed.

By January, Craven's language had become more colourful. The racial non-discrimination clause was a 'dog' of a proposal that was bound to create legal uncertainty, he said: 'there's an almost infinite category of things that can be connected to ethnicity, race or colour and if you're saying to the High Court that you have a blank cheque to decide that something is a problem you have no idea where that provision will go'.[2] By February he'd ramped it up further, writing in the *Australian Financial Review* that the panel's report was 'pathologically flawed', the panel members had 'suffered a fatal attack of enthusiasm', and the recommendations were 'reckless constitutional stupidity'.[3]

Reckless constitutional stupidity? That was our year of work. I was mortified.

Indigenous leader Warren Mundine built on the 'dog' metaphor and added others: the proposals were a 'dog's breakfast' and a 'lawyers' picnic'. They went 'a hundred steps too far' and opened 'a Pandora's box'. He took aim particularly at the panel's proposed use of the word 'advancement' in the proposed new section 51A. Otherwise supportive former Liberal prime minister Malcolm Fraser agreed that the term was too subjective and uncertain, and possibly paternalistic. I'd tried to warn Noel about the word before the report was finalised—he'd realised too late. But Mundine's commentary was vicious. 'I'm concerned about the impact the advancement clause will have on the cultural practice of taking child brides in some Aboriginal communities,' he said. 'Some could argue it is about cultural rights, it could be used under the advancement clause. I raised this with Tony.'[4]

Child brides? Seriously?

Tony Abbott stepped out as if on cue. This must not become a 'one-clause bill of rights', he cautioned. And, we should also be wary of anything that 'might *turn out to be* a one-clause bill of rights' (my italics).[5] We would deal with similar lines of argument in the years to come for the different and far more modest proposal of an Indigenous voice to Parliament, which Malcolm Turnbull would facetiously warn would 'come to be seen as a third chamber of Parliament'. I was quickly learning that it's not just the rational fears one must fight in a referendum campaign: one has to guard against conjured ones as well. The irrational evils—the ones that don't exist, but that people fear might one day materialise (even if out of thin air)—these are hardest to fight: like trying to punch a ghost or exorcise a demon. Logic does not defeat them. They need holy water: a generous dousing in goodwill and good faith.

On the proposed racial non-discrimination clause, there was none to go around. Conservatives were murdering the proposal. It was relentless and unfair. For in reality, this was no 'one-clause bill of rights'. It was a guarantee against racial discrimination, similar to that contained in Western liberal constitutions the world over.

They didn't cease, however. The metaphors used—*a one-clause bill of rights. Dog of a proposal. A dog's breakfast. A Pandora's box. A lawyers' picnic. A blank cheque. Child brides*—these were all in reality variations of the same dog whistle. The message conveyed: if we give black people any legal power to challenge laws, it will lead to grave and unknown danger beyond Australia's wildest nightmares.

Who knew something as simple as a guarantee of equality would give rise to such vicious fearmongering? Was it really so outrageous to propose that Australia's Constitution, our highest rulebook, should require that parliaments treat all Australians equally, without unfair discrimination on the basis of race? Was it so unthinkable that Parliament should be held accountable to this principle by the High Court, performing its constitutional role? Given the history of discrimination, particularly against Indigenous people, wouldn't such accountability be warranted? Most other Western liberal democracies held themselves accountable to such a guarantee—the USA, Canada, South Africa, and many more—so why not us? And what did it say about Australia's democracy when 80–90 per cent of Australians across the political spectrum supported the equality guarantee, and yet it was getting successfully vetoed by a powerful conservative elite?

I struggled to comprehend it, but we needed bipartisan support for a successful referendum. So far we didn't have it. The Coalition was not on board. I asked Noel what we should do. He was blunt: 'Convince them.'

First, we tried to persuade Mundine his opposition was incorrect. He was influential and could help convince the Liberals, we thought. We invited him up to Cairns and sat around at an excruciating breakfast. Noel was interminably quiet. Mundine had flown up to see him, but Noel just wouldn't speak.

I didn't know it then, but Noel was very sick, and the others around the table weren't versed in the constitutional reform policy. Eventually, I took a stab—one of the first times I tried my hand at verbal persuasion of someone who had publicly stated an opposing view on a particular constitutional reform. I made the case to Mundine: equality. Stop racist laws. Equal rights and equal responsibilities. No more hard racism, and no more soft bigotry. Equality before the law for all Australians. You get the gist.

When I finished Mundine was positive. 'I agree with everything you've said,' he told me and the table. Noel was hoping Mundine might take more of an active role in advocating for substantive reform, so Noel could step back and focus on his health. At least, I guess that's what must have been happening.

I didn't know until later, but Noel had been diagnosed with cancer.

In February 2012, we had a meeting with Abbott and George Brandis, the shadow attorney-general in the Liberal Party, at David Jackson QC's Sydney chambers. In preparation, we'd sought legal advice from Jackson, and were attempting to modify the proposals to address the conservative objections. We altered the non-discrimination provision to become an 'equality before the law' clause, refining the CYI approach the panel had not run with. Noel hoped this would make the proposal more palatable to conservatives.

Jackson's advice approved our revised provision with some minor wording suggestions. He said 'equality before the law' could be a value that Australians could decide should be included in the Constitution, giving us 'lofty ideals' to aspire to. He acknowledged that inevitably litigation would follow, but what's wrong with that? It's part of our constitutional system. (I hadn't yet grasped that no amount of tinkering with a racial non-discrimination clause could address the fundamental conservative objection about giving the High Court power to veto Parliament's discriminatory laws.)

Jackson was to act as mediator and was present at the meeting. I thought I'd be sitting quietly and taking notes while Noel led the advocacy. But when I got to Jackson's chambers in Sydney, Lew told me Noel wasn't coming. I froze. We should cancel the meeting, I said. Lew refused: Noel's instructions were that it should continue. Yet without Noel, I was the only one with knowledge of the reforms and the arguments. And I wasn't well myself. I would be in hospital for a minor operation the following week.

The meeting went ahead. I put my physical discomfort on the backburner for later attention. Brandis and Abbott were understanding of Noel's absence and I focused on the task at hand.

On our side were Mundine, who'd agreed to attend with us, consultants Tony Golsby-Smith and ex-CYI policy team member and Aboriginal advocate Dean Parkin, Lew (Noel's trusted media expert) and me. On their side were Abbott, Brandis and Peta Credlin, Abbott's chief of staff. They had copies of the letter I'd prepared from Noel.

Right off the bat, Abbott and Mundine appeared to be closer than I'd first realised. 'I think you're on the wrong team,' Abbott joked to Mundine, a longstanding Labor man, and all but winked salaciously. Mundine seemed pleased at the overture. This was not starting well.

Jackson gave a rundown of the provisions. Abbott liked the CYI proposed preamble and was especially turned on by the articulation of the three parts of Australia. Abbott and Credlin then began suggesting that the equality principle be included in the preamble, as a symbolic sentiment rather than a substantive legal protection. They started drafting on the fly. To my dismay, Jackson (who, though a terrific legal mind, seemed a less proficient political strategist) joined in: 'in the spirit of equality?' he suggested. *Stop it, mate*, I thought.

Abbott and Brandis agreed with removing section 25—but so what, that would change nothing substantive. They didn't, at that stage, see any reason to amend the race power. And, of course, they were utterly opposed to a racial non-discrimination clause. Minimalists, just like Abbott's email the year prior had indicated.

Though Abbott said he wouldn't 'instinctively' have an issue with equality before the law, he worried the clause would create a 'lawyers' picnic' (endless litigation), placing too much power in the hands of 'activist judges' and taking power away from Parliament. It might have stopped the Northern Territory Intervention, he objected.

And they might not have been able to suspend the *Racial Discrimination Act*—God forbid!

I listened to their arguments, rather stunned.

Abbott was also worried that refugees might mount an argument that they are being racially discriminated against, thus affecting immigration policy. (*Hopefully*, I thought.) Or maybe, gay people might argue for marriage equality, Abbott said. Such a clause went far wider than Indigenous recognition, they objected. It did not address the objective of fixing the Indigenous omission of 1901, and they were concerned that Indigenous people would get trapped in 'the quicksand' of 'broader identity politics' and that the referendum would fail as a result. Therefore, all things considered, they did not support a general equality provision.

In other words: they wanted Parliament to retain its power to discriminate.

To his credit, Jackson tried to interject that equality before the law was a value Australians could support, reassuring them that litigation was a necessary part of our constitutional process that already occurs. He was right, but it was to no avail.

'The glory of our civilisation and culture is that we *instinctively* regard people as equal,' Abbott said, as if that settled the matter. 'We don't need the value of equality in the Constitution. These matters are dealt with by Parliament.' Yet only a few minutes before, Abbott and Brandis, parliamentary representatives themselves, had talked about the need to retain the power to suspend the *Racial Discrimination Act*.

Abbott had conspicuous ears, but did he hear himself? Did they think about the two Aboriginal guys in front of them, men whose ancestors had likely been booted off to missions in chains, told they couldn't vote, told who to marry and paid unequal wages? These laws were clearly made by politicians who, instinctively or otherwise, regarded people as unequal, and enacted unequal laws, under the auspices of a Constitution that contained explicitly unequal and discriminatory race clauses.

I looked at Mundine, dismayed. He wore a puff-lipped grin and seemed to be nodding in agreement with Brandis and Abbott. When

Abbott became prime minister, he would appoint Mundine as his chief adviser on Indigenous affairs, and I could never shake the fear that we'd unwittingly played matchmaker, though in fact Mundine and Abbott had a friendship that dated back to 2008.[6] To my alarm, Golsby-Smith seemed to be nodding at Abbott's and Brandis's arguments too. No one was pushing back. I wished Noel were there.

I spoke, because there was no other choice. 'Okay, you've made your arguments,' I said. 'I'd like the opportunity to respond, if that's okay?'

I argued the history of discriminatory policies and laws, the fact that the majority of Indigenous people want more than just symbolism, the need for a principle of equality that works both ways—against the hard bigotry, but also against the soft bigotry of low expectations. I did the best I could on the fly. Bizarrely, Abbott was writing notes as I spoke. If I've misremembered my arguments, Abbott probably has a better record of them—he wrote it all down.

I allowed myself to argue more animatedly, enjoying the rush of standing up to the big men. Brandis's jowls began to shake. Steam seemed to gather around his ears and his complexion adopted a pinkish hue. He didn't like my arguments and launched a haughty refutation. I recall vigorous theatrical head-wobbling and a steadily increasing pitch. I later read that Brandis had been photographed reading a book of classic Australian poetry in Parliament.[7] Thinking back, I wonder if he was a frustrated thespian after my own heart. 'I don't know who wrote these provisions,' Brandis huffed, looking at me pointedly and crescendoing as he spoke, but that equality clause is 'contrary to the central thesis of the letter!' His last shrill note echoed through the opulent chambers. This was constitutional melodrama at its best.

For a second no one moved. I decided to keep going.

I began addressing their points one by one—for I too had been taking notes. My pushback must have shifted something, because at one point Brandis floated a compromise solution. If the aim was to prohibit discrimination against Indigenous people, why not 'just say that'? He suggested words to the effect of: 'No law of the

Commonwealth, state or territory shall treat a person less favourably than other Australians by reason of him or her being Aboriginal or Torres Strait Islander.' A racial non-discrimination provision that applied to Aboriginal people only. I pointed out the paradoxical nature of the proposition—a non-discrimination provision that is in itself discriminatory. Brandis in any case backed away from the whole idea quickly upon realising it would still be up to judges to decide what is 'favourable'. I tried to pull him back on it, as it seemed like a glimmer of hope (paradoxical or not). But he declared it was not the Coalition's position (even though the Coalition did not have a position, he noted)—he'd realised such a provision would still allow legal challenges to the Intervention and every other Indigenous-specific law. It therefore wasn't going to fly.

Tellingly, Brandis said there were three goals of constitutional recognition:

1. the symbolic element
2. getting rid of obsolete things (cleaning up the race clauses)
3. enshrining rights.

He could support 1 and 2, he said, but not 3. So there it was: the minimalist package outlined in clear-cut terms: a symbolic statement plus getting rid of references to 'race'.

This would not be acceptable to Noel, or to the majority of Indigenous people. I knew that much.

They went immediately on to matters of procedure. They wanted a bipartisan agreement about the mission, before Reconciliation Australia started promoting the panel document. Abbott said he would write a letter to Gillard urging her to wait until the reform package was decided before embarking on any public education campaign.

We said polite goodbyes. On shaking Abbott's hand, I tried to make one last attempt at persuasion. 'The equality guarantee is very important to Noel,' I said. Abbott wouldn't look me in the eye. He was more interested in Mundine and the other men.

CYI was expected to comply. We were expected to submit.

'She had him by the balls,' Lew told Noel after the meeting. I was pleased. I knew I must have done okay, even though I'd lost the argument.

I emailed Noel later, concerned that our efforts at trying to modify the panel's provisions by tinkering with the constitutional drafting to accommodate conservative objections were going to fail. 'There is a risk that we are slowly but surely getting cornered into the Coalition's minimalist "symbolic" position,' I wrote. 'Our negotiations may yield a weak result.'

I also reported Mundine's equivocal behaviour. 'He spent most of the time, in the little he spoke, asserting that he agreed with their arguments around wanting Parliament to retain power, wanting to minimise litigation, wanting to avoid a "legal dog's breakfast",' I emailed. 'He seemed to me very quick to agree with whatever Abbott and Brandis were saying.'

I urged Noel not to hold back on his advocacy for the equality guarantee. I was worried that our efforts at formulating arguments that were appealing to conservatives like Abbott were rendering our positive advocacy impotent. 'We are so busy trying to frame our argument in a way that the conservatives can swallow it, we don't end up coming out and demanding what we really want … it must be demanded by Aboriginal people, in no uncertain terms. They are successfully bullying us, and often I feel I am speaking out of turn, because I am not Aboriginal.' I'd let slip my true underlying concern. I felt I lacked legitimacy and authority to speak on the issue. I worried that I would be dismissed as a crackpot Indian who was verballing Noel. 'They probably think I'm secretly just concerned about my refugee rellies!' I wrote jokingly, thinking of their response to my advocacy for a racial non-discrimination clause. 'I could see Brandis almost rolling his eyes a few times …'

Noel responded from somewhere on the Sunshine Coast, in the midst of dealing with chemotherapy. He must have been feeling terrible, but he engaged with each of my points and gave direction on how to proceed.

He considered how we might get Mundine to 'harden up a bit' with Abbott and Brandis. 'Warren has pitched his flag at the furthest tactically right position,' Noel surmised, 'which puts him in a strong position to drag Abbott a bit more towards the centre.' Problem was, it seemed to me then that Mundine was not interested in substantive constitutional reform. At that stage, he seemed basically a minimalist, like Abbott, though he would shift to more ambitious positions in years to come. Mundine was a self-described 'treaties man' and would show himself to be an influential voice in the debate.

Noel also wrote something that has stuck with me ever since. In response to my concerns about illegitimacy, being a non-Indigenous advocate for Indigenous constitutional recognition, he made his position clear. 'Shireen: Don't hold back on your advocacy in this process,' he wrote. 'You're the one who understands the issues and arguments. You're responsible for the CYI position and you're a player in this process, both on the basis that you're as Australian as anyone, and you're the responsible person within CYI. This is about getting an Australian Constitution right for all Australians, not just between indigenous people and the Anglo-Celts.' Noel concluded our exchange with some encouragement on my legal drafting: 'I'm amazed David Jackson approved your draft of the equality provision without much change! Constitutional drafting might yet be your forte!'

I get teary thinking back on Noel's words. How is it that a guy grappling with his own serious illness could bother offering me such encouragement? His words were the reassurance I needed. I've never forgotten them: Don't hold back on your advocacy ... you understand the issues and arguments ... you're a player in this process ... you're as Australian as anyone ... Noel has never resiled from that position. Not even under great pressure, from both black and white.

Who would have guessed it would take an inspired descendant of the country's original owners to assure me of my place in Australia, as an Australian? I resolved to work hard to achieve the reforms Noel wanted—the reforms he felt his people, and his country, deserved.

5

To the Right and Up

WHILE NOEL WAS sick, I kept advocating the equality guarantee. But the political dynamics were not shifting. I needed Noel's direction. I'd also lived in Cairns for two years by now, and wanted to go home.

My move was sped up by a break-up. Distraught and without close networks up north, I sought the permission of Fiona Jose, a dynamic and intelligent Indigenous leader who was then CYI's CEO, to move back to Melbourne and work from there. She agreed. Melissa Castan also rang, having read my few publications in legal journals advocating a racial non-discrimination clause, and urged me to do a constitutional law PhD under her supervision, together with the supremely brainy legal philosopher Dr Patrick Emerton, at Monash. I used the enrolment as an extra excuse to flee the tropics. At the end of 2012 I left Cairns and returned to Melbourne to work remotely.

My mates rallied around me when I got home and I realised how much I'd missed their company. They helped redecorate my Richmond apartment, promoting a fresh start. We ditched Mum's old brown furniture (to her dismay) and purchased crisp white decor from Ikea. Jason, a fashion designer, painted my chairs a sparky blue. I was ready for 2013.

Noel slowly recovered and came back into action. He and I had dinner with Melissa in Melbourne. Her father, the late Ron Castan QC, had mentored Noel when he was a young lawyer, and the families remained good friends. Ron and Melissa, like many Jewish lawyers (I would come to learn), empathised deeply with the plight of Indigenous Australians, for their people, too, had suffered horrific discrimination. Accordingly, it was often Jewish lawyers who courageously stood up for social justice and Indigenous rights—Mark Leibler, Ron Castan, Jim Spigelman QC and Ron Merkel QC being prime examples among the many. Jewish lawyers fought for Indigenous people during the land rights struggles, stood up for multiculturalism and tolerance in the vicious 18C racial vilification debates, and would back Indigenous people again in the struggle for Indigenous constitutional recognition.

Noel's insight into the need to 'hunt on the right' was gleaned largely from his old mentor Ron. In 1998, in search of a better solution to the *Wik* controversy, Ron had taken Noel to meet the far-right leaders of the Country Liberal Party of the Northern Territory, to discuss a compromise solution: how could Indigenous rights to land be practically and fairly reconciled with pastoralists' rights, which the High Court had said could coexist? To Noel's great surprise, Indigenous leaders were able to find productive common ground with the right-wing pastoralists. They formed an extraordinary agreement that Noel later described as 'substantive and practical, generous towards indigenous concerns and aspirations, and reassuring in the certainty its terms gave to pastoralists'. It was an agreement that 'gave parties on both sides a shared sense of unity, compromise and common purpose'.[1] Noel realised that there might be more common ground between Indigenous people and right-wing Australians than is usually assumed—a lesson he applied in his thinking about Indigenous constitutional recognition.

Over dinner, Melissa, Noel and I looked back on the time since the Expert Panel report. A year in, there was still no official response from government, though both Gillard and Abbott had given speeches supporting the concept of constitutional recognition when enacting the *Aboriginal and Torres Strait Islander Peoples Recognition Act*—basically an Act to set up some committees to progress recognition—on 13 February 2013.

I had been sitting in the balcony at Parliament House when the speeches were delivered. Abbott's was notable for its moral generosity. He rushed into the chamber at the last minute with what looked like hand-scribbled notes. What he said, coming from someone on the far right like him, gave me goosebumps:

> Australia is a blessed country. Our climate, our land, our people, our institutions rightly make us the envy of the earth; except for one thing—we have never fully made peace with the First Australians. This is the stain on our soul that Prime Minister Keating so movingly evoked at Redfern 21 years ago. We have to acknowledge that pre-1788 this land was as Aboriginal then as it is Australian now and until we have acknowledged that, we will be an incomplete nation and a torn people. We have only to look across the Tasman to see how it all could have been done much better. Thanks to the Treaty of Waitangi in New Zealand two peoples became one nation. So, our challenge is to do now in these times what should have been done 200 or 100 years ago: to acknowledge Aboriginal people in our foundation document.[2]

Tony Abbott, using the T-word? I was shocked.

In the years to come Noel and I would be told by people in the know that even uttering the T-word around Liberal and National Party circles could send shockwaves of terror through the Coalition. Yet here was arch-conservative Abbott saying the word himself. Abbott also commended several prime ministers, including many Labor ones, on their efforts towards reconciliation, signalling a bipartisan approach. Perhaps he harboured more goodwill than I thought—just like those conservatives back in 1990s rural Queensland. Maybe Abbott could be our Nixon, despite the bad meeting with Mundine and Brandis the previous year. We just had to persuade him to back substantive reform over mere minimalism.

At dinner, we discussed Abbott's influencers. Professor Greg Craven was one. The 'one-clause bill of rights' catchphrase had been propagated by Craven, and Abbott had adopted it. 'You need to go and meet with him,' Melissa advised. Noel sought out a mutual contact, who helped set up a meeting.

We ran a forum in Cairns at which Noel and I spoke, along with Tim Gartrell. Gartrell was most known for running Kevin Rudd's 'Kevin 07' election-winning campaign. He began as a unionist, then became a Labor ministerial adviser before becoming national secretary of the ALP Secretariat. He later became CEO of market research firm Auspoll, before heading Twiggy Forrest's Indigenous employment charity, GenerationOne. In 2012, Reconciliation Australia employed Gartrell to run Recognise—the government-funded campaign body charged with raising awareness on Indigenous constitutional recognition.

Cape York Institute applied to Recognise for funding to continue our work in the area. The funding received was limited, however, and for six months in 2013 I was forced to go down to part-time hours due to lack of money for my position. I took on work as a casual tutor in Administrative Law at Monash to supplement my income. By now I'd completed my practical legal training and had been admitted as a lawyer to the Victorian Supreme Court—no one could say I wasn't a real lawyer anymore. Uni tutoring assisted in broadening my knowledge.

As time went on, Gartrell grew increasingly wary of my presence. Though I tried my best to work productively with Recognise, I felt I was regularly brushed off. I don't know what the source of their worry was. Perhaps that I wasn't Indigenous. Perhaps that I was a youngish woman and thus was viewed suspiciously. Their attitude wasn't warranted, however. I was just doing my job.

At a Cairns constitutional forum jointly run by CYI and Recognise on 6 February 2013, Noel made his passionate case for Indigenous constitutional recognition. Gartrell talked about the campaign. I talked about the specific constitutional reforms, and a racial non-discrimination clause. At least I think I did. My memory of the day is blurred.

On that same day, Lew Griffiths, Noel's trusted confidant and a stalwart supporter of Indigenous struggles, died suddenly in Cairns. I heard Noel's roar of grief when he was told the news. He disappeared. All the Indigenous people in the room got up one by one to shake the hands of the late Lew's colleagues. I sat, continuing my work, unsure what to do. It didn't seem appropriate to join in the handshaking. I hadn't known Lew as long as the Cape York people who'd worked with him for years. And certainly, I wasn't close to him like Noel was. I left them to their grief and kept to myself. I think my response was probably inappropriate, looking back.

I recall when I was about five, my parents came back from the hospital to inform us that my little brother Neeraj had died. The family were all around, and everyone started crying and hugging. I didn't know what to do, so I ran around doing somersaults on the couches and whooping, probably trying to cheer everybody up. 'It's nothing to be happy about,' the neighbour boy said. I don't think I ever learned how to respond appropriately to tragedy.

Things with Recognise got worse, and it seemed Gartrell was trying to limit my involvement. I was told I was not funded to take part in strategy discussions on how to persuade conservatives—this was Noel's job, together with strategist Mark Textor. Don't interfere with the work of the big men seemed the subtle message. But Noel's instructions were the opposite: I was to work on strategy, advocacy and policy. I carried on, aware of the latent tension emanating from this organisation that was supposed to be an ally.

In May 2013, Recognise kicked off its 'Journey to Recognition' campaign in Melbourne. I remember sitting with Melissa Castan and Marcia Langton on the banks of the Yarra River, explaining the exclusion I felt. Recognise had flown Cape York traditional owners down to Melbourne for the event. They were all going to the Indigenous Round AFL match at the MCG. I wasn't invited. I wondered what I'd done wrong.

On 18 July, we held another seminar for the Cairns public at the Pullman hotel. Professor Megan Davis, Fred Chaney and Noel all spoke. I MC-ed. The room was full and the event was a success. All advocated passionately for a racial non-discrimination clause.

We were plugging away. But I was still worried about Recognise.

I tried to confide in Zoe Ellerman, our hardworking CYI head of policy, and Fiona Jose, our CEO. Both were empathetic and encouraging, but thought maybe I was paranoid. I didn't blame them. I told myself to stop being so sensitive.

My research into right-wing objections was informing both my analysis of the problem at hand and the direction of my PhD research.

In June I cold-emailed Waleed Aly after reading his insightful Quarterly Essay on conservatism. I could tell he was insanely intelligent and wanted his take on our roadblock with conservatives. We met near the ABC Centre at Southbank. He'd been up all night writing; nonetheless he engaged generously with the issue. His advice was clear: he doubted we'd convince them to shift their position. Conservatives are fundamentally cautious about change, he explained. They will not endorse what they view as a radical change to the Constitution. They take the view that the common law system and the parliaments are best placed to effect slow, evolutionary change. 'So how do we persuade them?' I asked. Aly didn't think we could, but wished us luck. It was an enlightening conversation.

I wasn't convinced, however. *There must be a way*, I thought.

I cold-contacted Professor James Allan at the University of Queensland. Allan was strident in his denunciation of the supposedly activist High Court, and had publicly warned of the potential for legal uncertainty that came with constitutional reform. His emails helped clarify the conservative concern. Allan explained his view that the top High Court judges were wayward in their approach to constitutional interpretation. That's why he opposed a racial non-discrimination clause: because it would give those judges greater scope to make mischief. I didn't give up, however, and emailed back:

> Does this mean that if the High Court were different, and had employed the proper method of constitutional interpretation, your view on this issue would be different? You say the High Court

is now wayward. So if the Court was not wayward, would you support the sorts of changes being discussed?

The reason I think it's a bit of a flimsy objection is because Parliament is already bound by a written Constitution that judges must already interpret ... our Constitution gives courts that role. Unless you want to get rid of the Constitution, or courts, altogether ...

I think that it is possible to draft something well. Yes there will still be unknowns, but as you have noted, these exist already with the Constitution as is. What we have to gain though, to me, seems so much more: a legal system that does not treat Australian citizens differently on the improper basis of 'race'.

Politics aside, if you were a lawyer entrusted with this problem-solving task, how would you fix it in the most responsible way possible? I think that is a really interesting question, and I think conservative constitutional lawyers are best placed to answer it!

Allan was not persuaded, despite my unbridled enthusiasm. He said we would have to agree to disagree about the 'flimsiness' of his objection, and drew out the difference in position between Canada and Australia to show how things could go when a Constitution gives judges more licence to creatively make law. He concluded that he did not want Australia to be governed by the 'moral sensibilities' of activist judges.

The exchange was instructive. This was about who decides. Who decides what's right and wrong; who decides what laws are allowed and not allowed—judges or Parliament?

It was becoming clearer why our advocacy for a racial non-discrimination clause was falling on deaf ears with the conservative right. These objectors were not necessarily racist (though some of them may have been). They may or may not have lacked empathy for Indigenous Australians and the history of injustice they'd suffered. Fundamentally, many of these individuals were dead set against further empowering the High Court, and the legal uncertainty this would entail. They wanted Parliament to retain all its power, unchecked and unfettered by unelected judges.

The bottom line: they had faith and trust in the current constitutional system, and particularly Parliament, to deliver good law and policy overall. Indigenous people, understandably given the history, did not. This was the key difference in perspective, the empathetic gap that was proving difficult to bridge.

Meanwhile, however, Brandis appeared to be shifting. A joint committee with senators Brandis, Rachel Siewert of the Greens, and Trish Crossin of Labor was considering the issue and held a roundtable on 30 April 2013. At the roundtable, Brandis seemed to suggest that a racial non-discrimination clause might not be so bad. He preferred an 'unlimited' head of power, he said, 'just like every other section 51 head of power'. 'Head of power' clauses in the Constitution give Parliament its authority to make laws about certain matters. Section 51 of the Constitution gives the Commonwealth Parliament the power to make laws about a variety of things, from taxation to marriages, immigration to external affairs, and Indigenous affairs under section 51(xxvi), the race power, which was amended in 1967. Rather than limiting the head of power, Brandis indicated a preference for a standalone prohibition against discrimination, as proposed in section 116A by the Expert Panel. 'Without committing myself to that view,' he said, responding to an Indigenous advocate, 'from a technical point of view I think that would meet the concern you have.'[3]

I read the transcript and wrote eagerly to Noel: 'we should not give up on non-discrimination just yet. Not when Brandis is turning. Equality before the law is still the *political key* to winning this referendum.' I urged Noel that the equality principle was needed to tie all these reforms together and make them coherent and fair. It was also the reform that would make the most practical difference to Indigenous Australians, I argued.

Brandis may or may not have been shifting. Perhaps he was just pontificating. On a racial non-discrimination clause, conservatives such as Abbott and Craven would likely not shift. And Abbott was soon to be prime minister.

On 16 August 2013, not long before the election that would see Abbott into power, Noel and I caught a taxi to North Sydney, to the Australian Catholic University to meet Professor Greg Craven.

I remember the drive. We were nervous. Craven's language had been so negative and fierce, showing little respect for the intellects on the panel. He had written about our ideas as if they were trash. And now we were going to meet him. Would he blast us? Sneer at us? Would he be racist? Would he dismiss me as some kind of flaky foreign interloper?

I stressed about my clothes beforehand. What could I wear to make me more appealing to this terrifying Catholic arch-conservative? I was still traipsing about like a law student to all the meetings and didn't even own a suit jacket. I knew the image I presented: female, dark skin, long curly hair (which to this day I can't seem to find the motivation to brush), typically dangly earrings. I had PROGRESSIVE written all over me. I ditched the jangly Indian jewellery and attached fake pearls to my lobes, hoping they might soothe something deep in Craven's middle-aged aristocratic psychology. It was worth a shot.

We discussed our approach on the way. 'You lead the meeting, Noel,' I said. He too was more dressed up than usual. No jeans today: shirt and tie. He admitted later he was also scared. 'This is not about making the case,' he advised. 'No advocacy. This is about establishing the relationship.'

Craven greeted us cordially, more genteel than I had imagined from his ferocious columns. The office was plush and elegant, situated in the expensive rooms of the ACU Vice Chancellory. Craven had been on the 'Yes' team with Malcolm Turnbull fighting for a republic referendum but losing in 1999. He was experienced at referendum campaigns and politics, and particularly at referendum defeat. On Indigenous recognition, he was lining up to be on team 'No'—despite being philosophically inclined to support the cause—because he felt the proposed racial non-discrimination clause and other Expert Panel recommendations would lead to legal havoc. They would empower activist judges. And they would fail.

It was this last criticism that annoyed me most. What was it about these influential Catholic commentators (Craven, Abbott, Mundine, later Frank Brennan) and their penchant for omniscient political predictions? While their Catholicism tended to instil an admirable commitment to social justice, it also seemed accompanied by a certain arrogance about their own assessment of politics and future political outcomes. I was baffled: did they have crystal balls or magic mirrors stashed away that no one knew about, perhaps beside their Bibles—or were the political prophecies handed down by God himself? Yet the subtext of the predicted failure was clear: Craven himself, and people like him, would ensure failure with their advocacy and powerful influence. It wasn't just a prediction: it was a threat.

We sat on opulent brown leather couches and were offered cups of tea. There were some pleasantries. Finally the proposed reforms arose. Craven delivered his assessment calmly, soft-spoken, critiquing them as if they were someone else's ideas, not largely mine and Noel's. I don't know if this was a kindness intended to take the heat off us, or if he thought there was no way Noel Pearson, an intelligent and sensible Indigenous leader, could propose such idiotic changes to the Constitution. But Craven was non-confrontational. Indeed, he seemed a thoughtful and considered, wise person—to my surprise.

His position on a racial non-discrimination clause was clear: he felt it would fail abysmally, and took pains to convey how soul-crushing such defeat would be for reform advocates. Such a failure, he said, would also be terrible for the country and for reconciliation.

He went on to explain the kind of 'No' case that would be galvanised. Any reform that handed power to the High Court, or tried to implement a back-door bill of rights, would galvanise concerted opposition from the right, he said. Constitutional conservatives would rally against it, leading to sure defeat. By this stage I already understood the objections: I just didn't agree with them. I was itching to argue and watched Noel for signs of impending pushback. He was listening intently. I stayed quiet.

Craven gave one piece of seminal advice that stuck with us: don't try to do everything in the Constitution. Instead, put the hook into the Constitution, then use that hook to achieve the reforms we want in legislation. He floated the idea of an Act of Recognition, outside the Constitution. A Declaration, as it were. Imagine what could go in that Act, he urged. Perhaps such an Act could achieve much more than could ever be achieved in the Constitution. It was an interesting idea.

The meeting ended cordially. 'This has been very useful,' Noel said. Rapport had been established.

I was angered by Craven's easy dismissal of our key constitutional reform, however, and vented in the taxi back. 'He's saying a racial non-discrimination clause will fail—*he's* the one who's gonna lead the "No" case. He's already started!' I said. 'What about the history of discrimination? These people talk as if Parliament has always done the right thing by Indigenous people. Do they think about why Indigenous people want such a protection?'

Noel was quiet a moment. 'He does have us over a barrel on this racial non-discrimination clause,' he said.

What does that mean? I wondered. I imagined a busty wench with her skirt hoisted up, being bent over a drum by a grunting, be-stubbled sea captain. I googled the phrase later: Americans, evidently, would drape each other over barrels to empty the lungs of drowners (the sea-captain image was right) or to give floggings. It imputed powerlessness. Being at someone else's mercy. That was us.

Craven and his right-wing constituency indeed had us over a barrel. The infuriating thing was that those objectors, in their positions of power, had no need to properly contend with our substantive argument. They didn't need to answer *why* Parliament should be constitutionally allowed to make racist laws. They didn't need to justify their refusal to be held to account to as basic and fair a principle as equality. It was enough to predict referendum failure, with the omnipotent and omniscient confidence that failure would be guaranteed, because they would ensure it.

These were, it seemed to me, the white male custodians of the constitutional status quo, the moral and spiritual descendants of the colonial founding fathers, who in 1901 had shared out power among themselves, and given Indigenous peoples none. They still didn't want to share. The objectors had the power. They knew it. They'd use it to kill the reform proposal.

I later learned that the same political dynamics had played out in the lead-up to the 1967 referendum. Liberal MP Billy Wentworth had proposed a racial non-discrimination clause to ensure that the to-be-modified race power, which would be used to legislate with respect to Indigenous matters, would not be used to discriminate against Indigenous people—or any people. A qualified power was also considered—the same alternative that both George Brandis and, later, the joint parliamentary committee headed by Indigenous Liberal MP Ken Wyatt would toy with unsuccessfully. Prior to the 1967 referendum, the government rejected a racial non-discrimination clause, stating that while such a guarantee would 'provide evidence of the Australian people's desire to outlaw discrimination', it would also 'provide a fertile source of attack on the constitutional validity of legislation'.[4] The proposal fizzled.

A racial non-discrimination clause wasn't part of the referendum proposal in 1967 because of concerns about empowering the High Court. After the Expert Panel, history was repeating itself. Craven's predictions of political failure, as annoying as they were to me at the time, were supported by the historical evidence.

On 13 September 2013, Noel asked me to attend a meeting with him in at the airport lounge in Sydney. He was to meet with Tim Gartrell, Mark Textor and Tanya Hosch, the deputy director of Recognise. I knew Gartrell and had met Hosch a few times, who seemed an imperious Indigenous woman and was intimidating to me back then.

Noel gave me the background on Textor. He'd been John Howard's key pollster: the brains behind Howard's populist use of wedge politics back in the 1990s, having learned the tricks of the trade working under Ronald Reagan's far-right strategist, Richard Wirthlin. Textor imported these tactics into Australian politics during the Howard era. At the time, Noel had slammed him for fanning the flames of racism, rightly so, and Textor had smarted—he'd been copping a lot of criticism for his ruthless tactics. Noel's theory was that Textor now harboured a desire to make up for his past sins, particularly in relation to provoking racism against Indigenous people.

He thought Textor was a crucial player, key to winning over the Coalition on substantive constitutional recognition.

I'd met Textor with Noel a few times before: he came across more clown than evil genius. He evidently enjoyed theatrics and would leap to his feet to mimic a politician or act out a point. He seemed like a decent guy, I thought.

The meeting was strange. It was me, Noel, Gartrell, Hosch, Textor and Textor's adviser. First off the bat, Gartrell told me pointedly that any notes I was taking must not be emailed to anyone. He didn't say this to the others—it was directed at me only. I put my pen down and didn't write anything, thanking God, yet again, for the surplus melanin hiding my shame. What did they think I would do? Leak to the press? (The irony is not lost on me that I'm writing reflectively on this meeting now, four years later—from memory, not notes. Given all that has happened, I feel the real story must be told.)

There was some talk of Brandis and Indigenous Affairs Minister Nigel Scullion possibly shifting their position in favour of a racial non-discrimination clause. I nodded enthusiastically. Textor and Gartrell seemed to think the Coalition might be persuadable.

But at this point Noel sighed deeply. They stopped talking. He explained to them that he'd spoken to Craven. 'That meeting was really a cold shower for me,' he said. 'We are not going to be able to convince them on a racial non-discrimination clause. It's not going to fly.'

My heart sank. Was Noel giving up? What did it mean? Minimalism?

He pulled out a serviette and started drawing diagrams, as he often does, trying to convey his analysis of the political picture. Gartrell interrupted to suggest the advisers leave the room for this high-level strategy discussion. He looked at me. 'Oh,' I said, heart pounding. Big Brother had spoken. I got up to leave. Textor's adviser got up too, though it seemed I was the problem, not him. Noel stayed silent. I couldn't read his face.

I left and sat in the lounge with Textor's man, discussing drafting options for the contentious clause. I hid it, but felt humiliated. Rightly or wrongly, I felt I'd been kicked out so my work could be rejected. So they could plot a minimalist proposal without my overambitious and naive interference. I felt dumb and inept, and worried I'd lost Noel's support.

The meeting ended and I flew back to Melbourne, but I didn't hear anything more about what had happened until the next day, Saturday. Noel called in the morning. 'Strange meeting,' he said.

'Yep,' I said, still smarting. The impending capitulation had me gutted. How was I supposed to work on a minimalist proposal? What would be the point? Drafting a miserable symbolic preamble and nothing else would be unutterably boring! I was already thinking about quitting.

'I rang Gartrell,' Noel continued. 'I had a go at him for making you leave the room. I told him he can't tell *me* who I'm allowed to bring to a meeting.'

I felt some smidgen of relief. But there was still the substantive issue: our reforms. 'So what did you guys decide? What was the outcome?' I asked.

Noel sighed deeply. 'We are not going to get these conservatives over the line with a racial non-discrimination clause. They have us over a barrel. They will kill the thing. It is not going to work. I told them this was my view,' he said.

I was devastated, and found myself grasping at straws. 'I would just urge, Noel, that constitutional reform has to deliver something tangible for Indigenous people,' I said. 'If it's just minimalism, it might be a feel-good win. But what would it mean in the long run for Aboriginal people? Right now there are leaders like you who can fight for change and better outcomes. But what about when you're gone? Will the next generation be in a better position after this reform? What's the legacy you're leaving for future generations?'

'Yeah, minimalism is not the solution,' Noel said, and I was flooded with relief.

Then came the challenge: 'What I need you to do, Shireen, is take an Apollo 13 look at the whole problem. I mean go into outer space and look at the problem from a completely different perspective, from the other side of the universe, from a new and different angle. We need to come up with an alternative solution. Our challenge is to step to the right and up—this is what I told Gartrell and them. I drew this diagram. Wait, I'll send it ... Hang on, I'll call you back.'

That morning, Noel sent me a single PowerPoint slide. It was a graph depicting a narrow window of constitutional opportunity. Left and right were on the horizontal axis. Great and bad were on the vertical axis.

He rang again to explain. 'If it's too far to the left, conservatives won't support it and it'll fail, see? But if it's too minimalist, and sinks too low, Indigenous people won't support it and it'll fail. The panel's proposals, in hindsight, were too far to the left. We need to figure out how to step to the right and up. To move to something great, not minimalist, a proposal that truly excites Indigenous people, but that allows Nixon to go to China. A proposal the right can support too. We need to find the radical centre on this problem. So that's what you need to think about.'

That's what my job became. Figuring out how to step to the right and up.

6

In Search of the Radical Centre

I WENT ON A spy mission to the Samuel Griffith Society, the organisation of right-wing constitutional conservatives chaired by former High Court judge Ian Callinan. Together with Dyson Heydon, Callinan had been one of the most conservative members of the court. The motto of the Samuel Griffith Society is 'Upholding the Australian Constitution'. My aim in attending was to discern the key players we needed to get on board, to figure out how to step to the right and up.

The November 2013 conference was at the North Sydney Rydges hotel. I was immediately struck by the demographic: predominantly old white men. Wrinkled, pale and bent was the look. War medals and walking sticks.

I couldn't help but feel nervous. Gary Johns was giving a speech on Indigenous recognition, and I'd read his opinion pieces. He had been an elected member of the Labor Party until he lost his seat in 1996. He then drifted to the far right, working with the Institute of Public Affairs and the Bennelong Society, which advocated paternalistic and, in my view, prejudiced approaches to Indigenous issues. I'd read Johns' opinions on Indigenous recognition and found his arguments disconcertingly bigoted—not to mention illogical. Recognise alerted us that

Johns was speaking, which is why I went: know thy enemy, I figured. Recognise said they'd send someone along too, but there was no one I spotted. A sprightly young 'R' campaigner would have stuck out.

I would have stuck out too. In this crowd, people under fifty were scarce, women were even more scarce, and non-white people were scarcest of all. I don't know what those conservatives thought of me—the younger, dark-skinned imposter prattling uncontrollably about constitutional reform and Indigenous people to anyone who'd listen. I wonder if some secretly turned down their hearing aids to tune me out over those lunches and dinners. Some engaged in vibrant discussion. Others suffered me politely.

An exception to the age demographic was the young-looking Julian Leeser, constitutional arch-conservative and Jewish-Australian lawyer, a former Menzies Research Centre executive director and now convenor of the Samuel Griffith Society conference. Dressed in impeccable suit and spectacles, Leeser was obsessed with the Australian Constitution. Seriously obsessed. On his tenth birthday he asked his parents 'not for a BMX bike or a cricket bat' but for a copy of the Constitution. 'I think the Latin term for such behaviour is nerdus maximus,' he joked in his maiden speech to the Australian Parliament in 2016, three years later.[1] The self-deprecation prompted warm-hearted guffawing in the audience. I was there at Parliament House that day, with his many multicultural constituents, friends and family. Leeser had invited me and I was, by this stage, a fan. I observed him to be a consummate politician with a good heart.

To say Leeser took the Samuel Griffith Society motto dead seriously is an understatement. He loved the Constitution. He loved it passionately. And he loved it just the way it was.

Accordingly, Leeser was a prominent constitutional defender who had successfully fought against many attempts at reform. In 1998 as a committed constitutional monarchist, he led the 'No' case that vanquished the push for a republic—defeating Malcolm Turnbull and Greg Craven's 'Yes' campaign. In 2009, he helped defeat an Australian bill of rights—to keep the unelected judges at bay. In 2013, he led what was in his own words a 'scrappy but successful insurgency'[2] against Labor's attempted local government referendum (WA Liberal senator and constitutional conservative Dean Smith gave a speech on this defeat at the conference).

One might have expected Leeser, being a zealous constitutional upholder, to be wary of me, the upstart wannabe constitutional reformer. But he was polite and welcoming. He shook my hand and then, pulling me aside, offered a private warning. 'You might hear some not very nice things said about Aboriginal people at this conference, Shireen,' he said. I looked nervously at the bustling crowd of grey-suited men. 'I just want you to know we're not all like that. And I'm not like that.'

It was an unexpected and welcome kindness. I'd been regularly opting to hide in the toilets, due to sporadically faltering confidence. I was never very good at networking with strangers, let alone a throng I feared may harbour prejudices about someone like me, not to mention my absent Aboriginal boss. But Leeser's comment steeled my nerve. I resolved to seek out the good-hearted conservatives, of which he (I then suspected) was one.

He was right to warn me, however. Racism was a vivid and largely accepted part of the discourse at this conference.

Gary Johns, in his address on Indigenous constitutional recognition, recounted violent crimes by Aboriginal perpetrators and read out harrowing statistics on violence in Aboriginal communities, using such examples as the basis of his argument against any constitutional recognition of Indigenous culture. He spoke in a stilted, deliberate cadence—almost as if restraining himself from saying much worse. Aboriginal culture had a 'genius' for 'surviving in isolation', he said. 'Any more complimentary description than that, however, is, with great respect, gilding the lily. Hunter-gatherer societies were among the most violent societies in human history. Australian Aborigines were no exception to the rule. To preserve a violent culture would seem wholly unsavoury.'[3] At this point the old men, who had been grumbling in quiet approval, let out a triumphant 'Hear, hear!'

Johns' message was clear: there is no point recognising a culture that has only violent and negative traits. I cringed at his argument's blatant prejudice. Ancient British culture was violent too—indeed, there was extensive violence perpetrated throughout colonisation—but that doesn't stop Australia cherishing its British history and heritage. For this crowd, bloodshed wrought by British swords and guns, if acknowledged at all, would likely be viewed as chivalrous and heroic. Bloodshed wrought by spears and clubs, however, was barbaric and to be condemned—notwithstanding the fact that white people's superior weapons facilitated far more efficient mass killing, which is what made their colonisation so successful. Yet here were these old white men calling Indigenous people violent.

Johns was evidently trying to revive his career, which had begun on the left, by dog-whistling to the hard right. He had to go *far* right to prove his credentials—like the born-again Christian who hams up their evangelism to prove their bona fides to fellow believers. Johns was in favour of a one-line historic statement in a new preamble—a super-minimalist model (indeed, a 'Why bother?' model)—but nothing else.

He also warned that if we recognised Indigenous culture in the Constitution, it would lead to more lenient criminal sentences for Indigenous perpetrators, based on the argument that Aboriginal culture should be respected. It was a weak proposition but, unconstrained by logic, fed more freely on imagination and fear. The recounting of Aboriginal violence had its desired effect—it conjured a sense of disgust and loathing for Aboriginal people, to make the idea of their recognition seem absurd. Though ostensibly about unintended legal consequences, Johns' speech had a barely disguised subliminal message: these people are simply not worthy of recognition.

His dog whistle resonated, and the dogs howled back.

A former National Party senator for Queensland stood to declare his passionate agreement with Johns. 'What have Aboriginal people ever contributed to Australia? They are a Stone Age culture, who were basically wiped out. No trace of their culture remains in Australia. So what are we recognising?'

No trace? *What about their boomerangs, art, languages and songs?* I thought. *What about the word kangaroo, taken from the Guugu Yimithirr word* gangurru? *Or the ancient songlines that are still practised today?* I wondered about speaking up, but stayed silent.

The former politician went on to agree that Indigenous culture should not be recognised because it was a violent hunter-gatherer culture of little worth. His disdain for Indigenous people was savage, yet he was oblivious to the uncivilised, caveman-like thuggery he himself was demonstrating. I thought of Gandhi, who, when asked what he thought of Western civilisation, replied: 'I think it would be a very good idea.' The former politician was red-faced and spitting with hatred. He all but called for Aboriginal scalps.

Not all the speakers were so atrocious.

Damien Freeman was an eccentric-looking young philosopher and writer, a Jewish lawyer and reverent monarchist like Leeser (and, I'd later learn, his close friend). With bobbing curls, bow tie and waistcoat, and rainbow socks glinting out from under shortened grey trousers, he reminded me of a spritely Gene Wilder playing Willy Wonka in *Willy Wonka & the Chocolate Factory*. Damien was jaunty and fabulous, yet formal and conservative at the same time. A lecturer in aesthetic and art philosophy at Cambridge University, he was the kind of conservative I thought I could like. He gave an eloquent but cryptic speech advocating a Declaration of Recognition instead of constitutional alteration—like America's Declaration of Independence, carrying cultural and moral power but sitting outside the Constitution. I recalled Craven's similar idea. *Interesting*, I thought.

Craven spoke too, about federalism, advocating a statement of 'the ethics of federalism' that could be passed in a symbolic Act or document with the concurrence of all the states. It sounded similar to the Declaration of Recognition he thought could be enacted by all Australian parliaments and got me wondering: if there were a similar Act or Declaration on, say, the ethics of reconciliation, enacted by all Australian parliaments, and Indigenous peoples assented to the Act through a representative body, that might in essence be quite like a treaty—depending on its contents, of course.

Leeser, who worked for Craven at ACU, suggested something similar but different during a lunchbreak chat—a document containing five simple historical statements about Indigenous peoples that would have symbolic and moral force. Freeman, Leeser and Craven seemed to be thinking along similar lines.

As I got to know him in the months to come, Leeser came to represent in my mind the epitome of constitutional conservatism. When it came to the High Court, he was the most paranoid person I encountered in my seven years working at Cape York Institute. I imagined him in fitful sleep, clutching his dog-eared copy of the Constitution, addled by nightmares of unelected judges misusing uncertain constitutional words. Leeser was the benchmark: the good-hearted conservative, non-racist, and genuinely concerned to uphold the Constitution. Though he was in principle a supporter of Indigenous recognition and empathetic towards Indigenous causes, he opposed a racial non-discrimination clause and the insertion of uncertain poetry in his beloved rulebook, because he didn't want to further empower the High Court.

If we could win Leeser's support, that would be a good indication that we'd addressed constitutionally conservative concerns and had successfully stepped to the right and up. The challenge was: how might Noel and I, would-be constitutional reformers, find common ground with this dedicated constitutional upholder, and with people like him? Where might the synthesis of our competing concerns lie?

Esteemed constitutional law professor Anne Twomey from Sydney University spoke about states' rights under the Constitution. I noted the way the audience respected the voices and intellects of Freeman, Craven, Leeser and Twomey, who, unlike Johns, said nothing even remotely racist.

There were two kinds of conservatives at this gathering, I surmised: rational, genuine, good-hearted conservatives, and those who used conservatism as a smokescreen for their irrational bigotry. The serious conservatives seemed to be lending the racists their legitimacy. But perhaps there was a way to sort the wheat from the chaff—to bring the genuine conservatives on board by addressing their rational concerns, leaving the bigots isolated and exposed.

I wrote to Noel after the conference:

Hi Noel,
Conference this weekend was enlightening (and depressing) …
There is a lot of genuine racism. But there are also elements

that are interested in what we are trying to do and want to help us ...

I suggest we find ways to work with this group to workshop our package so that it is acceptable to both sides ...

I have joined the Society in order to infiltrate them as much as possible!

Shireen

I discovered something weird about myself at my first Samuel Griffith Society conference. I enjoyed talking to people with polar-opposite views to my own. I enjoyed arguing, challenging and persuading them, and sometimes getting them to like me. I enjoyed bringing them round and finding a compromise. And even when they didn't come round, I kind of enjoyed that too.

We identified Twomey, a highly respected black-letter lawyer, as the star legal mind. In February 2014, Noel and I met her at Sydney Uni. She agreed to help us with legal advice in our development of an alternative set of constitutional reforms that might address the concerns of Indigenous advocates as well as the concerns of constitutional conservatives.

I started working on a paper exploring the ideas Craven had raised—an Act or Declaration outside the Constitution, to give effect to the symbolic statements—plus the constitutional and legislative reforms Noel and I wanted to include as part of the package. What structural reforms might hang from the hook in the Constitution? And what was the hook itself?

I was thinking through whether the Act could be semi-entrenched by being enacted with the concurrence of all Australian parliaments. I was also exploring whether the Indigenous power might incorporate a requirement that Indigenous people be consulted in laws made about them. The idea of an Indigenous representative body had arisen in my conversations with Noel. I was trying to figure out how to ensure such a body wouldn't be struck down, like the Aboriginal and Torres Strait Islander Commission (ATSIC) had been.

In March, I met with Craven on my own, to get his feedback on the alternative ideas in development. We met at his Melbourne office, where the walls are beautifully painted with Christian art. I'd emailed him my draft paper. 'Did you write it?' he asked, after reading it. I told him I had. He nodded approvingly. 'Who taught you constitutional law?' he asked.

'Melissa Castan at Monash,' I replied.

Craven looked nonplussed. 'Well, she taught you very well,' he said politely. As a constitutional conservative, or 'con con' as Craven dubbed them, he was probably nervous I'd been taught by such a human rights progressive. 'I assume you are on the left, politically?' Craven asked me at one point in our meeting. He saw through the fake pearls, evidently.

'Depends on the issue,' I replied ambiguously—which was probably accurate. On welfare reform and alcohol management, I tended towards conservatism. On a racial non-discrimination clause, my outlook was obviously progressive. Yet my position was not so simple.

If Noel's radical centre philosophies were a dialectical synthesis of Adam Smith's self-interest-driven liberalism on the one hand and Johann Herder's patriotic cultural conservatism on the other, perhaps I could be the constitutional love child of Castan and Craven: progressive constitutional ambition tempered by hard-headed constitutional conservatism. Castan, following in her father's footsteps, had taught me to think of the law as a tool to assist those who are oppressed and disempowered—traditionally progressive causes. But from Craven I was learning about political realism and the importance of constitutional caution. I'd had a progressive teacher at uni; now here was my conservative one. I was enjoying the balance. Rights *and* responsibilities, ambitious yet sensible, or, as Craven would say of the reforms we would in coming months co-design, 'modest yet profound'. Finding the radical centre was all about finding common ground where you expected there to be none, bringing together the best of competing philosophies to uncover the hidden congruence—the hidden brilliant idea that synthesises competing concerns.

Craven was generous and encouraging, and gave thorough and detailed feedback on my draft paper. He made three preliminary points. First, there is probably only one model (accepting minor variations) that is going to succeed at a recognition referendum—not like the republic debate, where a variety of models might have succeeded. Later, I realised how accurate this prediction was. There was indeed only one model capable of succeeding: it wasn't a racial non-discrimination clause, and it wasn't a minimalist model, so what was it going to be? Second, Craven advised that the success of the referendum would turn on constitutional politics, not constitutional law or technicalities. Third, he had learned from the republic referendum that complexity entails opposition and thus failure. So: keep it simple.

On the idea of an Indigenous representative body to have input into Indigenous affairs—a longstanding theme in Indigenous advocacy for self-determination—Craven initially took some pushing. He urged us to leave it for later, after achieving the extra-constitutional Declaration. I resisted that suggestion. I said it needed to be part of a package deal, because if Indigenous people gave up a racial non-discrimination clause, they needed to get something decent in its place, some substantive reform. They wouldn't accept minimalism. He conceded the point. Eventually Craven said he personally would not be opposed to a body to review laws and make recommendations—like an Aboriginal Law Reform Commission, he said, getting clearer in his own mind on what was proposed. But while he could support a body, we'd need to test Abbott, he advised. He also encouraged us to meet with Leeser, who was close to Abbott.

He issued a warning, too: 'Just note that Abbott, like myself, might be a bit overoptimistic about this referendum. He and I are both Catholic, so we are concerned about social justice and have more compassion than some other conservatives. Make sure you get other people's advice as well.'

Not all Catholics are the same, though, as things turned out. Just like not all Indians or Indigenous people are the same. As the years passed, I came to see Craven as a true man of principle and a man of his word. A steadfast ally who was indeed highly compassionate.

Some Catholics are more compassionate than others, however.

Noel and I crossed the bridge to North Sydney a second time, this time to meet Julian Leeser at ACU. Leeser brought his old friend Damien Freeman.

They kicked off the meeting presenting to us a paper they'd prepared on how Indigenous recognition should be achieved—it called for a Declaration outside the Constitution. I was somewhat taken aback. We'd asked for the meeting, and here they were presenting their predetermined solution before we'd even had a conversation.

Their favoured symbolic Declaration would be like the Declaration of Independence. Inspiring poetry. Richer than any preamble. But they just didn't seem get it: how would a Declaration fix anything practical for Indigenous people? How would it empower them? How would it prevent discriminatory laws? Where was the substantive reform?

Noel sat silently, leaving me to ask the hard question. 'A Declaration sounds okay, but what about the Constitution?' I asked. 'Indigenous people are looking for more than just symbolism. They're looking for serious constitutional reform: some kind of guarantee that they'll be treated more fairly than in the past.'

Leeser and Freeman were supporters of Howard, and Howard had proposed a preamble, was their reply. They were also supporters of Abbott, which is why they were trying to find a sensible solution and didn't want to oppose it—because Indigenous recognition was Abbott's project. They wanted to make it happen without damaging his reputation, and also without damaging the Constitution.

With Howard and Abbott as their only frame of reference, it was unsurprising that for Leeser and Freeman this seemed just about symbolism. They hadn't yet properly considered Indigenous views.

I told them about the history of Indigenous advocacy, and pushed the need for substantive reform to address Indigenous concerns. In response, they raised the usual arguments against a racial non-discrimination clause: unelected judges, activist High Court, Parliament must be supreme. Noel listened all the while.

I started getting frustrated. They had a completely different and, in my view, seriously impoverished understanding of the problem we were trying to solve. We ran out of time and ended with no common ground achieved. 'Why were you so quiet?' I asked Noel in the taxi back.

'I was fighting the urge to blast them,' he said. 'I think you need to keep engaging. Without me. It might go better if I'm not there. Maybe they were showing off a bit in front of me, not wanting to concede anything?'

I asked for a follow-up meeting with just me. Leeser and Freeman agreed.

This time I allowed myself more dramatic persuasion. It got more heated. Freeman and I started to clash. Leeser stayed cool. Then I made a plea about perspective: 'You have to try to understand where Indigenous people are coming from here, guys. Try to develop some empathy. Understand *why* they are asking for substantive reform. Don't just dismiss what they're saying. Indigenous people are not stupid or crazy ...'

Freeman seemed to take offence at this. 'We're not saying they're stupid or crazy,' he interjected. 'If that's the way you're going to characterise what we're saying, you won't get very far.'

I pressed on. 'You are, actually. You're dismissing what Indigenous people are asking for, instead of thinking about *why* they might *rationally* be asking for constitutional reform. Why do you think they're asking for a racial non-discrimination clause?' Leeser and Freeman looked at each other. They weren't sure. 'Because the Constitution has allowed laws and policies that have treated them so unfairly,' I said. 'Because they were carted off to missions in chains, because they were told they couldn't vote, because they had their kids taken away, because they were paid unequal wages. Because the Constitution enabled them to get treated like dirt ...'

Something started shifting for Freeman. A light bulb flickered on. There was a moment of pause. 'I suppose I see what you're saying,' he said slowly. 'I guess in a sense, Indigenous people are looking for a guarantee that the future will be better than the past ... in the same way the Jews might seek a guarantee that the Holocaust doesn't happen again.'

Breakthrough.

Suddenly there we were: human beings seeing an issue from other human beings' points of view. Empathy. Leeser stayed silent, thinking hard.

'Help us find another way,' I urged. 'A different reform that gives Indigenous people the fairer go they seek, but that doesn't ignite the concerns you raise about the High Court.'

The conversation was more productive after that. We went on to discuss the possibility of a more limited non-discrimination clause—still wouldn't fly, as it still empowered judges. I'd covered this terrain already with Abbott and Brandis. Then we discussed a power qualified with a word like 'benefit' or 'advancement'—no chance, same problem. What about an Indigenous power that referred to an Act, I suggested. And what if the Act set up an Indigenous body? Like a guarantee of consultation? Seemed uncertain.

Leeser said he'd have no problem with an Indigenous body set up in legislation. Okay, I said, but what about the constitutional guarantee? That's why we are thinking about constitutional reform, after all.

We went around in circles, discussing possibilities. But something had broken through. Now we were problem-solving together. Australians who shared empathy for Indigenous people, and the Indigenous predicament. Australians who wanted to see Indigenous people guaranteed a fairer go.

I was told that Tim Gartrell had called CYI to raise concerns about me. He'd rung to ask why they didn't have an Indigenous person in my role, instead of me—the white male campaign director of Recognise, the government organisation campaigning for Indigenous constitutional recognition, called an Indigenous organisation to suggest they shouldn't be employing a non-Indigenous Australian.

At the time, I couldn't find words to adequately explain the offensiveness of Gartrell's apparent complaint. I have found them now: it was a combination of hypocrisy, chauvinism and political correctness gone so mad that it needed a white politics whiz to advise my

Indigenous bosses on the appropriate way to be politically correct. That is, it's okay for a white man to work on Indigenous recognition—indeed, to head up a multimillion-dollar public campaign on Indigenous recognition—but an Indian-Australian woman should, ideally, not even be an adviser in the process. It was bizarre.

'What ethnicity are you, Tim?' was the question fired back by my superiors.

I was deeply rattled. If there was one thing I was sure of about myself, it was that I was a diligent and hard worker. I took all my instructions from Noel and executed them to the best of my ability. I took pride in my work, and it was hurtful to hear that big boss Gartrell seemed to want me out.

It also seemed wrong in principle. While I was all for getting as many Indigenous people into employment and advocacy as possible, shouldn't Indigenous people and organisations also be able to hire whoever they want? Recognise might have been funding our constitutional recognition work at that time, but why was some white guy from an external organisation trying to tell CYI, run by Noel and Fiona, how to manage their affairs?

Noel told Gartrell off, further souring the already guarded relationship. Noel commented to colleagues later: 'If Shireen was a white man advising on Indigenous issues, no one would think twice.' It was true. No one objected to Gartrell, Mark Textor, Mark Leibler, Henry Burmester, Frank Brennan, George Williams or the multitude of other qualified and intelligent white male lawyers and political gurus who were regularly sharing their knowledge, input and opinions for the cause. So why did they object to me?

Partly, it was a boys' club. But partly, it was the established Indigenous affairs culture: almost as if you needed to be either coloniser or colonised, but nothing in between, to have a valid legal or political view. Yet where was the wisdom in Indigenous people getting legal and political advice predominantly from the direct descendants of the original oppressors? Wasn't it fundamentally a conflict of interests? Surely a more objective third party—the descendant of a random mix of Indians, for example—was a better choice? I smiled dumbly at the thought. The silly musing was little consolation.

The Recognise people should have been allies. We should have been working together to achieve a good result for Indigenous people, and for Australia. I deeply regret this conflict, which ended up lasting years, because we might have done better in the end had our powers been combined from the start. Instead, we were fighting among ourselves, wasting time trying to get each other sacked.

The Indigenous leadership at CYI stuck up for me, though. And after this debacle, Noel resolved that we could no longer be affiliated with Recognise. So long as I had his support, I carried on.

Damien Freeman and I started to become friends. We began to call each other regularly to talk about ideas. I shared with him the draft paper I'd discussed with Craven. He took to commenting on my work and helping me think through concepts and arguments. He was a smart guy and became a mentor.

I was still grappling with whether you could use a semi-entrenched Act, outside the Constitution, to ensure that an Indigenous representative body would be more stable than the legislative bodies of the past that were abolished as soon as governments changed, or as soon as they became politically unfashionable.

Then one day Damien and I had an extraordinary conversation. He rang me and we repeated the points about the need for stability for the body, the need for a guarantee for Indigenous people that the future would be fairer than the past. 'Why don't you put the body in the Constitution, if you want it to be guaranteed?' he said.

I was taken aback. Damien was an obsessive constitutional conservative—the guy who, when we first met, had not even understood why Indigenous people were seeking constitutional reform or constitutional guarantees. Yet he had now proposed a solution I never imagined might be acceptable to him and his constituency. That's why I was tinkering around with semi-entrenchment—because I'd assumed constitutional entrenchment would be a bridge too far for these right-wingers.

I was wrong. About Damien at least.

'Would there be a way to constitutionally guarantee a body that doesn't empower the High Court?' I asked, barely able to contain my excitement. 'Because that is the main issue—you "con cons" don't want to empower the High Court to strike down laws.'

'Maybe there is a way,' Damien said. 'It could be a clause saying Parliament must set up an Indigenous body, I suppose. That would be far simpler than semi-entrenchment.'

'This is going to require a complete rethinking,' I declared. I got off the phone and danced around my living room. I'm pretty sure I whooped out loud.

I called Noel. 'You'll never guess what Damien just said to me ...' I filled him in. 'So maybe you can have a constitutionally guaranteed body, then a Declaration outside the Constitution, which could—depending on content—be something akin to a treaty? And, you know, a settlements commission operating under it, set up in legislation?'

Noel listened intently. 'You need to organise a trip to New Zealand, asap,' he said.

7

Forging the 'Con Con' Alliance

Forging common ground between parties of oppositional views usually requires both parties to shift. The shift can be small but profound, and requires an intellectual and emotional journey that presents the other party with a different and compelling way of looking at a shared problem. The persuasion often becomes an exchange: in getting them to see your point of view, you come to see theirs. Building empathy across political, ideological and cultural divides. That was my favourite part of trying to forge consensus with the right.

The process at its best felt like reconciliation in action. A shared journey of discovery.

In June 2014, CYI obtained government funding for a research trip to New Zealand, to investigate the ways Maori are recognised in New Zealand's constitutional arrangements.

The delegation included Cape York Aboriginal and Torres Strait Islander woman and CYI's CEO Fiona Jose; Bardi man from saltwater country on the Dampier Peninsula and CEO of the Kimberley Land Council Nolan Hunter; the boy who began at Brewarrina mission and as a man became CEO of Darkinjung Local Aboriginal Land Council, Sean Gordon; Cambridge philosopher and director of the governor-general's constitutional essay prize at the Constitution Education Fund Australia Damien Freeman (Noel's brainwave); and me. The five of us went for a week, visiting Wellington, Hamilton and Auckland. I prepared a research/briefing paper, booked the meetings and organised the schedule.

The trip was jam-packed full of meetings and learning opportunities. Sean has never since let me forget how much I crammed in. I exhausted everyone.

On recognition and reconciliation, we found New Zealand was miles ahead of Australia. Maori were richly, inclusively and substantively recognised in the national and institutional life of their nation. And it wasn't just about symbolism. In New Zealand, Maori recognition was expressed through working structures, processes and democratic systems. New Zealand taught us that Indigenous recognition is not just a static thing. It is not just a statement or a 'plaque' or a preamble that makes people feel good. It's a process. It's operational. A big part of Maori recognition in New Zealand occurs through political representation, through having a voice in the systems governing the nation and in their affairs.

First, there was the Treaty of Waitangi, which was signed between Maori and the Crown in 1840. It established principles of partnership and biculturalism in the relationship between Maori and the Crown, which is seen as New Zealand's founding constitutional relationship. The day the treaty was signed is celebrated as Waitangi Day, New Zealand's national day. In contrast to Australia, where our national day commemorates a unilateral moment of British-asserted dominance that excluded, ignored and dispossessed Indigenous peoples, New Zealand's national day commemorates a moment of partnership and peacemaking. As Abbott described somewhat romantically in his 2013 speech, the signing of the Treaty of Waitangi was the moment 'two peoples became one nation'.

New Zealand has also had specific Maori representation in Parliament, through dedicated Maori seats, since the 1860s. The seats have come to be seen as an extension of treaty partnership principles. There is also the Maori Council, which grew from the Maori Parliament movement—a consultative and representative body for Maori people, empowered under legislation to advise government on Maori affairs.

New Zealand has embraced settlements and agreement-making between Maori and the Crown to redress historical grievances and breaches of the treaty. The Crown has committed to resolving all settlements, which include cash compensation (though the Crown admits this can only ever be nominal), documenting of history, return of land and cultural recognition. Settlements also include a formal Crown apology for wrongs done. The cathartic settlements process enabled truth-telling about history, allowing both parties to have their views heard, to come to terms with the past, and agree on a stronger partnership for the future. We were lucky to visit a settlement signing ceremony, replete with Maori song and dance, that was a joyous occasion of tears and healing. The Crown Apology was read out by the attorney-general in both Maori and English. These moments of reconciliation and recognition were evidently taken seriously.

Perhaps the most impressive aspect of Maori recognition in New Zealand was the way the nation incorporates and celebrates Maori heritage and culture as New Zealand's heritage and culture. The *Maori Language Act* recognises Maori as an official language of New Zealand and set up the Maori Language Commission to promote and revitalise Maori language. New Zealand rugby teams proudly perform the haka, which is embraced as a national expression of New Zealand culture (compare the way some Australians reacted when Adam Goodes performed a two-second Aboriginal war dance on the Aussie Rules football field). New Zealand has also embraced dual place-naming, which flows from the settlements as a form of cultural recognition. The nation itself now carries its Maori name: Aotearoa.

By the time we met Chris Finlayson, then New Zealand's attorney-general for the liberal-conservative National Party, we had been blown away by the difference in attitude and political culture in matters of Indigenous rights and reconciliation. 'How is it that New Zealand's political culture is so much more open and positive towards Indigenous rights?' I asked. 'In Australia conservatives are scared to utter the word "treaty". How is it that your conservative government championed the process?'

I was thinking about Nixon going to China. Stepping to the right and up.

Finlayson said he viewed the Treaty of Waitangi settlements process as deeply aligned with conservative values. Fair compensation shows respect for the rule of law, he said. Which made sense: if the Crown does not make good on past breaches of its treaty promises, what does that say about Crown accountability? It also shows respect for property rights, Finlayson explained—a deeply conservative value. If the Crown respects property rights, then Maori property rights should be respected, and justice must be done where people's property rights have been undermined.

Damien sat next to me, nodding quietly. Conservative values supporting a treaty. Supporting compensation and just redress. I was staggered at the sheer difference in attitude.

We met Sir Edward Durie, co-chairman of the Maori Council, the first Maori appointed as a justice of the High Court of New Zealand and a leading legal expert on the Treaty of Waitangi, together with Donna Hall, an experienced Maori affairs lawyer, who is married to Durie. Hall is a fiery woman. She noted Nolan Hunter's baldness—the bald black man was usually the 'big man' of the tribe, it seemed. Hall's sassy commentary reminded us of Marcia Langton's cynicism regarding black men in their black hats. Amusingly for us, however, the gentle and soft-spoken Nolan is nothing like the usual 'big man'—he is a total softie. Hall also identified Damien as the 'white brains' of the group. In New Zealand, too, it seemed a white adviser was an anticipated accompaniment to any tribal delegation.

The substantive discussion with Hall and Durie was about the Maori Council. In Australia, Indigenous people have only ever had a representative voice sporadically, and not since ATSIC was abolished. 'Don't underestimate the intelligence of Indigenous people to be able to choose their own representatives for a body,' Hall advised us. We heeded her counsel.

We also met Te Ururoa Flavell, the Maori Party co-leader; Judge Craig Coxhead, a Maori Land Court judge who sat on the Waitangi Tribunal; Dame Claudia Orange, a Treaty of Waitangi historian and expert at the incredible Te Papa Museum; and a heap of academics and lawyers. We even met the Maori king, Kiingi Tuheitia, and his advisers—and took to calling Nolan 'King Nolan', as it seemed an appropriately bombastic and ironic title. Often the meetings were preceded with song and ritual from our hosts, in Maori. We were granted a half-day audience with the members of the Waitangi Tribunal, who explained in fine detail how the settlements process worked. The members of our delegation learned a huge amount about this nation so close to our own, yet so far ahead.

The five of us bridged gulfs between each other, too. We discussed and debated extensively what reforms might be appropriate for Australia. The trip cemented relationships and alliances in support of substantive constitutional recognition that would last for years, across organisations. Aboriginal leaders King Nolan, Fiona and Sean got to know a conservative monarchist Jew in Damien. And Damien, who had probably never hung out with Indigenous people let alone travelled overseas with them, through our nightly group debriefs and on-the-road chats came to better understand why so many Indigenous people seek substantive constitutional reform.

Damien became stimulated by the legal and political problem at hand and would send me emails at about 4 a.m. each day of our trip. He read my New Zealand briefing paper carefully. 'I'm really interested in the stuff about the Treaty of Waitangi as a source of national pride, pride in Maori culture as a national culture of New Zealand,' he wrote. He suggested we go back to Australia with recommendations about how recognition 'could instil pride in Aborigines as first Australians' but also in Australians generally—pride in 'Aboriginal culture being Australian culture'.

We were coming to see that a Declaration of Recognition, if properly written and negotiated, could carry a place of shared honour for Australians, perhaps akin to the time-honoured place of the Treaty of Waitangi in New Zealand.

Damien's thinking about an Indigenous advisory body was also progressing, particularly after our meeting with Durie and Hall on the Maori Council:

> I think her comment on a policy advisory body fit very much with your thinking about an advisory body. She seemed to think it was important that the advisory body not have any financial role (unlike ATSIC), and that balance would work if it were funded by the state but elected by Indigenous people. I am ever more inclined to think that this is achievable. The issue is whether it can get constitutional sanction. On this point, I think it is probably going to be important to link it to the head of power ... *surely, if the Parliament is going to be given power to make laws about Indigenous policy, it ought to be required to consult with Indigenous people before enacting such laws* ... It also explains why it should be in the Constitution: if the Constitution is the source of the power, it ought also to be the source of the procedural qualification on how the power is exercised.

Damien's logic was compelling. He was the shining diamond unearthed amid the old-fogey followers of the Samuel Griffith Society. We found common ground through mutual give and take and mutual respect. 'Julian and I thought you were just a typical lefty human rights lawyer,' he told me one day, evidently impressed with the way I took on board their ideas and concerns, and how I opened my thinking to new ideas. And now he was doing what I had done.

We were also discussing the possibility of a settlements commission for Australia inspired by the Waitangi Tribunal, which Noel and I envisioned being part of the reform package. To my astonishment, Damien as a conservative and monarchist had no issue with the idea that the Crown should justly settle historical grievances with Indigenous peoples. He viewed this as an important part of the honour of the Crown, and in years to come would publish his support for such a process in Australia.

Abbott was a monarchist and Anglophile, like Damien. I gathered they were relatively close; later Damien would write a book about

Abbott. And Abbott had an affinity with New Zealand too, through his wife, Margie. Margie had even once visited the Waitangi Tribunal, like us. If Damien could be moved by the New Zealand experience, perhaps so could Abbott. He had mentioned the treaty in his speech, after all. 'We only have to look across the Tasman to see how it could have been done so much better,' he had said.

Why did things happen so much better across the Tasman? In my view, it is because New Zealand confronted and dealt with its colonial conflict, rather than repressing it. It did so through the treaty, which despite persisting power imbalances established New Zealand on a foundation of partnership rather than simple conquest and oppression. The Crown, acknowledging its past mistakes, has continued to address this history and strive for its 'more perfect union'—through settlements, Maori political representation and other proactive measures that encourage a fair relationship. Australia, by contrast, has tended to opt for repression over proactive resolution, and silence over honest discussion of past pain. Thus, our nation's unhealed wounds bubble up on the footy field or on Australia Day. Moments that should be about national unity instead lay bare the soul of a country still largely divided and troubled by an unresolved grief.

I think we will remain divided until we honestly address the past, and make amends through a constitutional promise for a fairer future.

While I was in New Zealand, Noel received a text from Abbott asking for his thoughts on the idea of an extra-constitutional Declaration. Julian and Damien had sent Abbott their concept paper, and Abbott had instructed Damien to forge common ground with Noel. Like Greg Craven, Abbott evidently knew that for Indigenous recognition to succeed, Indigenous leaders and constitutional conservatives needed to find agreement on the way forward. In a real sense, the 'con con' collaboration with Noel and me proceeded with Abbott's blessing. Indeed, it was what Abbott asked Damien and Julian to do.

Noel told me to draft a letter responding to Abbott's question. I did it from my hotel room. We exchanged emails agonising over the words, not wanting to concede anything too early. Finally we settled it and the letter was sent on 11 June 2014:

Dear Prime Minister,

I write in response to your recent text asking for my thoughts on the proposition that Indigenous recognition might be achieved in a non-legal Declaration voted for by the Australian people, rather than in the Constitution. In this matter, alongside Shireen Morris, my constitutional reform adviser, I have engaged with Julian Leeser, Damien Freeman, Anne Twomey and Greg Craven.

There is possibly merit in Julian and Damien's proposal, but only as part of a broader package of reforms. On its own, a Declaration would be rich in symbolism but light on substantive reform. Symbolism is important, but we also need to make a *practical difference to the problems we face in Indigenous affairs*.

Conservatives like Julian and Damien, in their eagerness to get judges out of the equation, tend to forget the Indigenous views and history that have driven this conversation about constitutional recognition.

Conservatives are concerned about judicial activism and do not want 'rights' clauses added to the Constitution. As a result, they oppose a racial non-discrimination clause. While I do not accept that these anxieties about judicial activism are justified, in the spirit of mutual understanding, I have come to some appreciation of conservative concerns about giving unelected judges too much power.

However, conservatives reciprocally need to understand that Indigenous people see constitutional recognition as being fundamentally about achieving *constitutional protection and recognition of Indigenous rights and interests within Australia*. Symbolism is only part of it. *Substantive change in the national approach to Indigenous affairs* is the other part.

Conservatives, too, need to understand our legitimate anxieties. Our people have lived through the discrimination of the past. We therefore have a legitimate anxiety that the past not be repeated, and that measures be put in place to ensure that *things are done in a better way*. If conservatives assert that a racial non-discrimination clause is not the answer—then what is a better solution?

Julian and Damien argue that the Constitution is a rulebook, a practical charter of government that sets out power relationships, like that between the Commonwealth and the states. It is not a vehicle for aspirations and symbolism: these can be articulated in a Declaration, not in the Constitution. But if the Constitution is a practical rulebook governing national power relationships, as conservatives assert, then it should also be acknowledged that there is one very important, national power relationship clearly not addressed in the Constitution.

Arguably, the rulebook should be amended to make provision for Indigenous people to be heard in Indigenous affairs.

After all, if unelected judges should not decide what is in the interests of Indigenous people, then who should decide? Indigenous people are only 2.5% of the population, and hardly get a fair say in Parliament, even on matters directly concerning them. Parliaments have never been good at listening to Indigenous people. This is the elephant and the mouse problem that has characterised Indigenous affairs.

Perhaps we can find a way to make democracy work better for Indigenous people. Perhaps we can find a way of ensuring that Indigenous people get a fair say in laws and policies made *about us*, without compromising the supremacy of Parliament. Perhaps we can create a mechanism to ensure that Indigenous people can take more responsibility for our own lives, *within the democratic institutions already established*, and without handing power to judges.

We don't want separatism: we want inclusion. We want to be inside the decision-making tent. We want our voices to be heard in political decisions made about us. A mechanism like this—guaranteeing the Indigenous voice in Indigenous affairs—could be a more democratic solution to the racial discrimination problem. You have already begun down this path with your Indigenous Advisory Council. Our Empowered Communities work is also heading in this direction. I am interested in how we can enhance and build upon your IAC in a way that excites Indigenous people and all those interested in Indigenous wellbeing and justice.

I ask that you keep an open mind. We are in the process of trying to reach some consensus on these ideas with Anne, Greg, Julian and Damien. A Declaration and removal of the 'race' clauses alone will not be acceptable to Indigenous people. We need to all work toward a package of reforms that have the potential to excite Indigenous people and con cons alike.

Yours sincerely,
Noel Pearson

Damien and I had begun trying to draft the constitutional clause requiring Parliament to set up an Indigenous advisory body that would engage with Parliament on Indigenous affairs. We were leading up to a crucial workshop with Anne, Greg, Julian and Damien, together with me and Noel. The workshop would be a chance to float the idea with these key constitutional conservatives to see if it could be supported by the wider group.

On Noel's instructions, I shared our letter to Abbott in confidence with the workshop participants.

Leeser's response to the argument in the letter was cautious, but showed he had shifted a lot from our first meeting. His email back acknowledged the need for substantive changes in the national approach to Indigenous affairs, and suggested that much could be achieved by legislation and policy. Crucially, he also acknowledged past racial discrimination against Indigenous people and the anxiety to see that it was not repeated—which Leeser said he shared. He said he didn't have any 'magic solutions' about ensuring Indigenous people a voice in Indigenous affairs, but suggested the solution might be legislative rather than constitutional. He resolved to think more about this before the workshop.

Damien warned me that getting Julian on board with an Indigenous body in the Constitution would be hard: Julian was more conservative than his friend. But we agreed that he was the key. He was still the benchmark.

I was so nervous I couldn't sleep the night before. It was the day of the 'con con' workshop, Thursday 19 June 2014. Noel and I were crossing the bridge yet again.

'How are we going to do this?' I asked.

'I'm going to let you lead it all, Shireen,' Noel said. He sounded chirpy.

The workshop was at the ACU Vice-Chancellory in North Sydney—the usual meeting place. I'd prepared a PowerPoint presentation of our reform argument that included constitutional drafting prepared with Damien. There was no slide projector—the secretary printed off copies for everyone: Anne Twomey, Greg Craven, Damien Freeman, Julian Leeser, Noel and myself. Jimi Bostock was there too—CYI's nuggety comms adviser, whose theatrical hand gestures and exaggerated 'mmmmm' thinking noises were a constant source of entertainment.

First up, I sought to reflect back to them each of their conservative arguments. I quoted Craven and affirmed his position: 'Greg is correct, we don't need to achieve everything in the Constitution. This can be a package of reforms. The Constitution can contain the hook. Greg is also right that we need to find a consensus between Indigenous people and the "con cons". Hence this workshop.'

I quoted Twomey and affirmed her position: 'We acknowledge that a certain amount of legal uncertainty arises in relation to the proposed racial non-discrimination clause. Your paper, Anne, provides some good options for qualifying the replacement power. My only concern is that Greg and Julian and others are still dubious about a High Court–adjudicated qualification, so we may need to find a different solution.'

I quoted Julian and Damien, and affirmed their position: 'We understand what you are both saying about the danger in having a new preamble in the Constitution. We also take on board your advice that the Constitution is a rulebook: a pragmatic and practical charter of government, not a vehicle for poetry … we've been largely persuaded by that point.'

I told them we now better understood conservative concerns about giving too much power to unelected judges through a racial non-discrimination clause. They listened, pleased at the validation.

Having appropriately conceded some ground, I then presented the Indigenous perspective on behalf of Noel—as characterised by an Indian-Australian relative newcomer to the debate. I reminded them of the history of Indigenous advocacy: Indigenous people seek constitutional protection of their rights and interests, I emphasised. I quoted Patrick Dodson and the great Yolngu elder Galarrwuy Yunupingu, who in their Vincent Lingiari lectures had both noted the importance of constitutional stability and guarantees. I told them about our New Zealand trip and what we had learned there. Symbolism is not enough for Indigenous people, I said. They listened.

I set up the challenge for the workshop: to reconcile the competing concerns. The conservative concern was that we should maintain the integrity of the Constitution as a practical and pragmatic charter of government: we should not give more power to judges or create uncertainty by putting abstract phrases or rights clauses into the Constitution. The Indigenous concern was that we find a certain and stable way to protect Indigenous interests and prevent unjust discrimination against Indigenous people. Our challenge was to find the correct synthesis of the competing philosophical ideals.

I then presented our political hypothesis: we needed to step to the right and up. We needed to find the radical centre.

I used Noel's favourite metaphor to point to the solution. In Australia, the 97 per cent elephant of government makes all the decisions about the democratically powerless 3 per cent Indigenous mouse. Instead of a racial non-discrimination clause, is there a way to constitutionally guarantee that the 3 per cent Indigenous mouse has a voice in political decisions made about it? Instead of empowering the High Court to decide what's good or bad for Indigenous people, can the Constitution empower *Indigenous people themselves* to have a fair say in laws and policies made about them and their rights?

I proposed three drafting solutions that could guarantee an Indigenous voice in their affairs, as discussed with Damien. The first two solutions were deliberately unworkable. The third was Damien's suggested drafting, which I had helped refine (and which he had told me not to frame as his, in case that clouded the politics in the room). It was the most sensible. I summarised the suggested package of reforms: an Indigenous body in the Constitution, appropriately remove references to 'race' while retaining an Indigenous head of power, and a symbolic Declaration outside the Constitution.

Vigorous discussion ensued.

Twomey wanted to clarify that we weren't advocating reserved Indigenous seats in Parliament. All agreed this would be politically unviable. But there was no outright opposition to a constitutionally guaranteed Indigenous advisory body. The vibe was constructive and positive.

Greg, Anne and Julian immediately began discussing how to make the drafting of constitutional option three more workable. How do you ensure the body cannot hold up Parliament through withholding advice? This needed to be fixed. Julian was concerned about justiciability: he wanted to be absolutely sure there could be no High Court uncertainty. 'You need to add a "no legal effect" clause,' Greg advised. Julian agreed.

Despite such technical concerns, they were basically persuaded by the concept. Greg even had an interesting suggestion regarding the name of the body: rather than calling it a Commission or something that would ignite misplaced fears about ATSIC, why not adopt an Indigenous language name? This would have the added advantage of incorporating an Indigenous word into the Australian Constitution, giving it contemporary use in national and political life. What a suggestion! An ancient Indigenous word, in a constitutional amendment guaranteeing forevermore the Indigenous voice in Indigenous affairs.

Now that we had addressed their rational concerns, these conservatives were turning out to be surprisingly imaginative. Who would have guessed?

We resolved to meet again in a few weeks. Noel remained mostly silent throughout, but in closing offered advice for next steps. Anne should refine the drafting and come up with a solution we all could sign up to, he suggested. I was to work with her. We would then all agree on the words of the amendment.

'Good work,' Greg said as we left. 'Very impressive work, Shireen,' said Julian. Damien and I smiled privately at each other. He emailed me later to confirm that Julian was on board. He was extremely impressed with the solution, Damien said, and was 'keen to do what he can to help promote the package' by working with other conservatives and Indigenous leaders.

I was so elated that I thought I might cry. I did later, on the phone to a friend.

On 14 July, Noel spoke at a dinner celebrating the fiftieth birthday of *The Australian* newspaper. His speech was effusive in its praise for the conservative broadsheet and created a splash. The words had their desired effect: conservatives were now paying attention, primed for discussion of constitutional recognition. His inclusive rhetoric drew them in.

I don't recall having input into that speech—it was all Noel. I teased him afterwards: 'That was some serious arse-kissing, Noel!' He did one of his roaring laughs. 'And it's working,' I said. 'The response from the right has been positive!'

'You know what they say, Shireen,' Noel replied. 'Anyone who says flattery doesn't work has never been flattered.'

Most striking in the speech was Noel's characterisation of the three parts of Australia:

> Our nation is in three parts. There is our ancient heritage, written in the continent and the original culture painted on its land and seascapes. There is our British inheritance, the structures of government and society transported from the United Kingdom fixing its foundations in the ancient soil. There is our multicultural achievement: a triumph of immigration that brought together the gifts of peoples and cultures from all over the globe—forming one indissoluble commonwealth.
>
> We stand on the cusp of bringing these three parts of our national story together: our ancient heritage, our British

inheritance and our multicultural triumph, with constitutional recognition of Indigenous Australians. This reconciliation will make a more complete commonwealth.

We stand in good stead. Never has the time been more propitious. The planets are moving into alignment. With a large enough lever, we can even nudge the stars.[1]

Noel drove home the message that this was not about recognising one group—this was about recognising each other. Mutual recognition, bringing Australians together. Uniting the nation.

Afterwards, he got an email from Tim Wilson, an Institute of Public Affairs (IPA) right-wing Liberal who had become a human rights commissioner; he had been dubbed 'Freedom Commissioner' at the Human Rights Commission after being appointed by George Brandis to 'rebalance' the discourse by defending 'classical human rights' such as free speech. The IPA wanted to get rid of, or at least water down, section 18C of the *Racial Discrimination Act* (in order to give greater freedom to bigots, according to Brandis's unwise characterisation). The IPA was also stridently opposed to Indigenous recognition.

True to his IPA platform, Wilson was also an advocate for amending section 18C to bolster free speech at the expense of protection from racial vilification. When it came to racial vilification law, we were opponents: I wrote CYI's submission to the 18C parliamentary inquiry, opposing any repeal or watering-down of current protections.

Because of his stance on such issues, Wilson was commonly assumed to be an enemy of Indigenous rights. His email to Noel, however, indicated that he might not be as hard-hearted as his IPA colleagues. He praised Noel's speech as 'exceptional'. On property rights, too, he supported stronger rights for Indigenous people. As 'Freedom Commissioner', he was working with Mick Gooda and other Indigenous leaders, including Noel and Patrick Dodson, to discuss how to strengthen Indigenous property rights. Perhaps there was more compassion in him than people assumed.

In the following years, Wilson became a supporter of Indigenous constitutional recognition. He later worked with Damien and me to produce an essay on an extra-constitutional Declaration for our 2016 essay collection, *The Forgotten People*. And behind the scenes, he began putting forward his own constitutional drafting ideas for how to recognise First Nations voices, urging that the Constitution should guarantee local Indigenous bodies, rather than a national body.

In our engagement I got the sense that Wilson, as a gay man, had more empathy for Indigenous struggles for recognition and equality than some of his right-wing counterparts. Noel's characterisation of the recognition project being about unity rather than division ignited Wilson's liberal instincts. He was also moved by the inclusive comments made by Rachel Perkins, filmmaker and daughter of 'freedom rides' activist Charlie Perkins, at a dinner run by Recognise. And, just as the Jews could relate to the history of discrimination and exclusion Indigenous people shared, so too, it seemed, could some gay people. Empathy, I was discovering, was the key. Without it, common ground remained elusive.

It felt like the planets were indeed aligning. The journalists and editors at *The Australian* were glowing from Noel's praise. After the workshop, the 'con cons' were coming on board. And now a hard-right Liberal had reached out to constructively join the conversation. It increasingly seemed that good-hearted conservatives and liberals could be persuaded with the right combination of respect, noble compromise and, yes, flattery.

Crucially, we hadn't stepped right only to slide down into minimalism. We were still aiming high. We'd stepped right and were shooting for the stars.

Noel was madly drafting his Quarterly Essay, to be launched in September. It would float the idea of an Indigenous body in the Constitution publicly for the first time. I was helping with some writing and editing.

Anne, Julian, Damien and I were refining the drafting of the constitutional amendment over email—by this stage Damien was away lecturing in aesthetic philosophy at Cambridge University, his yearly stint. A second workshop was held on 15 August 2014.

Updated wording was critiqued by the group. Discussions ramped up in the lead-up to a group meeting with Abbott to present our ideas. We wanted the drafting finalised by then.

I developed a paper that sought to draw out the constitutional issues for resolution. It canvassed, in excruciating detail, the concerns of each expert in relation to each version of the proposed amendment. We needed to agree on every word, comma and semi-colon.

I was grappling in particular with a version that included, at Julian and Greg's insistence, versions of a 'non-justiciability' or 'no legal effect' clause. Julian was digging his heels in about it because of his deep-seated High Court paranoia. The group, aware of the need to keep him signed up, was thus contemplating a subsection along the lines of: 'A failure to comply with this Chapter in relation to any Bill that becomes an Act does not affect the validity, operation or enforcement of that Act or of any other statutory provision.'

The proposed section was grating on me, and I sensed it would be a make-or-break issue. Through this drafting process, I saw myself as the lawyer representing Noel, acting on his instructions and trying to secure the best deal for him and, by extension, his people. So I decided to push back. I told Noel I didn't like the clause, and he agreed, then I rang Anne to discuss it. 'It seems disingenuous,' I said. 'Other constitutional clauses don't include such expressions of bad faith. Why does this clause need to? Isn't there another way?' She went away to think about it.

I also raised the concern strategically in the paper. With Noel's advice, we framed it as a concern of the Indigenous constituency, who we needed to keep on board, so that Julian and Greg wouldn't try too hard to persuade us otherwise—a 'no legal effect' clause simply wouldn't fly with the mob was the angle. It is a common tactic in attempts at law reform—verballing various constituencies, when actually you don't really know what they think until it's been properly tested. Politicians do it all the time. (Note how, in 2017, Tony Abbott claimed his opposition to same-sex marriage reflected the position of the 'silent majority'. When the postal survey results came back, his own electorate demonstrated 75 per cent support for same-sex marriage. Malcolm Turnbull would similarly verbal the Australian people that year, claiming they wouldn't accept an Indigenous voice in the Constitution, a concept that had by that time gained serious Indigenous and non-Indigenous support.) Us declaring that Indigenous people wouldn't accept a 'no legal effect' clause was the same annoying 'it won't fly' political prediction roadblock that objectors like Greg had used on us in relation to a racial non-discrimination clause. Now we were using it on them, in order to nut out the best constitutional amendment possible for Indigenous people. I was enjoying the karma.

Our political prediction was correct too, however, and supported by strong evidence. Noel knew the Indigenous constituency well, and we'd run Cape York workshops and summits testing our revised ideas. Plus, the Expert Panel after its consultation had found that a 'no legal effect' clause (for a preamble) would not be accepted by Indigenous people because it was viewed as tokenistic. While we had a good sense that Indigenous people would likely be attracted to a constitutional voice as a vehicle for self-determination, we also knew that if the whole thing became too weak we would probably lose them. This reform had to be modest enough for conservatives, but also substantive and meaningful enough for Indigenous people. The constitutional drafting was all about balancing the competing concerns. It had to be strong yet sensible. Empowering yet practically workable. Modest yet profound.

In the end, our objection to a 'no legal effect' clause was accepted by the 'con cons' with little fuss. Julian immediately attempted redrafting the clause to take on board our feedback. He also advised that the Indigenous-body amendment should be up the front of the Constitution, not hidden away at the back. These conservatives were perpetually surprising: once they were on board, they were bold about it.

By this stage we were playing with the name 'Delak' (sometimes spelt 'Dilak'), a Yolngu word that had been used by Galarrwuy Yunupingu's people in their petition to Prime Minister Kevin Rudd calling for 'serious constitutional reform'. The word meant 'council of elders'. We had sought preliminary permission to use it privately in our drafts, but it didn't make it into any final public versions for fear it might be controversial. As a concept, I felt it worked. I still think incorporating an Indigenous language name for the Indigenous body is a great idea, if people can agree on what word or words to use.

Finally Anne came up with the breakthrough draft amendment. She emailed me on 22 August to tell me she had cracked the non-justiciability problem. My question to her—why do we have to have a non-justiciability clause when none of the other constitutional provisions have one—had triggered something in her vast reservoir of constitutional knowledge. She realised that sections 53 and 54 of the Constitution are considered non-justiciable without any express clause specifying so, due to the terminology used—'proposed law', rather than 'law'. It indicated that these clauses concerned the internal workings of the Houses: matters for Parliament to manage, not the High Court. Anne used the 'proposed law' terminology to construct a provision that would be non-justiciable without an ugly express clause saying so.

Her final drafting, a new Chapter 1A establishing an Indigenous advisory body, was agreed to by the group and made public in 2015, with only slight variations:

> 60A(1) There shall be an Aboriginal and Torres Strait Islander body, to be called the [insert appropriate name, perhaps drawn from an Aboriginal or Torres Strait Islander language], which shall have the function of providing advice to the Parliament and the Executive Government on matters relating to Aboriginal and Torres Strait Islander peoples.
> (2) The Parliament shall, subject to this Constitution, have power to make laws with respect to the composition, roles, powers and procedures of the [body].
> (3) The Prime Minister [or the Speaker/President of the Senate] shall cause a copy of the [body's] advice to be tabled in each House of Parliament as soon as practicable after receiving it.
> (4) The House of Representatives and the Senate shall give consideration to the tabled advice of the [body] in debating proposed laws with respect to Aboriginal and Torres Strait Islander peoples.[2]

As Anne explained, the non-justiciability of the draft amendment meant that whether advice was tabled, whether it was considered, and whether advice could be given on particular matters were all issues for Parliament, not the High Court. Anne had also eliminated any risk of parliamentary delay. Under this proposal, the group was confident that parliamentary supremacy would be totally upheld, and High Court uncertainty eliminated.

Noel and I met with professors Marcia Langton and Megan Davis to ascertain their views on the proposals. We hoped they too would be part of the coalition, to engage in further refinement of the package and to own and champion the proposals. We knew it was important that this reform be advocated by Indigenous leaders other than just Noel. Though we had received very positive feedback from the Cape York people we'd spoken to, there were no resources available to consult around the country with Indigenous people (at least not yet). Ventilating the idea with Davis and Langton was a good start.

They responded cautiously at first, but considered the proposal with open minds. Davis immediately set to work applying her sharp constitutional mind to the idea. Though she wasn't immediately sold on the example drafting, she came to view the concept as a robust and attractive reform that would empower Indigenous people with a much-needed voice in the policy process, and help Australia to implement the principles of the UN Declaration on the Rights of Indigenous Peoples, which emphasised the importance of Indigenous consultation, political participation and self-determination in decisions made about them. From her extensive international law experience with the United Nations, Megan knew of many examples of other countries where Indigenous political representation and mechanisms for consultation had worked well to ensure the Indigenous voice was more effectively heard by settler democratic systems. She added academic rigour to our discussions.

Langton and Davis came with us to a third meeting with Greg, Julian and Anne on 10 September 2014 (Damien was still in the UK, following the process closely via emails with me). I tended to always run these workshops, and was nervous about how the two professors might react to the role I was playing. I raised my concern with Noel. 'I think it'd be better if you run this meeting,' I said.

'No, you run it,' he replied dismissively. I later realised that he consistently chose to take a back seat in these workshops so he could retain the authoritative effect of his sparsely chosen words and interventions. It meant that when he pressed a point, it had impact. I was the frontline; Noel was the heavy artillery. It was a way of saving up his powerful influence for when it was really needed. In the same way, he left me to prosecute the constitutional detail while he kept his eye on the strategic big picture. We worked well as a team in this way.

I ran the workshop as per usual. Anne explained her drafting logically and concisely. Amazingly, we obtained endorsement from the wider group on the proposed constitutional drafting, without a 'no legal effect' clause. Even Julian agreed this practical machinery clause, to guarantee Indigenous people a voice in their affairs, was a safe and sensible solution. More safe than inserting a racial non-discrimination clause. More safe than inserting symbolic words that the High Court could misuse.

The 'con con' alliance was forged.

It was settled that a group letter explaining the proposal would be written to Abbott and signed by all present. Then the group would attend a meeting with the prime minister at Parliament House to make the case for the reforms.

On 11 September, Noel launched his Quarterly Essay, *A Rightful Place*, at the Sydney Opera House and floated publicly, for the first time, his shift in position. It was big news. Noel Pearson no longer advocated a racial non-discrimination clause, which we had pushed since 2011. He was now advocating an Indigenous constitutional voice, in the form of a constitutionally guaranteed advisory body to Parliament. The landmark essay described his engagement with the 'con cons' and the noble compromise position that had been reached.

There was an immediate negative response—not from the public, but from government. Indigenous Liberal MP Ken Wyatt, who was by now chairing a parliamentary joint select committee on the issue, didn't appreciate Noel's intervention and told the press Noel should make a submission to the committee 'like everybody else'.[3] Don't step out of line and propose new ideas was the clear message. Once again, we were being told to submit.

It was an oddly authoritarian response from Wyatt. Since when did politicians reprimand civilians for expressing ideas? As Noel commented later in *The Australian,* it was 'as though blackfellas can't write an essay without permission. Did Wyatt want to proofread my essay to ensure it was aligned with his Liberal Party line?'[4]

Stranger still was the fact that when a white lawyer, Father Frank Brennan, later promoted his book, *No Small Change,* which argued only for minimalism—it opposed a racial non-discrimination clause and an Indigenous constitutional body—government representatives did not complain. Nor did they tell him to make a submission 'like everybody else'. It seemed odd that an Indigenous leader's public ideas were chastised, yet a white man's were not. Either Wyatt had a personal issue with Noel particularly speaking up, or it was starting to seem as if the government had a predetermined outcome in mind (despite the fact the committee was still taking submissions) and that outcome didn't include the ideas we were proposing.

We sent every committee member a copy of Noel's essay, and Noel instructed me to write a submission explaining the proposed reforms. In the end we made three submissions to Wyatt's committee, including a report on the New Zealand research trip.

The day after the essay launch, our broader 'con con' group co-signed the letter to Tony Abbott to inform him of the newly forged consensus and ask for a meeting.

Noel also spoke to Abbott on the phone and explained the proposal. Strangely, Abbott expressed a preference for Indigenous reserved seats instead, like they have in New Zealand. He thought that would be a simpler solution than a constitutional advisory body. A day later, as Noel would subsequently describe, *The Australian* reporter Dennis Shanahan 'floated the anonymous balloon and exploded it himself, in the same article'.⁵ Abbott's reserved-seats brainwave, which I assume was leaked deliberately by the prime minister's office, died the same day.

It at least showed that Abbott was not closed-minded about substantive constitutional reform, however. Though he'd indicated preferences for minimalism previously, it seemed he was now grappling with how substantive reform might be achievable. Perhaps he was feeling ambitious. If he was, the negative reaction to his reserved-seats idea must have dampened his spirits.

Abbott was up in Arnhem Land in September 2014, doing one of his remote community stints. Yolngu elders, probably influenced by our policy work and their respect for Noel's ideas, used the opportunity to advocate to the prime minister regarding constitutional recognition. As *The Australian* top-end journalist Amos Aikman reported, the group of Yolngu leaders pragmatically indicated to Abbott that they did not wish the constitutional recognition debate to become 'mired in arguments about racial discrimination', an acknowledgement that seemed to heed the warnings of constitutional conservatives against the Expert Panel's proposed clause. In any case, they seemed more concerned with practical action to address their disadvantage. As Aikman reported, the Yolngu elders told Abbott they needed a stronger voice for their people and their land—for their land was 'unable to speak for itself'. The Yolngu wished to empower their 'Dilak, those adults who have traditional authority, but who struggle to be heard in the wider world' and argued for constitutional change to enable the 'Dilak to speak for their people, and ensure their opinions are heard'. The Yolngu were sending a simple message: listen to our voices.⁶

Listen to us. Recognise our traditional Dilak. It was a message Abbott needed to hear.

Our proposed meeting with Abbott didn't happen until three months later, in December 2014. Members of our 'con con' alliance met with him and Peta Credlin, together with prime ministerial adviser Bennie Ng, at the prime minister's Parliament House office, to make the case for an Indigenous voice in the Constitution. Abbott listened to the arguments from the constitutional experts and the

Indigenous leaders, then proposed his own revised, weaker drafting for the Indigenous advisory body, on the fly—just like he had in our 2012 meeting in response to our proposed equality guarantee. I thought it odd that he could think his off-the-cuff amendments superior to the ones that experienced constitutional experts had spent months negotiating word by word. Just as he had impulsively floated reserved seats, so too would he impulsively draft a superior Indigenous body amendment, it seemed. It was an insight into how Abbott's numerous foot-in-mouth moments as prime minister, which were costing him politically, had come about. It seemed he didn't take enough time to think things through.

This didn't instil much confidence. Constitutional reform required a leader who could pursue a smart, considered political strategy, not someone who made rash, impulsive moves and comments.

Nonetheless, Abbott wasn't totally opposed to the idea of a constitutionally enshrined advisory body. He was, however, worried about the political difficulty of achieving it. As he complained to Noel earlier in September, having copped the negative response to his hasty reserved-seats idea, he was worried that today's conservatives lacked compassion—the unspoken implication being that he had loads of it and it was others who were the problem. A subtle version of the old 'blame the constituency' trick. It's not me: it just won't wash with these other bastard right-wingers.

Yet here we were, demonstrating that some conservatives indeed had compassion and could support and champion an Indigenous body in the Constitution. Couldn't Abbott, as the self-proclaimed Prime Minister for Indigenous Affairs, be one of them, and help champion the reform in his party room? Instead, he asked our 'con con' friends to help build consensus for the proposal so he could then lead. They agreed.

Looking back, the sad irony of Abbott's 'conservatives lack compassion' observation hits home. In the time he had left as prime minister, he never showed any real leadership on this issue. He never did the hard work and the hard thinking, and never did any real consensus-building.

I'm writing this in 2018. Malcolm Turnbull is now prime minister, after knifing Abbott for the job in 2015. Perhaps not for long. An embittered Abbott, having retired to the backbench, has been the Liberal Party's resident spoiler ever since, despite promising not to be. This remains an unstable government, riven from within.

No wonder Abbott was nervous about the politics and ultimately unable to show leadership on Indigenous recognition. He was desperately clinging to his job and trying to maintain control of his party, just like Turnbull would be when he obtained the prime ministership. That's not an excuse for what they did. Ultimately, for these men, it became all about holding on to power rather than wielding it for the national good.

Just recently, Abbott complained about the 'toxic egos' on 'both sides of Parliament' being detrimental to politics. 'Too many people have put themselves first and not their country,' he complained.[7]

Abbott could have been talking about himself, not just his usurper. And the Yolngu still wait for their voices to be heard.

8

Low Expectations

IMAGINE THE POLITICAL spectrum is a clock face, divided in half: left and right. Progressive middle around twelve o'clock, spanning across both Labor and the Liberals. The Nats and One Nation at four and five o'clock, further to the right. The Greens at seven o'clock, around to the left. Both sides get more radical as they get closer to six o'clock.

With our 'con con' alliance, we'd placed a small stake in the ground at around 4.30 on the political spectrum, with our group on the conservative right. The theory was that everyone to the left of that stake should be easier to get on board, because progressives, by definition, are more ambitious about reform than conservatives. The further left you go, the easier it should get.

That was the theory. In practice, it didn't always play out.

Personalities, egos and partisan politics had a huge role in influencing what the various players would or would not support. While it was crucial to have conservative allies, for constitutional reform bipartisanship (and indeed multi-partisanship) was just as important.

Noel had the unusual talent of appealing to both left and right, but he could infuriate left and right too. In mid-2014, he enamoured the political right with his fiftieth birthday of *The Australian* gala speech, but probably annoyed the left, who might have interpreted it as simply sucking up to Rupert Murdoch. In November that year, he ignited progressive passions with his groundbreaking eulogy speech at the funeral of former Labor prime minister Gough Whitlam, rightly praising his reform legacy, but in doing so he may have alienated the right.

Each move had its ramifications. Advocacy and persuasion were balancing acts, just like the constitutional drafting. We knew the right would need the most persuasive work. But we also knew our work with the right might turn off the left.

We'd built our 'con con' alliance. But plenty of people weren't happy about it.

The Joint Select Committee on Constitutional Recognition of Aboriginal and Torres Strait Islander Peoples was chaired by Ken Wyatt, with Indigenous Labor senator Nova Peris as the deputy chair. It was a cross-party committee charged with taking constitutional recognition forward, building on the work of the Expert Panel.

The committee was exploring variations on the Expert Panel's proposals. But these variations were essentially more limited racial non-discrimination guarantees and retained uncertain symbolic language in the Constitution—reforms that still empowered the High Court. They did not address the crux of conservative objections.

Noel and I could see where the committee was heading. It was failing to step to the right and up; instead, it was trying to move right by watering down the Expert Panel's proposals, but sliding down to minimalism in the process.

Instead of addressing the crucial question of justiciability and High Court uncertainty, and adopting a non-justiciable yet substantive and empowering reform—being the Indigenous constitutional body—the committee's attempts at trimming the panel's proposals were pulling the whole thing downward towards nothingness. Once a racial non-discrimination clause (and variations of) was derailed by the political right and therefore abandoned, as we predicted it would be, the only thing left would be a symbolic insertion and some tidying-up of the race clauses—minimalism—unless the committee adopted an alternative substantive reform. To avoid a minimalist result by default, we had to persuade it of the merits of the Indigenous body proposal we had nutted out with constitutional conservatives.

It was proving difficult.

Wyatt and the Labor members on the committee were initially sceptical of the Cape York Institute proposal. The natural left–right tribalism was readily apparent.

On 6 November, Fiona Jose and I addressed the committee at a public hearing in Cairns. Labor Shadow Minister for Indigenous Affairs Shayne Neumann was dismissive of the criticisms of constitutional conservatives in relation to a racial non-discrimination clause—he said they didn't understand the constitutional role of the High Court. Neumann was also critical of the body proposal and the idea of a Declaration. He argued that the High Court would use any extra-constitutional Declaration to make implications about the constitutional body, leading to legal uncertainty.[1] Surprisingly, Neumann, though on the left, was conjuring a fear about unintended judicial intervention that not even the most paranoid constitutional conservatives, such as Julian Leeser, had entertained. Neumann's argument was far-fetched. I defended our position, but things were not beginning well.

On 19 December, Noel, Marcia Langton and I attended a private hearing with the committee at Redfern in Sydney.[2]

Langton advocated strongly for the Indigenous body. She explained that the proposed racial non-discrimination clause had unearthed a political 'minefield' of opposition, and contended that the correct alternative solution was the proposed constitutional body. A voice for Indigenous people would 'complete the Commonwealth', she said, evoking Tony Abbott's rhetoric. 'It establishes First Peoples, the British traditions and the emergence of a democratic multicultural society with a very strong democratic polity in which all ethnicities, including the first peoples, are treated with respect and honour … I love the concept.'

On political viability, Langton was optimistic. 'I think we can achieve it and I think it is very attractive to all Australians,' she argued.

'It resolves the problem of parliamentary sovereignty because the Indigenous body, whatever it turns out to be, would advise Parliament. It would provide a parliamentary consultation process that enables the Parliament to be apprised of Indigenous views on legislation that affects their interests …'

Noel contended the body was urgently needed to improve Indigenous affairs policies and ultimately close the gap. '[T]he good intentions of the wider community will never meet our determination to make those things work until we have a proper voice in the system,' he said, urging the committee to envisage how such an Indigenous voice might add rigour, accountability and empowerment to the failing Indigenous affairs system.

He also noted the proposal seemed to carry favour with the Cape York people we'd so far engaged with, but needed wider national testing. He proposed a series of Indigenous regional meetings or conventions so Indigenous people could grapple with the ideas and issues. Langton agreed.

At that second hearing, it was Labor committee member Stephen Jones who pushed back hardest. 'I am an advocate of the Expert Panel's propositions,' he said. 'I see whatever we do thereafter as a necessary political compromise and not a virtue in and of itself.'

Jones suggested that the proposed constitutional body would be too weak—no different to the current Human Rights Commission, which was toothless and mostly ignored. Noel noted that the Human Rights Commission is not a representative voice for Indigenous Australians. (Nor is it, as I later pointed out, a constitutionally recognised institution.) Jones acknowledged this fact, but maintained scepticism. 'I know the way that legislation is formed,' he said. 'I sit in Parliament; I see those bills come before it. If the answer is to have one of your mob stand up and read a report in Parliament before we vote on a bill, it would be pretty powerful at first, but over the years it would be diluted, I can tell you.'

It was the inverse of the 'may become a one-clause bill of rights'–style arguments. Instead of the worry that the reform might evolve into something scary—the right-winger's fear of unintended radical change—this was the left-winger's worry that it might evolve into something weak and insipid. Yet we were pushing a noble compromise, a sweet spot between the two extremes.

Jones wanted us to convince him that the advisory body would carry authority before he would consider it an acceptable alternative to judicial review. It seemed the proposal had to be all things to all people: we had to prove to conservatives it would be modest and risk-free, and we had to prove to progressives it would be authoritative and paradigm-shifting.

In reality, the proposal as intended—if designed, legislated and implemented well—could be all these things: that's why it was a radical centre idea, modest yet profound. But how do you inspire leaders to imagine success when on a particular matter they seem pessimistically predisposed to imagine failure? We were talking about the future of the nation, after all. That future couldn't be proved. It could only be created—with political will, leadership vision and collaborative action—by working together constructively to achieve a shared goal.

The hearing was a wake-up call—I'd always assumed progressives to be more generally optimistic than conservatives. But our engagement with the committee exposed a particular progressive attitude that seemed to bubble up in constitutional recognition, and perhaps in Indigenous affairs in general: progressive pessimism, derived out of well-meaning benevolence. What Noel described as 'the soft bigotry of low expectations' that sometimes infects leftist thinking. The assumption that Indigenous people will not succeed, leading to predictions of failure. The trouble is that such low expectations, when harboured by powerful politicians, can become self-fulfilling prophecies.

Jones pessimistically predicted the proposed Indigenous body would be 'bureaucratic' and 'ineffectual', but he didn't seem to be worried that a racial non-discrimination clause might also be costly, cumbersome and ineffectual—which was a genuine risk. It's not as if litigation is ever quick, certain or easy.

The fact is that both proposals had their pros and cons. I tried to explain this to the committee. I don't know if I did a good job.

Neither an Indigenous advisory body nor judicial review under a racial non-discrimination clause was a failsafe solution for Indigenous people. Both had strengths; both had risks. The High Court doesn't always hold in an Indigenous litigant's favour, just as an Indigenous body's advice won't always be heeded by Parliament. But the proposed body, though carrying no veto, would be a proactive approach—an Indigenous voice and input before a law is enacted, right at the start when the bill is being debated. A racial non-discrimination clause is a retrospective, reactive approach—you go off to court after the law has already been passed and try to get it struck down, with no guarantee of winning. Some Indigenous advocates describe a racial non-discrimination clause as more like a shield—a passive protection—whereas an Indigenous body in the Constitution is more like a sword—a proactive voice. I pointed out that the proposed voice would carry the moral and political authority that arises from being an institution of the Australian Constitution—created by the powerful collective endorsement of the Australian people through a referendum.

Weak, strong; ambitious, modest—it was all about perspective. Ultimately, choosing what reform to advocate for was a call Indigenous people had to make, keeping in mind political viability, risks and potential gains.

While the concerns regarding the body proposal were valid and answerable, an underlying paternalism in the conversation began to grate on Noel and Marcia. I could see them trying not to lose patience. They'd endured right-wing paternalism, which advised Indigenous people not to be too ambitious lest the referendum fail. Now here was the progressive variety: advising them not to aim low, lest their preferred reform achieved too little for their people. Jones was trying to look out for Indigenous best interests, but these Indigenous leaders could do that for themselves. And they were not aiming low: minimalism was the very outcome they were trying to avoid.

The committee didn't seem to get it.

Noel worked hard to refute the argument that the Indigenous body would be too weak. It would need 'proper institutional recognition', he said. It should not be 'slinking around the corridors' like some lowly lobby group. 'It should be an institution in the Parliamentary Triangle that has an honoured place in the nation's democracy …

supported by good legislation. With the proper status and respect being accorded to this institution, it could be a powerful voice ...' Affirming there would be no veto, he argued that the body could nonetheless carry 'the moral power of a people's voice, which is a lot more than we have now'.

He was trying to paint the vision, but so far the Labor guys didn't seem inspired, though Nova Peris seemed cautiously curious. The women on the committee—Peris (Labor), Rachel Siewert (Greens, from Western Australia) and Bridget McKenzie (Nationals, from Victoria)—at this hearing seemed significantly more open-minded than the men.

I suspected the Labor members had received advice from some left-leaning human rights lawyers who were likely ideologically predisposed against the body proposal. Some, I gathered, seemed to feel betrayed by our shift away from racial non-discrimination. Human rights expert Professor George Williams, who had helped us draft the racial non-discrimination clause, had seemed initially unhappy about our change in position and argued publicly against the proposed constitutional body. He too initially felt it would be weak. Williams may have also felt put out that we'd worked with conservative constitutional lawyers—his natural adversaries. A long-time advocate of a bill of rights for Australia (which constitutional conservatives successfully opposed), Williams had an understandable affinity for rights-clause solutions. He was also affiliated with Labor.

Langton evidently carried a similar concern. At one point she told the committee she was worried they were 'being persuaded by a particular kind of constitutional advice' that was mixing up recognition with bill of rights issues. Her advice was pragmatic: 'either we want to win the recognition issue or we want to lose it. If you mix it up with all of these general human rights problems, then we will lose it. We will lose the referendum.'

'Lose!' Bridget McKenzie echoed, with a raised 'Hallelujah!' hand—like a sassy back-up singer to Marcia's gospel. She was nodding enthusiastically at much of our advocacy.

Jones wasn't convinced. He told us he 'needed to get excited' about the proposal. The irony was excruciating. The right had warned us that the Expert Panel's racial non-discrimination clause (which we had passionately pushed) was too strong, driven by caution and a desire for certainty. And now that Noel and Marcia, two former Expert Panel members, had adjusted to a noble compromise position that took on board conservative concerns, progressives were complaining their alternative proposal wasn't exciting enough and so were withholding their support.

It seemed like every side wanted it exactly their way.

There was a beautiful moment when Jones cautioned Noel and Marcia to 'beware the pitfalls of the existing architecture in what you are recommending to us'. The well-meaning white politician seemed to be warning these two seasoned Indigenous activists about the downfalls of the Australian constitutional system—the very constitutional system they were trying to reform for their people's benefit.

Langton couldn't stomach it: 'You think we don't know?'

'No, I am certain you do,' Jones replied quickly. 'I will leave it there.'

'Thank you,' said Langton. How we adored Marcia in those moments.

On the other side of the committee, McKenzie seemed intrigued by and amenable to our approach. She had spoken at the Samuel Griffith Society on the day of my first spy mission back in 2013, and appeared to be a down-to-earth, practical woman who was admired by the crowd. A steadfast constitutional conservative, McKenzie at the committee hearing seemed to indicate that she understood our 'radical centre' logic, describing it as a way of bringing Samuel Griffith Society types together with the Indigenous activist types of Redfern, where this hearing was being held. Her analysis was accurate: that's exactly what we were trying to do. Later, in a private meeting, she told us she thought our proposal was radical but in a good, smart way, and that she loved the concept. Senator Rachel Siewert was also amenable, indicating she was 'very attracted' to the idea of the Indigenous constitutional body.

So there it was: further right and further left, in the Nats and the Greens, there was support. On the committee at least, they seemed more in favour of an Indigenous body in the Constitution than Labor (Neumann and Jones) or the Liberal centre (Wyatt). Political dynamics are strange. As Noel would later describe, our proposal seemed to win support further right and further left, but suffered from a sagging middle.

Often, I learned, a lack of political tension could create the phenomenon of the sagging centre. Imagine a bouncy hammock tied between two sturdy trees, left and right. If both ends are pulled taut, a constitutional reform proposal might be hoisted up to a high position. The tautness, the robust struggle for resolution of the tension, pulls the proposal up and a high, radical centre position might emerge. But if one side sags, or worse, falls over and releases the tension, the proposal slides down to minimalism.

This was the flip side of the common call for bipartisanship in constitutional recognition. Bipartisanship was important, but you also needed a robust contest of ideas for a good result to emerge for Indigenous people. We needed Labor to stay ambitious.

At first, in the years after the Expert Panel, the political tension had been high. Progressives were pushing for a racial non-discrimination clause; the Coalition was pulling the other way, towards minimalism. There was a strong, productive tension, awaiting a radical-centre, noble-compromise resolution.

Our work offered that solution to the committee. Not a racial non-discrimination clause, not minimalism, but a substantive position nonetheless: an Indigenous body in the Constitution. For the solution to be realised, Labor needed to keep expectations for substantive constitutional reform high.

At that hearing in December 2014, the Labor MPs on the committee correctly maintained the tension. They were sticking to a racial non-discrimination clause, urging ambition. While they would ultimately need to shift to the radical centre for the body proposal to get anywhere, in the meantime staying ambitious was important. So long as they maintained the tension, a good result might yet be achieved.

In April 2015, Noel Pearson launched Julian Leeser and Damien Freeman's essay on a Declaration of Recognition, and helped kick off their new conservative organisation, Uphold & Recognise. The Uphold & Recognise philosophy was that it was possible to meaningfully recognise Indigenous peoples while upholding the Constitution. They argued for an Indigenous advisory body in the Constitution and a Declaration outside it, together with cleaning up the race clauses (the same reforms Cape York Institute now advocated). Their aim was to promote these reforms, particularly to the political right.

The NSW State Library was packed when Julian and Damien declared their support for an Indigenous constitutional body. Noel in turn declared his support for an extra-constitutional Declaration. This was the quid pro quo: substantive reform within the Constitution, symbolic language outside it. Conservative supporters immediately began to sign up. I sat proudly in the audience.

The media coverage of the event was extensive and the backlash immediate. It came at us hard from the left and the centre right—the progressive middle.

Ken Wyatt got on radio to criticise the proposals. They were too tokenistic, he argued: 'The message has been very clear: substantive recognition, not tokenistic.' (Note that in 2015 this Liberal Party representative was describing as too tokenistic the same approach Malcolm Turnbull, as prime minister in 2017, would reject as too radical.) Wyatt also suggested that Indigenous people did not support the proposals.[3] The next few years would prove him wrong.

Liberal pollster Mark Textor, who was working for Recognise, also got on radio to denigrate Julian and Damien for proposing new ideas, and urged that people must follow the proper 'process'.[4] He was furious about our shift in position and sent a text message to Noel expressing dismay that he had conceded to the constitutional conservatives. Textor seemed to view Julian and Damien as the enemy. We gathered this was about historical rivalries (possibly dating back to the republic debate in which Textor had worked as pollster for Howard) as much as anything else. Textor asked Noel to explain the logic and 'trade-offs' in his shift in position. Noel did—just as he had in previous meetings, just as he had in his Quarterly Essay, and just as we had in our three submissions to the committee. It didn't abate Textor's annoyance.

It was bizarre: two Liberals were bagging Noel for trying to forge a noble compromise with conservatives, and also criticising us for exercising free speech to float new ideas.

Textor was not the only disgruntled pollster. After the launch, Tim Gartrell of Recognise was so annoyed he withdrew a previous offer to fund Uphold & Recognise. He said it was because Uphold & Recognise didn't support 'constitutional recognition'—despite the fact it supported an Indigenous advisory body in the Constitution, a substantive form of constitutional recognition.

I could think of four possible explanations for these reactions. Either these pollsters had not read our submissions or Julian and Damien's submission to the committee; or for them and others, the phrase 'constitutional recognition' was code for symbolism in the Constitution and nothing else and they refused to open their minds to any other possibilities; or because Recognise and Textor were on the government payroll, they were simply adhering to a predetermined government position; or the pollsters had already decided that the body proposal had no chance of winning a referendum and were advising government accordingly, creating a kind of echo chamber of political low expectations. I suspect it may have been a combination of all four.

The decision to withdraw the small funding offer from Uphold & Recognise was a stingy, petty move from the head of Recognise, an organisation that had millions of dollars at its disposal. Julian and Damien had both contributed a few thousand dollars of their personal money to start the organisation. They didn't have to: they could have just sat back and done nothing. Instead they took responsibility and backed the cause, backed Noel and me, and helped push substantive constitutional recognition through an Indigenous body. I distinctly recall Julian announcing to the room of supporters that they should hand back their name badges after the event so they could be recycled to save funds. Now they would be reliant on private donations or personal cash to do the work.

For all its frugality, Uphold & Recognise achieved more to build support for an Indigenous voice in the Constitution than Recognise, with all its millions, ever did—for in reality, Recognise behind the scenes was working against the Indigenous body proposal. Damien especially would churn out work in support. Over the years he advocated, wrote articles, provided advice and organised many impressive promotional events—all on a completely volunteer basis. Never once did he ask for anything in return, apart from requesting Noel to launch his book, *The Aunt's Mirrors*, which Noel happily did before a beaming throng of Damien's Jewish supporters and family. Recognise, by contrast, was well funded by government. Perhaps that is why they were pushing minimalism. Everybody knew it. Indigenous people knew it—that's why they grew to distrust Recognise. The 'R' logo came to represent the meaningless, purely symbolic recognition that Indigenous people did not want but government seemed intent to impose.

Committee member for Labor Shayne Neumann also criticised the ideas presented at the Declaration launch, saying our proposals had come too late in the process—an excuse Turnbull would revive in 2017 to reject the Uluru Statement from the Heart. Strangely, Neumann argued lateness despite the committee process still being underway and submissions still being received. Both CYI and Julian and Damien had already made submissions, so why the pretence? And why was this proposal in particular being publicly trashed by the committee, and by Recognise?

A lot was low expectations: it's all too hard, so let's not try to think through the problems and find creative, substantive solutions. The pollster's mantra 'Keep it simple' was often code for minimalism, though as 1999's failure had showed, trying to insert symbolism in the Constitution was anything but.

As Noel suggested in *The Australian* that week, it was 'becoming clearer that the committee wants only miserly remnants of recommendations of the Expert Panel ... The matter is settled, and everyone else, including myself, needs to shut up.' He identified two groups trying to destroy our proposal: 'One demands the recommendations of the Expert Panel and nothing else. Then there is the committee, committed to a watering down of the panel's recommendations' who 'oppose ideas seeking to step outside their process-obsessed box'.[5]

The committee was unwilling or unable to embrace the radical centre. It seemed obvious it was being advised by Recognise, and particularly by Textor and Gartrell. 'There are more than one or two influential Indigenous leaders in this country', I recall Textor saying pointedly at a Recognise event. Such comments were deliberate digs at Noel and Marcia. (Ironically, when the Uluru Statement in 2017 showed there were indeed many more Indigenous leaders than just Noel and Marcia—and they formed a national Indigenous consensus behind the Indigenous voice proposal—Textor still wouldn't be happy and would still blame Noel.)

The beckoning dais was a propelling factor in these interpersonal rivalries. As is human nature, the promise of a legacy of lasting individual fame and glory propelled strangely competitive behaviour among the key players in this debate. Noel and I would joke that everyone wanted to get up on the dais. Everyone wanted to go down in history as the person who delivered the winning referendum model, but they were concerned the dais was only big enough for a few—and here was Noel, with his annoyingly brilliant brain and eloquent rhetoric, trying to wrestle them off it. Only he wasn't: there was enough room on the dais for everyone, if only people would work together. Sometimes people even worried I might try to ascend the dais too—and there was definitely not enough room for an over-enthusiastic Indian-Australian, let alone all the Indigenous leaders, politicians, white lawyers and pollsters who were trying to climb on.

Tall poppy syndrome and anti-Noel personal jealousy were undoubtedly factors in these dynamics. Constitutional reform was about changing the nation for the better, but there was a potential to make history in the process. This ignited rival egos—and there were some massive ones.

9

Black Robe

IT WAS MARCIA LANGTON who first alerted us to the impending catastrophe of Father Frank Brennan's interference. In May 2015, he was returning to Australia and had a book coming out on Indigenous constitutional recognition. 'Uh-oh,' she warned. 'We'll have to stop him before he screws this up.'

Brennan was a Jesuit Catholic priest and respected constitutional lawyer who worked at Australian Catholic University, where Greg and Julian also worked. A long-time human rights advocate, Brennan sat further left than they did. He was a bill of rights proponent and Indigenous rights activist. In 2017, he supported same-sex marriage.

Brennan descended from on high after a stint at Boston College in the US—where coincidentally I'd spent six months on exchange during my Arts degree at Melbourne Uni—and materialised on our continent like a dark archangel portending bad news. He promptly decreed any substantive constitutional change unachievable 'folly', proclaimed minimalism the only way forward, and basically advised Indigenous leaders to accept whatever miserable crumbs of acknowledgement the politicians were offering. Having been crucified in 2009 during his unsuccessful prosecution of a federal bill of rights, which was never implemented (even under a Labor government), now here was Lazarus risen from the dead, come again to bestow his infinite wisdom and pessimistic political prophecies regarding what the natives could and could not achieve.

Brennan's new book, titled *No Small Change*, argued for precisely that: small change.

It rejected an Indigenous constitutional body, dismissing the concept with one perfunctory prediction: 'there is no prospect that such a body would be included in the Constitution at this time'.[1] It also argued extensively against a racial non-discrimination clause. Instead of offering any substantive solution, the book argued for the insertion of some symbolic statements of recognition and cosmetic tinkering with the race clauses. Brennan spruiked this minimalist constitutional model at speeches and events and in the media.

No one from government or Recognise complained about Brennan's public push for minimalism.

It was my first introduction to a startling progressive phenomenon: the educated, white human rights lawyer who does not champion substantive constitutional reform to enhance Indigenous rights protections, but instead advocates low deals and minimalist solutions, driven by a mix of paternalistic goodwill, a weird faith in the healing power of symbolic gestures and political low expectations.

Brennan described himself as an Indigenous activist but championed constitutional symbolism, even though he knew Indigenous people wanted substantive reform. His public advocacy and behind-the-scenes manoeuvring played a significant role in letting conservative politicians off the hook: for here was a respected human rights advocate pushing minimalism and urging Indigenous leaders to accept it. It gave the politicians an easy way out.

When I think about it now, waves of fury still flow through me. I expected this kind of behaviour from the conservative right, not from a progressive human rights lawyer.

Brennan had historical form for such behaviour. His paternalistic interference in the *Wik* 'Ten Point Plan' native title negotiations in 1998 attracted the ire of former prime minister Paul Keating, who derided Brennan as a 'meddling priest'. (This was a reference to King Henry II's tirade against Thomas Becket, the Archbishop of Canterbury in 1170, who came into conflict with the king over church-versus-state quarrels because the laws of men and the laws of God were not yet constitutionally separated. In his frustration at the cleric's interference, King Henry is said to have proclaimed: 'Will no one rid me of this meddling priest!?' Four knights took the monarch's quip as a command—though this was not intended by the king—and murdered Becket.)

In 1998, contemporary Australia's own meddlesome priest had acted as an unauthorised go-between to prosecute a low-compromise solution to the *Wik* crisis. Brennan urged Tasmanian independent Brian Harradine to cut a deal with John Howard to resolve the high-tension conflict that was playing out. He did so without the permission of Indigenous leaders, whose rights were at stake and who were completely excluded from final negotiations, ostensibly to save them and the country from a divisive 'race' election. As Paul Kelly describes in *The March of Patriots,* Keating condemned Brennan for selling Indigenous people out and letting Howard off the hook, and also accused Brennan of second-guessing the electorate by assuming Labor could not win the forthcoming election—another pessimistic political prophecy. Kelly describes Brennan as 'worse than a meddling priest': he 'fought Labor's strategy of confrontation with Howard. He had opposed the strategy of Indigenous leaders. He had dined with Howard at the Lodge. He had consulted with Catholic Liberal politicians, among them Tony Abbott, to reach a settlement.'[2] Brennan was in everybody's business. Yet on whose behalf was he negotiating? And on whose authority?

Keating's final assessment was scathing: 'When Aborigines see Brennan, Harradine and other professional Catholics coming they should tell them to clear out.'[3] Noel at that time labelled the Howard government 'racist scum' for their discriminatory 'Ten Point Plan': for under Howard's rule, as Noel later described, 'kicking the black dog was not even politics, just sport'.[4] But if Howard's approach was to stoke racism, how then does one characterise Brennan's behaviour as mediator/facilitator of the 'Ten Point Plan'? My assessment: where Howard brought the hard racism, Brennan brought the soft bigotry—well-meaning, but perhaps more dangerous for its insidious undercover influence. Indigenous people never stood a chance.

Now he was doing the same thing on Indigenous constitutional recognition.

In 2015, Brennan did not seem to see his intervention as immoral. On the contrary: he seemed to view himself in impeccable esteem, as a supreme do-gooder—saving the Aborigines from their childish ambitions and the country from the pain of a failed referendum. He was saviour of us all, just like in 1998.

I asked Greg Craven for his advice. He's a 'lone wolf', Greg said simply. It was an apt description. Brennan seemed an independent operator who answered to no one and made his own political calculations.

Despite warnings against such damaging intervention from Noel and other leaders in the 1990s, Brennan was still aiming low. Though he may have meant well, his influence on the Indigenous recognition debate—like that of other good-willed political advisers like Gartrell and Textor—was ultimately counterproductive. Indigenous people should have been supported to negotiate an outcome directly with government, without the interference of unauthorised middlemen peddling low expectations (whether they knew it or not).

In 2015, Brennan went around opposing an Indigenous constitutional body, claiming it would undermine parliamentary sovereignty and raise issues about Indigenous identity. He also second-guessed the electorate, just as he had in 1998, predicting that the Australian people would not support such a body in the Constitution. Now, however, the opinions of respected Catholic constitutional lawyers were split. The world had gone topsy-turvy.

Greg Craven, the constitutional conservative, supported and publicly advocated for an Indigenous body, later describing it as the kind of referendum proposal that would 'gain support over time'—which was unusual, he said, as most referendum proposals lose support over time. Brennan, however, saw it as a proposal that would fail. And while Brennan was predicting failure, he was also actively ensuring it: his politicking was chipping away at the support we were trying to build. It was framed almost like a benevolent mercy killing: intended to put the poor unviable proposal out of its misery, and put Indigenous people out of their misery too, lest they hope too high and walk away disappointed. Because God forbid Indigenous people feel disappointed—how would they ever cope? And how would Australia ever cope with a failed referendum? Remember how the streets burned in 1999, when Howard's symbolic preamble was rejected? The looting? The civil unrest? The atrocity?

Only none of that ever happened.

Howard's preamble was pointless minimalism—many Indigenous organisations didn't support it, and the Australian people rightly rejected it. Why did Brennan want a rerun of that waste of time and money? Indigenous people had survived decades of colonisation. They would also survive the disappointment of trying to achieve constitutional justice but failing, of this I was sure. 'If we fail, so be it,' Noel would say.

Noel argued that we had to try for a good result, and that Indigenous people would be no worse off for having tried—the issue would remain open for future agitation and perhaps future generations might succeed. But if minimalism succeeded, then the constitutional recognition issue would be assumed resolved and taken off the table forever. They would have squandered their one shot at constitutional reform on a minimalist outcome that made no real difference to Indigenous peoples' lives. I agreed fully with Noel's assessment.

Some Indigenous leaders took to describing Brennan as a representative of the 'Catholic social justice mafia'. All they could do was try to mitigate the damage through their own advocacy.

Noel retaliated in the *Sydney Morning Herald* by highlighting the illegitimacy of Brennan's interference. 'This idea that somebody who has been out of the country ... can come back with his black robes on and determine what is right for our people is just completely inexplicable,' he said. 'I don't know where Frank Brennan gets off ... This is not black robe territory two centuries ago.'[5] Langton pleaded directly to the people. 'I implore Australians to listen to what Indigenous people want. Not Frank Brennan,' she said.[6]

But Brennan was well connected. The son of Sir Gerard Brennan, former chief justice of the High Court, he was respected in circles of power, affluence and prestige. He had the ears of politicians and a platform in the media. Thinking back, I am certain he influenced his fellow Catholic Tony Abbott, just as he had in the 1990s over *Wik*. It is likely that he advised Abbott to maintain, or indeed harden, his minimalist position.

Brennan was exactly why Indigenous people so desperately needed a constitutional voice in their affairs. So they could speak for themselves in matters concerning their rights, rather than having unauthorised white intellectuals cutting political deals on their behalf.

We asked Anne Twomey to make public our agreed constitutional drafting, under her name. We needed to get the words out there to respond to Brennan's claims of legal unworkability. Her article, published in May 2015, refuted Brennan's arguments and explained why the Indigenous body was a safe and modest proposal that was designed specifically to respect parliamentary sovereignty. Her drafting was also submitted to the committee.

That same month, Marcia Langton and I were invited to speak to the proposal at the Attorney-General's Department Constitutional Law Symposium in Canberra. I made the legal case, and explained why it was a constitutionally conservative model. Anne was also there, and she advocated in support. We took questions from the legal fraternity and fielded them well. We received positive feedback from many of the lawyers present, including representatives of the Attorney-General's Department, on the strength of our advocacy and ideas.

On 2 June, Noel and I met Malcolm Turnbull, then communications minister (this was before he became prime minister). Turnbull was accompanied by his then chief of staff Richard Windeyer, a descendant of the colonial barrister Richard Windeyer, a member of the Aborigines Protection Society who worked on the Myall Creek massacre trial, argued against land rights for Indigenous people, yet coined the phrase 'this whispering in our hearts' to describe the moral pain felt by Australians at the ongoing mistreatment of the original inhabitants, which historian Henry Reynolds later brought into popular Australian usage.

We explained to Turnbull the logic of our proposal, and why it was a sound alternative to a racial non-discrimination clause. He expressed sympathy with the 'one-clause bill of rights' arguments against what the Expert Panel proposed, and told us the Indigenous constitutional body alternative 'seems sensible'. He then asked, 'How can I help?' We discussed the possibility of a promotional event in his electorate, and he expressed a preference for pub events. It was a very positive meeting. Turnbull gave me his card and asked me to send him any material. 'Call me Malcolm,' he said warmly. I emailed him our policy papers that same day.

Noel and I also met privately with Ken Wyatt in early June. We'd sent him a detailed letter laying out the problems with the Expert Panel's approach and the more limited racial non-discrimination guarantees the committee was exploring. We were desperately trying to get him to see the political difficulties of sticking with a racial non-discrimination clause. The letter praised his work on the panel and as an Aboriginal man in Parliament, and reminded him of his comments in panel discussions that were published in the panel's report, advocating 'the need for public servants and parliamentarians to change their practices in dealing with ... communities' in favour of 'an approach based on negotiations with communities on a consensual basis'. We tried to get him to see that the proposed Indigenous body was a way to achieve this kind of empowering, relational shift.

Wyatt wasn't yet persuaded. He told us our proposal needed more work, and suggested the Indigenous body should be legislated first and possibly constitutionalised down the track—which was exactly what Frank Brennan was arguing.

On 12 June, CYI helped run a legal workshop, together with Anne Twomey, at Sydney University to critique and refine the Indigenous constitutional body proposal. Many respected constitutional lawyers gave papers on the proposal. There was robust discussion. George Williams' opposing arguments were refuted, as were Brennan's. The papers were published in a special edition of the *Indigenous Law Bulletin*. We invited committee members to attend but to my knowledge, none did. However, Tim Wilson made the effort to come, as did former Aboriginal Affairs Minister for the Liberals Fred Chaney.

Then, on 22 June, Noel and I met Christian Porter, former attorney-general of Western Australia and now parliamentary secretary to Abbott. We laid out the arguments for the Indigenous constitutional body proposal and the extra-constitutional Declaration. Porter was a constitutional conservative who had previously been a member of the joint select committee (though he was not present at the hearings I attended). He expressed concern about where the committee's work was heading and was rightly worried they were sticking with the doomed Expert Panel approach—an approach he said he did not support. Porter understood and was amenable to our alternative approach, so much so that Noel suggested he should be a 'champion' for the reforms in Parliament. It was a positive meeting.

Later that month, the joint select committee delivered its final report. As feared, it stuck with the Expert Panel. The committee recommended removing references to 'race' and proposed three variations of the Expert Panel's racial non-discrimination proposal, plus symbolic statements in the Constitution in the form of a new section 51A. It completely failed to step right, or up.

The report rejected Cape York Institute's proposals. That came as no surprise.

A historic Kirribilli meeting was to be held on Monday 6 July 2015, soon after the committee's report was delivered. Tony Abbott and Opposition Leader Bill Shorten invited forty Indigenous leaders to attend to discuss next steps for Indigenous constitutional recognition.

The weekend prior, the National Congress of Australia's First Peoples invited Indigenous leaders to convene in Sydney to prepare their position. I was asked to attend, together with CYI's head of policy, former bureaucrat Brian Stacey. The first day, Brian and I were kicked out of the room due to an Indigenous motion. I was used to this by now.

Later, I was invited to speak on the CYI proposals. As it turned out, I was on a panel with Frank Brennan and another (former) Catholic priest, Patrick Dodson. Luckily I had been drafting letter responses to Brennan's arguments, so had my arguments fully nutted out.

Dodson spoke first, urging the Expert Panel's proposals. He particularly saw a need to 'cut the cancer' of race out of the Constitution, and saw removing the race power and inserting a new section 51A power as a good way to do this. Of course, such changes alone would not prevent Parliament enacting racist laws. Without a racial non-discrimination clause, removing the word 'race'—or removing the race power and inserting a new power—was just a cosmetic change.

Brennan went next and outlined his arguments against CYI's body proposal.

Then it was my turn. In front of the Indigenous audience, I refuted each of Brennan's arguments and urged him to cease his negative advocacy and give Indigenous people the time and space to try to achieve a substantive outcome, instead of trying to kill every substantive proposal. The tension in the room was high and Brennan's pale cheeks were rosy with adrenaline. He nodded sagely at my refutations. I worried about how he may be influencing fellow Catholic Dodson.

The next day, on 5 July, Brennan sent Noel a letter. He noted his interaction with me on the panel and reassured Noel that he would stay quiet and out of the press—for the next few days at least. He signed off in good humour, referencing Noel's attacks on him: 'Frank Brennan SJ (Black Robe)'.

In the Kirribilli Statement of 6 July, Indigenous leaders demanded substantive constitutional reform, with the Expert Panel proposals as the benchmark. Brennan was trying to drag them low, but they were keeping the tension high. 'A minimalist approach that provides preambular recognition, removes section 25 and moderates the race power [section 51(xxvi)] does not go far enough and would not be acceptable to Aboriginal and Torres Strait Islander peoples,' the statement declared.

But walking into the meeting, Joint Select Committee Chairman Wyatt was doorstopped by the media. Astoundingly, after his committee had recommended three variations of a racial non-discrimination clause, Wyatt told reporters that such a clause was unlikely to succeed. I was gobsmacked. He later confirmed his position in *The Australian*. A racial non-discrimination clause would not get up, he said, because it was already being opposed, including by 'those in my own party' who saw it as 'effectively a bill of rights'.[7]

Just as we had predicted, Wyatt slid to the right and down, and political expectations followed.

This was exactly what we'd been trying to tell the committee since 2014. This was why we'd been pushing an alternative substantive solution. But on the proposed constitutional body, Wyatt at this stage remained dismissive. '[I]t has merit, but I don't think it will be embedded in the Constitution,' he said[8]—a pessimistic political prediction that sounded much like Brennan's perfunctory dismissal in his book. I noted the sense of powerlessness in Wyatt's words: as if these were the decisions of others, not him. Wyatt was, it seemed to me, yet to find his own voice on constitutional recognition. He would galvanise in years to come, but for now, he seemed stuck.

What did that leave, then, in terms of constitutional reform?

Having repudiated the substantive options recommended in his own committee's report, and having dismissed an Indigenous constitutional body, the manoeuvring left only one option on the table: minimalism—Frank Brennan's miserable position, which Indigenous people said they did not want.

It was a devastating blow. We had worked so hard to try to shift the committee to the radical centre, but had completely failed.

Noel was brutally honest in the media about the 'highly stage-managed' nature of the Kirribilli meeting, at which he said Shorten and Abbott 'pretended to listen' to Indigenous leaders when actually they had already decided a way forward themselves. He also condemned Wyatt's capitulation to minimalism upon entry into the meeting. Noel's criticisms were fair: the whole thing had been choreographed by Recognise. The pollsters were not perturbed by Wyatt's abandonment of a racial non-discrimination clause—they didn't criticise his capitulation in the media. Somehow when Noel had abandoned a racial non-discrimination clause in favour of an Indigenous body, they had been outraged, but when Wyatt abandoned a racial non-discrimination clause in favour of minimalism, nobody complained—except Noel.

It made me wonder: perhaps Wyatt's backdown was planned and timed. Had he been instructed to publicly concede that a racial non-discrimination clause would not fly? Were they hoping it would go unnoticed amid the feel-good festivities surrounding the Kirribilli meeting? Many other leaders were mostly swept up in the occasion. Noel, however, didn't let it slide. He slammed the meeting, Recognise and Wyatt.

Wyatt seemed untroubled, and dismissed Noel's criticisms as unstatesmanlike 'hissy fits'.[9] This was the beginning of a meme that would be used against Noel and our constitutional reform proposals to undermine Noel's intellectual authority and credibility by framing him as a bully and a sook who was upset that his body idea had not been adopted. Noel's criticisms of government would be dismissed as mere tantrums and tirades. This, I believe, was a deliberate strategy emanating from government.

Noel was standing up for his people and rightly calling out those in power. Given the committee's charade process and Wyatt's surrender to minimalism, his reaction was warranted. Noel had his faults, but the gossip that he was a bully was overcooked. While he was a passionate advocate and a courageous political fighter, in my experience he was also remarkably patient and forgiving. More than I was.

In the coming years he would try to work again with Textor, despite Textor's past behaviour and despite me voicing concerns. He was also more forgiving of Gartrell and Brennan than I was initially inclined to be.

As for the accusation that Noel was simply upset that his own idea was not getting traction, anyone following the debate and Noel's work would understand the reality as more complex. Noel did not tend to get intellectually attached to any particular idea. According to my observation, he simply wanted a good outcome for Indigenous people and was interested in good ideas in general. That's why he had been open to Julian and Damien's Declaration proposal. And that's why he had been quicker than everyone else to switch from a racial non-discrimination clause (a proposal we had championed) to an alternative solution (he was quicker to abandon it than me, for I was intellectually attached to my ideas, I admit).

For Noel, a good outcome was always more important than his idea winning. It was more about the correctness of the positions than intellectual ownership. Indeed, for people who know him, Noel's intellectual changeability can be infuriating—he is forever coming up with a new solution. That's because he is a seeker and a learner. A hunter of the radical centre. His is anything but a stagnant mind.

The 'egotistical bully'–type jibes were attempts at undermining our efforts to build consensus by undermining Noel's character. They floated around in the form of rumour and ridicule.

On the grapevine we heard some Labor committee members were calling the constitutional body proposal an 'Aboriginal House of Lords' when it was no such thing, and Noel saw himself as 'chief lord' was the joke. It was an early iteration of the 'third chamber of Parliament' caricature that would be used prolifically by Malcolm Turnbull in years to come to disparage the Uluru Statement from the Heart. I suspect that smear began with some Labor members. Talk about a bipartisan approach.

In 2017, Turnbull would signal the phrase in a private meeting about the Indigenous advisory body with Noel: he snidely referred to Noel as 'Lord Pearson'. I didn't know about this incident until Noel told me recently, and I felt sick when I heard. It was a schoolyard taunt that reminded me of my own childhood: the clever, dark-skinned geek getting sneered at by the pompous white rich kid. There is only room for one lord of the manor here, the sneer said.

There is something abhorrently racist about the 'Aboriginal House of Lords' meme that I detest. As if it's okay for white people to form committees, bodies and institutions, but if Aboriginal people want to do it, that deserves to be mocked. The derision spoke to something base and bigoted, and the far right joined in. Eccentric right-wing monarchist David Flint would in 2017 describe the proposed Indigenous advisory body as 'a cross between a House of Lords and a Raj Chamber of Princes'. The *Spectator* editor, Rowan Dean, used similar derisory language. The meme spread among the political elite, from left to right, and eventually to the Liberal Party and Turnbull himself.

And yet the proposal was simply for an Indigenous advisory body, to advise on Indigenous affairs. External to Parliament. Non-binding advice. No veto. Set up in legislation. Guaranteed by the Constitution.

There was no proposed change to the Houses of Parliament whatsoever. It was a modest request given the discrimination and dispossession Indigenous people had suffered at the hands of government for so many decades. A request, simply, to be heard in decisions made about them.

Despite its modesty, the proposal got slandered by politicians. And Noel, the model's chief proponent—who was born a non-citizen, who grew up in the mission at Hopevale under protection policies, whose people had endured racism, violence and dispossession, who came from poverty and got where he is only through his talent, intelligence, ABSTUDY support and sheer hard work—was mocked as 'Lord Pearson', a blackfella who was getting too big for his boots. And it was Malcolm Bligh Turnbull, multimillionaire ex-banking magnate, the prime minister of Australia, who did the mocking. Noel was arguing for a constitutional voice for Indigenous people—the most disadvantaged people in the country. Turnbull was preparing to reject the request.

Think about those power dynamics.

Noel was not the bully in this story. Not by a long shot.

I emailed Brennan in response to his letter to Noel, to set up a conciliatory meeting. On 10 July 2015, together with the constitutional conservatives, we attempted an intervention at ACU in Melbourne. Priest or no priest, the meddling had to stop.

Noel and I, together with Indigenous leader Richie Ahmat of the Cape York Land Council, sought to resolve our differences with Brennan and bring him on board with the body proposal. The meeting was hosted by Greg Craven at his ACU chambers in Melbourne. Julian Leeser was also present to show that conservative support for the proposal was indeed possible.

Greg asked Brennan to open with a prayer, to get us into the conciliatory spirit. We all diligently bowed our heads, despite the fact that a Jew (Julian), a Lutheran (Noel) and a non-practising agnostic Hindu (me) were around the table. I peeped at the men through lowered lids—all had their eyes closed as Brennan led the prayer, concluding with a group 'Amen'.

We had a productive discussion in which we asked for Brennan's input in refining the proposal and urged him to hold off on trying to kill it while we worked to build the necessary consensus. Ostensibly at least, he agreed to work with us.

Alas, despite our shared prayers, it was not to be. A week or so later he wrote antagonistically about Noel's advocacy around the Kirribilli meeting. Noel retaliated with a terse phone call and promptly handballed any other engagement with Brennan to me to avoid further angry altercations.

'Who will rid us of this meddling priest?' I emailed in exasperation. We were at a loss.

At the same time, the political landscape was changing.

There was a sense of impending change in our lobbying trips to Parliament House. We met with Queensland Liberal Mal Brough, among others, in early September 2015. He sat with me and Harold Ludwick, a Cape York man who was a passionate supporter of the reforms. Brough seemed amenable to the proposals and cryptically indicated that he thought the political situation might soon become more favourable for our cause. Abbott was the roadblock, seemed the implication. In retrospect, Brough's hints make more sense. It seemed he thought Turnbull would provide more effective and progressive leadership.

Later that same month, having squandered his political capital on a series of poor decisions that indicated a disconnect with the electorate—not least of which was that 'dumbass knighthood' for Prince Philip, as Noel later described it[10]—Abbott lost his prime ministership to Turnbull in a leadership spill, with Brough among Turnbull's supporters. Our potential Nixon was no longer prime minister. Maybe a more progressive prime minister would be better for Indigenous people, we hoped. And perhaps Abbott could be pulled to a better position on the backbench now that he didn't have his prime ministership to lose. This was how we mused in our more optimistic moments.

In our more pessimistic ones, we dreaded that things had gone from bad to worse, and that Abbott might not let Turnbull achieve anything easily. Noel told me to read John Milton's *Paradise Lost* and pay particular attention to the poetic descriptions of Satan and his squad of blood-hungry fiends. That epic poem, Noel surmised, provided an insight into the probable post-defeat mindset of Abbott and his far-right faction:

> … Him the almighty power
> Hurled headlong flaming from the ethereal sky
> With hideous ruin and combustion down
> To bottomless perdition, there to dwell
> In adamantine chains and penal fire,
> Who durst defy the omnipotent to arms.
> Nine times the space that measures day and night
> To mortal men, he with his horrid crew
> Lay vanquished, rolling in the fiery gulf,
> Confounded, though immortal; but his doom
> Reserved him to more wrath, for now the thought
> Both of lost happiness and lasting pain
> Torments him; round he throws his baleful eyes
> That witnessed huge affliction and dismay
> Mixed with obdurate pride and steadfast hate.

This was basically going to be Abbott and his far-right posse for the foreseeable future, Noel postulated hilariously. Ever the grand and literary thinker, he was seeking to prompt our creative interrogation of the strategic problem. He would often use biblical or Shakespearean analogies to elucidate vexing political challenges—now it was Milton, and the imagery was not far off.

Condemned to dwell in backbench hell, and harried by fitful dungeon dreams of escaping the inferno and ascending once again to power, Abbott would likely be single-minded about exacting vengeance. He would not, we feared, be thinking about how to conclude his public service by establishing for himself a lasting legacy of honour and dignity by helping to deliver meaningful constitutional recognition of Indigenous peoples—the most disadvantaged, disempowered and dispossessed people in the country. No.

If Milton knew anything about the forces of nature, humanity, the ways of men, and heaven and hell, Abbott would likely be thinking of only one thing: how to make Turnbull pay.

10

The Art of Persuasion

WHILE AUSTRALIAN POLITICAL leaders were knifing each other in the back in their struggles for power, a small army of Indigenous advocates was building, united by the desire to address their powerlessness. Led by the intellectual forces of Noel, Megan Davis and Marcia Langton, they were excellent persuaders: articulate, intelligent and, most of all, passionate—for it was their people they were advocating for. Each saw the immense value in Indigenous peoples having a constitutional voice in their affairs and was prepared to work to make it happen. I would help them prepare, providing material, writing support and offering persuasive tips.

In addition to our positive meetings with Turnbull and Porter prior to the spill, we'd been meeting several other politicians. On these lobbying trips, I would initially accompany Noel and sometimes Marcia. Later, other Indigenous advocates championing the Indigenous body proposal would come with me instead, among them Rachel Perkins; dedicated Cape Yorker Harold Ludwick; and bright young leaders Adam Bray and Nigel Craig. We would also be joined by (King) Nolan Hunter, who ever since our New Zealand trip had been a steadfast supporter of the approach. Sean Gordon began advocating in his own right. And Davis, as always, was using her ever-expanding national and international academic profile and cultural influence to make powerful speeches and write articles in favour of substantive constitutional recognition.

I usually joined Uphold & Recognise on their lobbying trips, too. In 2016, Damien hired an impressive young advocate, David Allinson, a law and philosophy student who demonstrated a passionate interest in Indigenous constitutional recognition from a conservative perspective. With his British accent and affable manner, David proved an energetic addition to the Uphold & Recognise team. Together, our two organisations were making a significant effort at pulling some Coalition members across the line. Others remained immovable. We also tried to persuade conservative commentators.

Prior to the leadership spill, journalist for *The Australian* Chris Kenny wrote a negative piece arguing that our proposed Indigenous body was too complicated. Noel immediately urged me to go meet with him. In June 2015, Kenny met me near the News Corp building in Sydney. We spoke in hushed tones in the cramped cafe and I laid out the problem: Indigenous people want substantive reform, but too many politicians think this is only about symbolism. There are dual conversations happening, I said, and they are clashing. I took him through the history of Indigenous advocacy and explained the logic of our proposal, why it was a conservative and sensible, noble compromise. Kenny asked me to send him as much material as possible. I did, and even pasted a chronology of the history of Indigenous advocacy into the email.

A week later, Kenny emailed to say he had written a 'pretty strong endorsement' of our approach for the Saturday *Oz*. He had turned from critic to supporter. Kenny thought an institutional voice for Indigenous people was 'the least we can do' and felt the proposal aligned with conservative themes of responsibility and equality. He was intelligent and capable of nuanced and empathetic thought, and on this issue, he was prepared to take a moral stand. His writing on the proposed Indigenous advisory body, a Declaration and even the fraught (for his conservative constituency) concept of a treaty was impressive for its nuance and sensitivity.

Kenny suggested I meet with other right-wing commentators Andrew Bolt and Greg Sheridan, and made email introductions.

I wouldn't change their minds, Kenny advised, but I'd likely take the hard edge off their 'No' case advocacy. He also introduced me to Chris Merritt, legal affairs editor at *The Australian*. Over time Merritt, too, became persuaded and wrote compelling legal arguments for the proposed constitutional advisory body.

Damien took to teasing me with the title 'Queen of Sheba', after the African monarch said to have beguiled King Solomon with her exotic spices and gifts—implying it was my feminine wiles that made me an effective persuader. I told him to stop being jealous, but suggested he refer to me with that title from now on—which he occasionally did. He and I had begun coediting a collection of essays to drum up right-wing support and propel discussion of the package of reforms. It was to be called *The Forgotten People: Liberal and Conservative Approaches to Recognising Indigenous Peoples*. Damien was accustomed to writing and publishing books. I was not. He graciously allowed me to coedit the collection with him, and also include an essay of my own.

The book turned out to be an excellent persuasive tool—a way of signing up supporters and getting them on the record. It was also a means for promotion, media and advocacy. Essay contributors would include Chris Kenny, Greg Craven, Anne Twomey, former governor-general Michael Jeffery, Cardinal George Pell, Tim Wilson and Julian Leeser, among others. Kenny, Craven, Twomey, Pell, Leeser, Freeman and I all used our essays to make the case for a constitutional body. Others argued for a Declaration or recognition generally. Australian Christian Lobby right-winger Lyle Shelton even wrote empathetically about frontier violence and the need for national atonement. Working on the book was a revelation. It showed me how much goodwill exists for this cause, even on the right.

Damien asked Nationals senator Bridget McKenzie to contribute an essay. She couldn't, but remained enthusiastic about the proposals. He also asked Christian Porter to contribute, due to his previously expressed support: Porter agreed. He later withdrew, citing lack of time, but still provided a written endorsement for the book. Damien and I met with Porter on 19 April 2016. At this meeting, Porter indicated even more enthusiasm for the advisory body proposal, describing it as an 'elegant solution'. We were so encouraged we asked him if he would launch our book in Perth, and we spent the next several months trying to organise a date that worked for him.

The Forgotten People was released in March 2016. Reverend Tim Costello, former head of World Vision, had agreed to launch it in Melbourne in June. Porter had agreed to launch it in Perth. Things were looking up.

Over these years, we met with senior staff and legal advisers in the attorney-general's office, who informed us that the Indigenous body proposal, something along the lines of Anne's drafting, was legally sound and their preferred constitutional approach. They had also been engaging productively with Julian, who was championing the merits of the reforms.

Some younger MPs in the Liberal Party began to come quietly on board, particularly up-and-comers like good-willed right-winger Alex Hawke and optimistic progressive Craig Laundy, both from Sydney, as well as the quirky and canny Andrew Laming of Queensland—each indicated they would be willing to support the reforms we were proposing, including an Indigenous constitutional body, over minimalism. They were impressed with our work and encouraged us to keep going. We got the beginnings of good vibes and indications of interest from newcomer conservative Andrew Hastie from Western Australia; and Liberal Tim Wilson, having contributed to our book, was demonstrating increasing enthusiasm about getting actively involved in the debate. Even ex-IPA Victorian senator James Paterson initially seemed to indicate some amenability to the logic of our proposal, while also mischievously suggesting that Australians were not free to candidly discuss the issue due to the supposed free speech restrictions imposed by section 18C of the *Racial Discrimination Act* (the baseness and dishonesty of Turnbull's rejection and the ensuing debate, however, has since demonstrated without a doubt that free speech in Australia—even fallacious and bigoted speech—is alive and well). With extraordinary impudence, Paterson seemed to suggest that if Noel came out in support of repealing 18C, then a free discussion could be had and he could think about supporting our constitutional reform proposal. *Yeah right*, I thought, and Noel agreed. Some older Liberal Party members, including Russell Broadbent of Victoria, also became increasingly supportive but noted that lowly backbenchers couldn't bring this home alone—it needed a party leader to champion the cause, so they could rally around him. It was sound advice.

In addition to McKenzie, we were finding pockets of significant goodwill among members of the National Party, including (at that stage) Nationals leader Barnaby Joyce, who, in our brief interactions, indicated general enthusiasm about the idea of recognition. This accorded with Noel's experience in the 1990s that good-hearted country people with significant Aboriginal populations in their electorates could often be persuaded to support fair reform proposals. Even the bombastic Queensland conservative George Christensen shocked us initially with a passionate statement about the need to protect Indigenous culture and heritage, though he eventually landed in opposition to the proposal.

As for crossbenchers, the Greens were supportive, and the Nick Xenophon Team was positive and understood our radical centre approach—they even began adopting the term. A few tense meetings with Pauline Hanson began to build some interesting rapport. On Noel's instructions, I'd written for him an opinion piece praising her defence of Julian Assange, which was published in the *Herald Sun* the day Damien, David and I met her for the first time. The olive branch from Noel had an impact. After initial hostility, Hanson in that meeting became drawn in by arguments that respected, rather than repudiated, Australia's British heritage, and she even told us that she felt Indigenous culture was special and should be celebrated. To our surprise, she said she thought we 'could bring Australians along' with these constitutional recognition arguments. Upon saying goodbye, she squeezed my arm and told me I looked 'beautiful in that blue dress'. Hanson, we discovered, was a striking personality: a strangely alluring mixture of vulnerability and rancour. Could we get her on board?

One of Hanson's senior advisers was in favour of our approach and began to attend our promotional events with her imprimatur, 'because it's important', we were told. These indications were positive, but a following meeting with Noel and me was not nearly so productive. This time, Hanson's opposition began to flow fiercely. By this stage her party was in trouble, which may have been a factor, or perhaps persuasion of her worked better with comforting white men by my side, rather than Noel. Were two brown faces a strategic mistake, causing Hanson to feel 'swamped', I wondered? We'll never know. Still, we got close. And it was worth a shot. I still wonder whether Hanson might find it in her heart to support this fair and sensible reform.

The model increasingly won favour among key respected monarchists. Initially, David Flint came on board with the idea of an extra-constitutional Declaration. Later, Damien and I lunched with him at the Australia Club and made the case for the Indigenous body. Flint listened attentively but cautiously. Eventually, however, he descended into public derision, with his own creative variations on the 'Aboriginal House of Lords' taunt.

One of our most enthusiastic monarchist supporters turned out to be Kerry Jones, who had succeeded Tony Abbott as executive director of Australians for Constitutional Monarchy and was close to Damien and Julian. She was joined by people like Major General Michael Jeffery, Dame Marie Bashir, and Lloyd Waddy, the first chair of Uphold & Recognise. Monarchists often had a propensity to support the proposals, we found. Many carried immense goodwill towards Indigenous people, and could see how at the very least they deserved a voice in their own affairs—a fact that is perhaps historically unsurprising.

In making the case, I would remind conservative audiences that in 1787, as his fleet sailed towards Botany Bay, Arthur Phillip, like Cook before him, carried secret instructions from his British king commanding him to 'endeavour, by every possible means, to open an intercourse with the natives, and to conciliate their affections, enjoining all our subjects to live in amity and kindness with them'.[1] These instructions were not followed. An English-Australian journalist Edward Wilson lamented in *The Argus* in 1856 that:

> In less than twenty years we have nearly swept them off the face of the earth. We have shot them down like dogs. In the guise of friendship we have issued corrosive sublimate in their damper and

consigned whole tribes to the agonies of an excruciating death. We have made them drunkards, and infected them with diseases which have rotted the bones of their adults, and made such few children as are born amongst them a sorrow and a torture from the very instant of their birth. We have made them outcasts on their own land, and are rapidly consigning them to entire annihilation.[2]

The force and violence of colonisation in Australian history cannot accurately be described as a relationship of 'amity and kindness'.

The monarch's historical injunction had contemporary moral impact, especially on monarchists. Julian, Damien and now Kerry and many other monarchists, through their support, advocacy and collaboration, were striving to forge a relationship of mutual amity and kindness not only with Noel and me, but with Indigenous people more generally. They saw the merit in sensibly transforming the Crown's constitutional relationship with Indigenous peoples, to ensure it would be fairer than in the past.

Kerry adored Noel, describing him reverently as 'Australia's Gandhi', and her involvement in our constitutional recognition work attracted the criticism of far-right stalwarts such as former National Party politician John Stone. Stone published a furious column in *The Spectator* in response to a promotional event, condemning Julian and Damien for their involvement, attacking the contributors to our book, including Tim Wilson and Chris Kenny, and slating me ('Shirreen Morris'—with my name misspelled): 'I do not know her personally,' Stone wrote, 'but have seen her interviewed on television. She strikes me as an intellectually arrogant young woman, clearly unwilling to suffer gladly any fool who disagrees with her.'[3] With characteristic intellectual arrogance, I still wonder if Stone realised he'd inadvertently conceded that people who disagree with me are fools (himself included), or if it was just part of his intentionally confusing writing style.

I began to grow a thick skin and we didn't let such outbursts dissuade us. This was part of sorting the wheat from the chaff: the reactionaries from the true conservatives. Stone's reaction told us we must be doing a good job—our opponents were getting anxious.

Julian and Damien had been trying to engage former prime minister John Howard, with little success. Julian attempted to persuade him that a new preamble to the Constitution was a bad idea that risked yielding unintended legal consequences through judicial interpretation, and that our approach—an Indigenous constitutional body and an extra-constitutional Declaration—was superior. Howard, however, was a committed minimalist. He had tried to implement a purely symbolic preamble in 1999 and Australians had voted no. Despite that failure, he wasn't budging.

It was a monarchist who alerted us to a prolific rumour regarding Turnbull's ascendancy to the prime ministership. The rumour in authoritative circles was that he had done a deal with Howard to secure his support in the spill against Abbott. Part of this deal was that Turnbull as prime minister would only support minimalist constitutional change—nothing more.

After the spill, Howard immediately expressed support for Turnbull's leadership, though he was philosophically more aligned to Abbott. I remember discussing it with Noel: Howard's endorsement felt too soon, almost unseemly. Abbott held Howard in great esteem as his political mentor and was stung by his hasty endorsement of his usurper.

In that June 2015 meeting prior to the September spill, Turnbull had told Noel and me that our proposed constitutional body sounded sensible, and offered his support. But perhaps it all changed when Turnbull became prime minister. And perhaps the deal with Howard was part of the reason. A monarchist ally seemed sure this was the case. Noel floated the theory in his Woodford Folk Festival speech in 2017. In early 2018, Howard wrote to Noel to deny the claim. Noel responded, accepting Howard's refutation, but explaining that his theory was based on information from a prominent conservative figure, and on Howard's 'unseemly' quick endorsement of Turnbull.

That Turnbull sold out his principles in order to obtain power fits with his inability to provide the kind of progressive leadership he promised Australians. Former Labor prime minister Bob Hawke, speaking in 2017 at the same Woodford festival, where he is a regular guest, suggested Turnbull's leadership was fundamentally afflicted by shame, due to the many concessions he had made to secure the top job. 'I have a theory that Malcolm is basically ashamed. By that I mean Malcolm had to give up certain issues that he believed in to get the numbers to roll Tony Abbott,' Hawke told the Woodford crowd.[4] Turnbull had to concede many of his principles to the conservative right of his party to obtain power. It is likely he also abandoned his support for an Indigenous body in the Constitution in favour of minimalism, to shore up his ascendancy.

It was bad news for our cause. Without a supportive prime minister, our work was likely to go nowhere, no matter what support we could muster lower down in his party. The only way we might change the situation was to persuade Abbott, who could persuade the right. If we could get Abbott to come out in support, this could give Turnbull the cover he needed to be able to support more substantive change. We resolved to keep trying.

Noel had done the groundwork in the relationship. Abbott had called Noel a 'prophet' of our times and mutual respect had been fostered. But while often supported by Noel, Abbott was also regularly taken to task by him. In 2014, when Abbott declared that the arrival of the First Fleet was Australia's defining moment, Noel rang and admonished him. He told Abbott that he couldn't take a narrow Anglophile stance as prime minister—he needed to govern for all Australians and embrace the three defining moments: the arrival of the First Peoples, the arrival of the First Fleet and the multicultural immigration that began with the end of the White Australia policy. In 2015, Noel strongly criticised Abbott's comments about remote Indigenous communities being a 'lifestyle choice', describing the debate as 'deranged' and 'substandard'.[5]

It was a love–hate relationship.

Sometime after the spill, Noel had dinner with Abbott to share commiserations. Together with Julian and Damien, we'd been trying to keep Abbott on side and thinking through the proposals. Then, at his Press Gallery speech on 27 January 2016, Noel told journalists he regretted the spill that had seen Abbott fall from power. He was trying to remain neutral while also showing Abbott support, but the comment made headlines. I later wondered if this was a factor in Turnbull withdrawing support for the Indigenous body proposal, or whether it was the alleged deal with Howard that did it, or simply the political difficulty of holding his party together amid continued pressure from Abbott and the right. Or perhaps it was his chronic inability to lead, or his basic disinterest in Indigenous affairs.

Maybe it was all these things.

Whatever the reasons, Turnbull after becoming prime minister decided to oppose the Indigenous constitutional body proposal he'd previously described as 'sensible'. He was supposed to be a progressive prime minister but he converted to minimalism, just like John Howard. He began to dog-whistle like Howard too. Australians had thought they were getting a reform-ambitious, innovative leader. We were duped.

He could don a leather jacket, but Turnbull was John Howard's boy.

I emailed Brennan on 29 October 2015, after the spill, to urge him to 'allow the political tensions to play out' and 'allow Indigenous people some time to *try* to negotiate and persuade a good outcome'. We then talked on the phone. It was a long and emotional conversation. 'Frank, would you be happy if Indigenous people succeeded and got an Indigenous body in the Constitution? You personally?' I asked.

Brennan, surprisingly, indicated he would indeed be happy with that outcome. I was shocked. 'Then why are you arguing against it?' I asked, baffled.

'Because it will fail,' he told me passionately. 'I can feel it in my bones!' I imagined those street-corner evangelists—*The end is nigh! The prophet has spoken!*—and considered the impact of such negative public advocacy on Australia's already reform-shy political culture. If a progressive human rights advocate was predicting doom, what hope was there? Brennan was reiterating predictions he had published and stated publicly many times before.

'Your political prediction may ultimately prove correct, Frank,' I said, containing my anger. 'But you are creating a self-fulfilling prophecy, and it's undermining our attempts, and Indigenous people's attempts, to achieve a good outcome.' I told him how hard Julian, Damien, Noel, Rachel and others were working to drum up support on the right. 'Think about it,' I said. 'If you keep doing what you're doing, we won't ever know whether your prediction was correct or not, because you are killing the proposal yourself! Why don't you let it play out?' I was attempting to snare him in his own logic, hoping he would want to see his political prediction independently proven correct so he could say 'I told you so'.

Brennan agreed to stop making the 'No' case. He stopped publicly arguing against the Indigenous body proposal and, to my knowledge, did not comment again until after the Uluru Statement from the Heart, in 2017. The sad thing was that by the time he ceased his negative advocacy, the damage was probably already done.

I often consider what our efforts, and the efforts of so many Indigenous advocates, might have yielded had Brennan been a supporter, rather than an opponent. Fighting him took time and energy that should have been spent persuading the political right, where the real work was needed.

Yet he was not the only human rights lawyer whose seeming acceptance of mere symbolism on Indigenous recognition took me by surprise. In 2016, on my first-ever appearance on the ABC's *Q&A*, Gillian Triggs, the prolific then-president of Australia's Human Rights Commission, while expressing her support for consitutional recognition seemed to suggest a merely symbolic outcome might be acceptable. 'We cannot have our First Nations peoples not even mentioned in our constitution,' she said—that word, a mere 'mention', to me always seemed to ominously suggest minimalism. Her following comments ignited my concerns: 'We've got to start with some of these changes. It may be more symbolic than anything else. We don't yet know what's going to be proposed.'[6] Triggs went on to note that the proposal must be accepted by Indigenous people, but I was baffled: if it needed to be accepted by Indigenous people, why was she predicting a symbolic outcome that Indigenous Australians were overwhelmingly rejecting? As a human rights advocate, why wasn't she advocating more forcefully that the Constitution should better protect Indigenous human rights?

The panel members in the green room had just witnessed the harrowing Don Dale abuse-in-custody report on *Four Corners*, and we each had acknowledged the need for urgent practical action in Indigenous affairs in our on-screen discussion. Yet Triggs seemed to frame constitutional recognition as a merely symbolic endeavour. To me it felt like it was a massive wasted opportunity. Triggs was a respected and influential human rights expert, whose voice might have made a difference. But Triggs had also been in fierce battles with the government over refugee rights, so perhaps her reticence on Indigenous recognition, at this stage of the debate, was understandable.

I pushed back, however. 'Indigenous people's views are absolutely crucial to this,' I said. 'I reiterate that I wouldn't support going ahead with anything that Indigenous Australians didn't agree to and … they've made it clear time and time again that they don't want mere symbolism. They want this to be practical … This is a big opportunity and it's one we need to think really carefully and strategically about. It's not just about saying, well, maybe we'll end up with symbolism and maybe that's okay. I don't think that would be okay.'[7]

On that *Q&A*, I refuted the arguments of conservative philosopher and theologian from the Centre for Independent Studies Peter Kurti, who seemed to argue for a symbolic preamble while at the same time complaining it would make no practical difference, and suggesting that practical action was more important. Well, exactly. I pointed out the nonsensical, circular nature of his argument: if practical action was important, then we should implement practical reform, not feel-good constitutional nothingness. I could comprehend why conservative Kurti needed to be pushed—this was expected. But the human rights left, in my view, should have been advocating for substantive reform, not conceding to political low expectations.

The lethargic attitude of acceptance of mediocrity on Indigenous recognition, demonstrated by some on the left, was becoming infuriating. I can sometimes be impatient, however. Building consensus takes time, and everyone must travel at their own pace. In years to come, after Turnbull's rejection, Triggs would advocate in favour of the Uluru Statement, particularly supporting its call for treaties.[8]

Still, Indigenous people could have used Triggs' respected influence and advocacy in fighting for substantive constitutional recognition, before the rejection. They could have used Brennan's influence and advocacy too. They could have used the support of many progressive commentators and lawyers who chose to withhold it until it was too late.

In June 2016, Julian Leeser and I argued for an Indigenous constitutional body and an extra-constitutional Declaration at an event at the conservative Sydney Institute, run by Gerard and Anne Henderson (who seemed increasingly supportive of our approach). Julian made an articulate case, and we both successfully fielded the grumpy 'humphs' and heckling from right-wing historian and Stolen Generations denier Keith Windschuttle, who was in the front row.

In August the previous year, I'd watched Julian stand up and advocate the proposals at the Samuel Griffith Society conference, prompting dismissive boos and heckling from half the audience and winning the quiet respect of others. He stood up for our proposals in front of the toughest of crowds, explained them and answered the aggressive questions with patient politeness and perseverance—a true man of principle. Chris Kenny would do the same at a right-wing *Quadrant* conference. He delivered a dinner keynote endorsing the proposals at a Samuel Griffith Society conference, in the same harsh conditions. Kenny too was brave and principled in the face of criticism from parts of his constituency.

While Julian and Chris were undertaking this kind of courageous advocacy, former deputy director of Cape York Institute Alan Tudge, who was parliamentary secretary to Abbott and then a minister for Turnbull, was going with the minimalist flow of his government. He went around advocating for minimalism, including at a Jawun Indigenous business dinner. 'Could you stop saying we support a preamble?' I asked him as he was leaving, assuming (incorrectly) some remnant allegiance on his part with Cape York Institute and Noel. 'I'm not saying *you* support it,' Tudge replied sheepishly. On another occasion I ran into him on the foyer steps at Parliament House and told him Indigenous people still wanted substantive constitutional reform. Tudge said something to the effect that most Indigenous people wouldn't know what's in the Constitution anyway, letting slip his disdain.

I was dumbfounded and called Noel to report his comments. In my experience, Indigenous Australians—like any Australians—could indeed understand the Constitution given the right information, explanation and support. Constitutional ignorance was certainly no excuse for trying to dupe people into accepting substandard reform. My sense of Tudge's latent prejudice was confirmed in a 2016 meeting in Melbourne together with David Allinson, at which Tudge grudgingly said he would probably support our proposal just to support Noel, but then went on to assert that there really were no decent Indigenous leaders who could sit on an Indigenous advisory body anyway, so the whole thing would be pointless. 'Who?' he challenged. 'Name one!' I was again stunned. Cape York alone boasted scores of intelligent, impassioned and responsible Aboriginal leaders who would do a stellar job at serving and representing their people and voicing their concerns to Parliament. I was repulsed by Tudge's views, but was sure he wasn't representative of sentiment on the right.

In the 2016 election, Julian Leeser and Tim Wilson both won Liberal seats. Their interest in this issue did not abate when they became parliamentarians. Julian advocated our approach to Indigenous constitutional recognition in his maiden speech in September. After boasting about his successful opposition to all other attempts at constitutional reform, Leeser urged that 'In important public debates, in a time of increasing polarisation of views, we need people who can build consensus and find the middle ground.' He told the spellbound audience how he had 'worked with Indigenous leaders and constitutional conservatives to find a constitutional way to make better policy about, and due recognition of, Indigenous Australians' while avoiding the uncertainties of 'inserting symbolic language into a technical document, which requires interpretation by judges'. Julian thus signalled his intent to keep advocating. His colleagues offered a standing ovation to his speech.

Wilson was one who stood in support of his colleague, and he was also becoming increasingly engaged in our work. Noel and I had conversed with him the previous year, and I'd met him at the Human Rights Commission to discuss the Indigenous body proposal before he got into Parliament. He scribbled furiously on the whiteboard in his office, trying to explain that the constitutional amendment should recognise local First Nations bodies rather than a national body. I tried to follow his thinking, but struggled. Still, it seemed like he was open to the concept of an Indigenous voice, or voices, in the Constitution. That was positive. His input grew from there.

In October 2016, Damien and I fronted an Australians for Constitutional Monarchy event in honour of Keith Windschuttle's new book, *The Break-up of Australia,* which presented his conspiracy theory that Indigenous constitutional recognition was really a secret plot by Indigenous activists to achieve Aboriginal separate state sovereignty—a claim I'd refuted as irrational in an article for *The Australian*. Damien and I sat on the panel after Windschuttle's speech to battle with him and editor of *The Spectator* Rowan Dean. We held our own with dignity and made the conservative case that would appeal to the monarchists. Some of the old ducks nodded enthusiastically, and one woman encouraged me afterwards to 'keep doing what you're doing'. For others, it fell on deaf ears—literally. I nudged Damien and pointed out five aged citizens in the front row who were sound asleep—perhaps lulled into slumber by Windschuttle's speech, I surmised, which had been like a fantastical bedtime story.

The ACM panel was a wasted opportunity for sensible, cross-partisan discussion. Instead of focussing on Damien and my constitutionally conservative, radical-centre arguments for an Indigenous advisory body in the Constitution, Windschuttle and Dean focussed on refuting the separatist sovereignty arguments of the far-left (who were not represented on the panel)—for those arguments were easier to sensationalise and therefore undermine. They barely engaged with our more balanced, middle-ground approach. I spent considerable energy on that panel explicitly affirming the value and success of Australia's Constitution and acknowledging the need to uphold it—hence the modest proposal for a voice, instead of the insertion of uncertain symbolic words. Instead of hearing my constitutionally conservative arguments, Rowan Dean mischaracterised my position: he said I was saying Australia had a 'racist Constitution' (words I did not say), essentially lumping me in the category of the radical left without engaging with my position. I pulled him up, and Dean apologised for the mischaracterisation. It demonstrated the deafness of the reactionary far-right, who tend to be more interested in sensationalism than genuine intellectual engagement, even when presented with conservative arguments.

Sometimes the far-right surprised us, however.

Lyle Shelton, staunch right-winger, then head of the Australian Christian Lobby and opponent of same-sex marriage (with whom Noel and I disagreed on many things, including amendment of the *Marriage Act*), was also coming quietly on side with the idea of an Indigenous advisory body in the Constitution. It took a few meetings and repeated explanation, but eventually he told David and me he supported the proposals and now would need to get his board on side.

Somewhere along the line, Damien and I convinced Noel to address the ACL conference in April 2016. He agreed, then pulled out to attend the funeral of Indigenous activist Tiga Bayles. I spoke in his stead, to 600 or so people; Julian and Damien helped me draft the speech. I painted a picture of Australia's British, Indigenous and multicultural heritage as strands irrevocably entwined, enriching us all. I made the moral case for an Indigenous voice in the Constitution as a way of ensuring a relationship of 'amity and kindness' as the Crown intended, quoting Paul Keating, George Pell and Jesus Christ, and even threw in a bit of my Hindu karma argument for good measure. I could feel the audience was with me and engaged. Afterwards I sold and signed a heap of books, and in talking to audience members, discovered this crowd carried genuine goodwill for the Indigenous recognition cause despite their discriminatory stance on same-sex marriage. 'You persuaded a lot of people, Shireen,' Lyle told me after. 'It really shifted them.'

It was a valuable lesson: just because a constituency opposes a particular progressive cause, it doesn't mean they can't be persuaded to support another—especially if the argument is presented in a conservative way. This was the value in prosecuting a truly radical centre proposal. It could win support in the most unexpected of constituencies.

We were criticised by some on the left, however, for attending the conference at all.

Our book launch of *The Forgotten People* was to be held at the Melbourne Town Hall in June 2016, hosted by Lord Mayor Robert Doyle. A few days before, our book launcher, Reverend Tim Costello, pulled out due to the death of his father. As chance would have it, I'd been trying to organise a meeting with former Liberal premier of Victoria Jeff Kennett.

Two days before the launch, I went to Kennett's Richmond office. We had a quick chat and I could see he was intrigued. 'You're on a mission,' he observed, and asked about my background. I told him and also explained the proposals. 'So what do you want me to do?' Kennett asked. I decided to be bold and asked if he would launch our book that Wednesday night. He looked sceptical, then told me to send him the constitutional drafting and some dot points explaining the proposals. I did. At 9 p.m. he called and agreed to be our launcher.

One hundred people turned up at the Town Hall to support the launch of my first-ever book (albeit coedited). Kennett met my parents, and tried to persuade them to ditch Labor and join the Tories. 'Shireen tells me you're rabid socialists,' he joked (but he was correct). He had advised me in our meeting that I should join the Liberal Party to pursue politics, because he thought I should change things from within. I wasn't convinced, but he seemed to respect me and I was quietly chuffed, for Kennett was clearly a charismatic and caring Liberal.

The following week Kennett published in the *Herald Sun* his support for the Indigenous advisory body in the Constitution, even endorsing Anne's drafting. I had no idea he would do this, but he put his support on the record. I couldn't have asked for a better outcome. He would publish his support again after the Uluru Statement from the Heart, in 2017.

Our persuasive work was paying off.

Supporters of our approach now included Liberal Party stalwarts such as former Australian trade minister Andrew Robb, former federal Opposition leader Dr Brendan Nelson, centrist military veteran Sir Angus Houston, and progressives such as author Thomas Keneally, who at a NSW Art Gallery event declared an Indigenous advisory body the way forward in the most theatrical and uplifting way I had yet witnessed. A growing number of constitutional lawyers were coming to see the merits in the approach, and Uphold & Recognise had run impressive promotional events at the NSW Gallery and the War Memorial in Canberra, and had been involved in a standout event at Parliament House at which Julian, Tim Wilson and Chris Kenny all made the case (Wilson noting he had his own original ideas to input), with Rachel Perkins and me on the panel.

Rachel spoke at many of these events and proved herself an eloquent advocate. I watched in awe as she altered her Parliament House speech midway through: she'd just seen Abbott walk into the room and paused to acknowledge his leadership in this debate, conjuring a sense of flattery and respect but emphasising the responsibility he now bore to take things forward. There were other Coalition members present, engaged, attentive and interested. At these events, members of the public were always moved and energised. Many found the proposals compelling.

We were slowly building consensus across the different sectors of the political right. These were the hardest sectors to crack, but we were gradually cracking them.

Turnbull in 2017 would claim the proposed Indigenous body in the Constitution would be unable to win the support necessary for a successful referendum. In our experience, the opposite would be true. With a bit of hard work, the proposal could win support—we had seen it time and again.

The problem was that there were only a few of us advocating, with too few resources. The political leadership was still missing.

There is another factor that may have contributed to Turnbull's abandonment of support for an Indigenous body in the Constitution: the changed positioning of Labor. This part of the story is not well known. Insiders know what really happened.

Previously, Labor had been advocating ambitious reform, sticking to the Expert Panel approach and keeping the political tension high. But somewhere along the line (after Wyatt's joint select committee report came out in June 2015, and Wyatt repudiated its recommendations) they released the tension—at least for a time. They didn't shift to the radical centre; they drifted down to minimalism just long enough for it to have an impact. It meant there was no strong progressive influence forcing the Coalition to a more ambitious position. Productive political tension, for a time at least, was lost.

Labor's brief descent into minimalism should be viewed in context, however, as should Wyatt's historical preference for constitutional minimalism over an Indigenous constitutional voice. Both Labor and Wyatt would shift to positions more supportive of an Indigenous constitutional voice in months and years to come. As this story shows, people change their minds over time. Noel and I changed our minds. Julian, Damien and Greg changed their minds. Building consensus is a journey, and each must travel at their own pace. As I came to learn, the ability to change one's mind shows humility and courage. It is an asset, not a flaw.

After the Kirribilli meeting in July 2015, Noel, Megan Davis and Patrick Dodson, together with Kirstie Parker of the National Congress of Australia's First Peoples, pushed Abbott to endorse an Indigenous-specific consultation process to determine a national Indigenous position on constitutional recognition. There would be no point proceeding with an Indigenous recognition referendum that Indigenous people did not support, they argued. After Wyatt's capitulation, the Indigenous leadership realised the whole thing was heading towards minimalism. The only way they could stop it was by forming a strong Indigenous consensus: a position that backed substantive reform and rejected minimalism once and for all.

I drafted a united opinion piece for Noel and Dodson, pressuring Abbott to allow Indigenous people a say. It was a historic moment, with both leaders rising above their historical personal and political differences. Both Noel and Dodson resolved to respect whatever came out of the Indigenous process.[9]

Abbott initially refused the request, saying it would lead to an Indigenous 'log of claims'. Indigenous leaders, especially Noel, pushed back.[10]

On 20 August 2015, the four leaders attended a seminal meeting with Abbott to prosecute their plan. Their conjoined advocacy was powerful and it won the day. Abbott agreed that an Indigenous process would be part of the planned consultation process. It was the 'rumble we had to have to get the ground rules right', Noel said.[11]

A month later, Abbott was no longer prime minister, but the plan they forged stuck.

On 7 December 2015, the new prime minister, Malcolm Turnbull, together with Opposition Leader Bill Shorten, appointed the Referendum Council to take constitutional recognition forward and advise government. They made Mark Leibler and Patrick Dodson the co-chairs, just like in Expert Panel days. The council included Noel, Megan Davis, Tanya Hosch, veteran Indigenous activist Pat Anderson, and, initially, journalist Stan Grant (before he left to take up an ABC position), plus Yolngu leader Galarrwuy Yunupingu and Torres Strait Islander Dalassa Yorkston. Among the non-Indigenous leaders were former NSW Labor premier Kristina Keneally, former chief justice of the High Court Murray Gleeson, lawyer Michael Rose, former Democrats leader Natasha Stott Despoja, and former Liberal Party Indigenous affairs minister Amanda Vanstone.

Due to the advocacy of Indigenous leaders, an Indigenous led and run Indigenous consultation process was part of the Referendum Council's terms of reference. The council was tasked with consulting with Indigenous people and concurrently with the broader community, to make recommendations on the way forward. Its Indigenous members began to organise a historic series of First Nations regional dialogues to ascertain Indigenous views and enable them to form a national Indigenous position.

As the work was getting started in 2016, the issue of treaties was also bubbling up in some states. Victoria's Labor government announced it would begin a treaties process, and South Australia followed suit. There was some talk of the Northern Territory doing the same. Renewed talk of treaties changed the debate.

Patrick Dodson, who previously had been passionately attached to a racial non-discrimination clause, after the Referendum Council was appointed publicly indicated a willingness to abandon the Expert Panel's key reform. A racial non-discrimination clause would 'have a hard time' succeeding, he conceded.[12] Wyatt had ditched the substantive reform. Now so had Dodson, it seemed—before the council's consultations on the options even began.

Dodson began advocating for a 'post-recognition settlements' process, to follow a more minimalist form of constitutional recognition. Some speculated that he might have been persuaded by representatives of Recognise to shift to constitutional minimalism. My own speculation was that it was probably Frank Brennan's influence. Maybe it was both.

In April 2016, Dodson was elected as a Labor senator for Western Australia and resigned from the Referendum Council. Then, when Bill Shorten appeared on *Q&A* in June 2016, his comments indicated that Labor was pushing a 'post-recognition settlements process' too.

'Do I think that we should have our First Australians mentioned in our national birth certificate, the Constitution? Yes,' said Shorten. Again: 'mentioned'? *What happened to substantive constitutional reform?* I thought anxiously as I watched. The 'national birth certificate' lingo smacked of Recognise. 'Do I think we need to move beyond just constitutional recognition to talking about what a post-constitutional recognition settlement with Indigenous people looks like? Yes, I do,' Shorten further stated.[13]

If there is a settlements process after the referendum, then constitutional minimalism may be acceptable, seemed Labor's new logic. Yet Bob Hawke had promised a treaty too and never delivered. What if Labor accepted constitutional minimalism on the feeble promise of a future treaty, and then the treaty promise disappeared like writing in the sand, as Yothu Yindi sang? Why not argue for substantive constitutional recognition *and* a treaties process, as a progressive party should?

The strategy was not well considered. But Shorten on this issue seemed to be taking his cues from Dodson, just as Turnbull was taking his cues from Wyatt, and neither Wyatt nor Dodson at this stage seemed amenable to Noel's suggestion of an Indigenous constitutional body as a middle-way alternative to constitutional minimalism. They would rather support minimalism than support the Cape York Institute model, seemed the sad truth.

But just as public views shift over time, so too can true leaders galvanise to match the passions of the people they serve. Both Dodson and Wyatt would down the track shift their positions to express support for the Uluru Statement's call for a constitutional voice. Dodson, in particular, together with Linda Burney and Malarndirri McCarthy, would become a passionate and impressive advocate, holding Turnbull fearlessly to account. Wyatt would even speak up against his prime minister in defence of the proposal.

For now, however, they seemed resigned to constitutional minimalism. This caused a momentary lapse in political tension, with devastating results.

Over the next few months, as the Referendum Council members would discover, the Labor Party's position on constitutional recognition slid down to the same level as that of the Coalition. By November 2016, it was clear the politicians had done a backroom, bipartisan deal for minimalism.

11

A Snowflake's Chance in Hell

To achieve national change, one must first be able to imagine that change and envisage its realisation. It requires optimism. One must have hope that change is possible, for without hope and vision, there is no driving force for action. Hopelessness breeds apathy: lethargic acceptance of the status quo.

Noel and I practised radical hope. Hope against the odds. Hope in the face of losing battles. Our hope is what drove us during these years—it's why we worked hard and why we often felt at the edge of victory, even as we teetered against heartbreaking defeat. We were in it for the long haul and every skirmish along the way bolstered our resolve. Referendum or bust. Substantive reform or nothing. 'We will get there,' Noel would say.

While engaging with compassionate conservatives, politicians on the left and the occasional far-left Indigenous radical to boot, I was also engaging with the reactionary right. Earlier that year, I met Andrew Bolt for the first time. It was the day after Australia Day: 27 January 2016. I was in Canberra to film my segment for the ABC documentary *I Can Change Your Mind on Recognition* with Bolt and Indigenous Labor MP Linda Burney. A symbolically appropriate time for the encounter, perhaps: the day after the British arrived at Sydney Cove in 1788.

The filming was at the National Press Club, where Noel had literally just given his speech. I sat in the audience of the fancy lunch but couldn't eat. Jimi Bostock, who was with me, quaffed wine, oblivious to my angst. Noel spoke of the radical centre and his regret at never entering politics. We were both realising you had to be inside to truly change things. Advocating from outside was feeling increasingly futile.

I sat dumb, riddled with nerves. I'd spent the past several years watching and reading Bolt and understanding his arguments. They were basically the same as those of the IPA. I'd met Chris Berg and Simon Breheny, two IPA advocates, was across their positions, and knew the reasons they were wrong. The night before, in my hotel room, I'd practised on a conference call with friends—studying several typed pages of my Andrew Bolt analysis. My mates played an even more annoying version of Bolt than Bolt himself, if that's possible. It helped.

Then the day came, and I went through some initial stress about a deodorant stain on my blue dress (I washed it in the sink, blow-dried it with the hairdryer, ironed it then donned it again). The producer rang to tell me Bolt was cranky. Noel had refused to be in the doco with him, and I had been put forward instead (an unknown replacement, but Jimi had pushed). But upon arriving at the Press Club to see that Noel was speaking at exactly the same venue on the same day, Bolt, apparently, was insulted. I hid in the toilets, mulling over this added aggravation, imagining his seething disdain at having to meet a mere adviser.

The pair arrived and we made a show of greetings for the cameras. Burney was for team 'Yes', coming from the left. Bolt, of course, was for team 'No', coming from the hard right. I was on team 'Yes', certainly, but was coming from the 'radical centre'. This meant I'd sometimes agree with Burney, and other times I wouldn't. Half the time I'd agree with Bolt, and the rest of the time I wouldn't.

The conversation was so long and intense that I missed my 5 p.m. flight. The debate was essentially between Bolt and me, with Burney interjecting intermittently. It wore on for hours, and as I became more exhausted, my impatience started coming through.

Bolt had one anti-recognition line that he repeated ad nauseam. 'Indigenous recognition will divide us by race. It will create apartheid,' he argued, like a broken record of the IPA. My response: the Constitution already divides us by race. There are already racist clauses in there. It has presided over decades of discrimination against Indigenous peoples. That's what constitutional recognition seeks to fix. We need to implement fairer constitutional rules. So what will the new rule be? An equality guarantee? Or the Indigenous right to have a say in their affairs?

I have a tendency to count off lists with my fingers when I argue. When the show went on air my mates put the segment into slow motion, highlighting my gawky gesticulation. First point: index to index. Second point: finger completely slips off other finger (was I having a stroke, they asked?) Third point: two witch-like claw hands appear either side of my face, as if I'm screeching 'Fly, my pretties! FLY!' and my eyebrows arch in villainous refutation. It was hilarious to watch back. Especially in slow motion.

The highlight came when Bolt said, 'I'm Indigenous', and I chortled involuntarily. *Excellent*, I thought—I'd prepared well for this moment. After explaining to Bolt why he was not Indigenous under Australian law (which imposes a three-part definition requiring ancestry, community acceptance and self-identification—Bolt only had one out of the three), I tried to get him back on topic. 'We are trying to have a conversation about the Constitution! And that means this practical matter of the law … I really, really want you to grapple with the technical problem, okay?' I implored, trying to get him to understand the need to replace the race power.

'I have been, all along,' Bolt interjected forlornly—the tired student, genuinely trying to understand. After two hours of intense conversation, I didn't blame him for being exhausted. I was too.

Perhaps my erratic, witchy hand movements mesmerised him, but Bolt and I developed a rapport after that. As soon as the cameras were off, he became a gracious gentleman. The meanness was mostly an act, I realised. He, Burney and I had a drink after the filming and he congratulated me generously on my advocacy, saying my PhD study was evidently paying off, because I knew a lot about the topic. 'You were very well prepared,' he said. 'It makes all the difference.' The producer rang Jimi the next day to tell him Bolt had been full of compliments on their drive back to Sydney. Queen of Sheba strikes again, I bragged to Damien later, and we laughed. Might the terrible Bolt possibly be turned from foe to friend, we mused?

Noel instructed me to continue to work on Bolt, so I arranged a further meeting. We had a docile chat at his home, I gave him our book and was baffled as I left. Here was a nice man, with a good life. Bolt led a comfortable existence in Melbourne's well-off eastern suburbs. Like me, he enjoyed all the benefits of his Australian citizenship—a citizenship many people around the world only dream of holding. We were two lucky Australians, in the luckiest of countries, both descended from immigrant parents and privileged to reap all the benefits and opportunities this nation has to offer. So why wasn't being Australian enough for Bolt? Why did he feel the need to claim to be Indigenous Australian, too? I wondered at the many losses Indigenous people had suffered so people like Bolt and me—whose ancestors were newcomers to the country—could prosper. They'd lost their land, often their freedom. Many lost their lives. Did Bolt really need to try to take their Indigenous identity as well? It seemed rather gluttonous.

Bolt took to inviting me on his show regularly, and seemed to enjoy our altercations. The first time, however, he spoke over me incessantly while claiming he was Indigenous. I couldn't refute him properly, so in May 2016 I wrote a piece for *The Australian* explaining exactly why he wasn't. Bolt was furious and attacked me in his blog, calling me 'rude, wrong and deceptive'. My parents freaked out. So did I. So did Noel. I was never the type to get into private fights with people, let alone public ones. I felt nauseated with worry for a few days, but then got over it. I survived and felt stronger for it, for surely I could handle whatever anyone threw at me now. I was no snowflake, I discovered.

Bolt's blog is still the first thing that comes up when you google my name. Shireen Morris: 'rude, wrong and deceptive'. At least he spelled my name right. The commenters under the video segments seemed to agree with Bolt's assessment. They called me 'arrogant', 'lecturing' and loud. 'Shireen Morris is such a fishwife,' said one comment. I had to google what that meant: a loud, unpleasant woman, often with poor hygiene.

Oh well, I reasoned.

I kept going on Bolt's show. As always, he was aggressive on camera and charming off—full of compliments and friendly advice. Off air, I even began to get the impression he was not really that opposed to our proposals. I got the sense he'd shifted, ever so slightly. It was his business model that kept his opposition going. This was his livelihood: he couldn't very well stop. But the fervour of his opposition decreased.

Three weird things happened after my 'rude, wrong and deceptive' row with Bolt in 2016. The first was that Lyle Shelton, who was usually on Bolt's side but who had contributed to *The Forgotten People* in support of Indigenous recognition, took to Twitter to defend me. Bolt usually has sensible things to say, Shelton's tweet noted, but on this issue 'Morris has his measure'. Later Shelton privately reiterated his support for our proposals to David and me. After Uluru, I urged him to advocate publicly. 'We need your support,' I said. But even when Uluru was rejected by the prime minister, Shelton said nothing. He was probably consumed by his advocacy in opposition to samesex marriage, which was unfolding at the same time. Still, that he backed me over Bolt when it counted stuck with me.

The second weird thing was that after one such Bolt TV altercation around the time of the Uluru Statement in 2017, I got a kind phone call from Paul Kelly, editor-at-large of *The Australian,* who took the time to congratulate me on my performance. It was a generous gesture from a stalwart of politics who could just as easily have said nothing. On a separate call I'd explained our proposals, and at that stage Kelly had seemed amenable (though he later seemed to agree with Turnbull's rejection of the Uluru Statement). Former editor of *The Australian* Chris Mitchell also wrote an opinion piece describing that debate with Bolt as 'riveting', and Chris Merritt, the paper's Legal Affairs editor, texted Noel to express his excitement about what he'd seen. The *Oz* was usually on Bolt's side, but the key players seemed to be enjoying watching these fights unfold. I was enjoying it too: it was helping to sort the right-wing wheat from the chaff.

The third thing was that Tim Gartrell of Recognise called me and commended my courage. I'd now earned my stripes, he said. Gartrell hadn't been in touch for what seemed like a long time, and the relationship was mostly cold by now. But by fighting Bolt, it seemed I'd proved I was not one of the bad guys. We rekindled our engagement and he even indicated that he found me easier to work with than Noel, who was evidently too intimidating. At this point I decided to talk openly with Gartrell about our unproductive relationship. I did, and we resolved to try to work more constructively in future. It seemed like a change in attitude. Some respect had been fostered.

I persuaded Gartrell to provide some minimal funding for Uphold & Recognise. Recognise did so—albeit far too late. Still, I suppose we have Andrew Bolt to thank for that. It's funny how a common enemy can unite.

Strange events were unfolding in the lead-up to the Referendum Council's consultations.

Turnbull and Shorten had asked the council to consult on all options: the Expert Panel recommendations, the joint select committee recommendations, and Cape York Institute's proposed constitutional body and extra-constitutional Declaration proposals.

But the prime minister let slip the minimalist outcome he wanted before the Referendum Council's consultations even began. Like the kings of the past, Turnbull issued secret instructions to his subjects—only these had nothing to do with amity and kindness. Turnbull's instructions were pure deception and deceit.

In a meeting at Parliament House in November 2016, Turnbull revealed to the Referendum Council that only minimalism would be acceptable. He indicated that a racial non-discrimination clause was not going to work, and said the Indigenous body proposal had a 'snowflake's chance in hell'. 'It's just my personal view,' he qualified—the omniscient wisdom of the guy who had led the losing team in the republic referendum.

Turnbull realised his mistake, however, when Noel challenged him to tell the Australian people his view on the reform options about to be discussed in First Nations regional dialogues around the country. Noel suggested it would be disingenuous for the government not to tell Australians, and Indigenous people particularly, if they'd already ruled the substantive options out: that would make them nothing more than sham consultations. Turnbull bristled at the word 'disingenuous'. But that's what it was. In 2015, he had told Noel and me that the body proposal was 'sensible' and offered to help promote it. Now, right before the dialogues were to kick off, he was saying it had no chance—essentially taking the substantive models off the table.

Noel tried to remind Turnbull of his expression of support at our 2015 meeting, but Turnbull denied it. Noel subsequently told me to find the email I'd sent to Turnbull after that meeting. Noel found it before I did (I'd forwarded it to Noel the same day) and I cringed when I read it. 'Dear Malcolm and Richard,' I'd opened with temerity (he'd told me to call him Malcolm, hadn't he?). 'It was great to meet you both this afternoon.' I went on to give Turnbull links to Anne Twomey's constitutional drafting and our committee submissions for their further reading. Then I confirmed our positivity about the discussed promotional event: 'It would be great to work towards an event in Wentworth.' I also saw fit, in my unrestrained enthusiasm, to invite them both to the constitutional law symposium we were organising at Sydney Uni on 12 June—as if that's what you did, invite ministers to attend law workshops just for their own mental stimulation and scholarly understanding. 'It would be great if you or someone from your office is able to attend,' I enthused. Reading back, I wince at how many times I used the word 'great'. They must have thought I was a complete pain in the arse.

Nonetheless, the email confirmed it: the meeting had happened and Turnbull had expressed support. Yet now he was saying the proposal had a snowflake's chance in hell. From the prime minister, this amounted to a death warrant.

It was an attempt to covertly bully the Referendum Council into toeing his minimalist line. Turnbull's coercion even went so far as to articulate exactly what his preferred constitutional reform model was: remove section 25 (a dead-letter provision), and remove the race power and replace it with a new section 51A, with symbolic statements incorporated. No body. No racial non-discrimination clause either. Minimalism. A model that Indigenous people had reiterated time and again they did not want, and that constitutional conservatives (such as Julian Leeser, Greg Craven and others) had vowed to oppose—because they didn't want unelected judges to wreak havoc with ambiguous symbolic words. A merely symbolic model had failed in 1999. Why would this time be any different, given the added factors of Indigenous and 'con con' opposition?

But Turnbull noted it was not just him who held this view. Bill Shorten agreed, Turnbull said. And so did the four Indigenous MPs: Patrick Dodson, Linda Burney and Malarndirri McCarthy of Labor, and Ken Wyatt of the Liberal Party were all present in the room and seemed to indicate their assent.

Labor had evidently abandoned its previous position supporting a racial non-discrimination clause. Now it supported constitutional minimalism. It was a bipartisan deal for a minimalist model and the Referendum Council was being told, essentially, what to recommend. They were being told to undertake pretend consultation.

I saw the council members' stricken faces after that November meeting. The Indigenous leaders congregated at the airport to compare notes and mull the path forward—Noel, Megan Davis, Dalassa Yorkston and Pat Anderson. (Anderson, the inspiringly dedicated Indigenous activist and co-author of the seminal *Little Children Are Sacred* report, which had so moved me back in 2011, by now had replaced Dodson as co-chair.) I sat with them, watching their lost expressions. Betrayal. Hurt. Anger. That was the first time Turnbull kicked Indigenous people in the guts.

After talking it through the leaders, to their credit, decided to fight on. Perhaps the power of a forged Indigenous consensus would sway things. Perhaps the politics would shift. Perhaps they could rally public support. They chose to fight back, because what other choice did they have? Their people were dying, languishing in jail, committing suicide at unprecedented rates, still subject to top-down policies that wasted money and didn't work. To give up would be to adopt a position of hopelessness, and they could not. They had to continue to push for a good outcome for their people. They had to keep fighting for substantive change.

The council members wrote to government for clarification that they were indeed to consult on all options, as previously instructed. In a letter response jointly written with Shorten, Turnbull in effect withdrew his private comments and said they indeed expected all options to be put to the forthcoming dialogues.

But now Turnbull's pre-determined minimalist position was clear, as was the minimalist position to which Labor had descended. The Indigenous leaders had to pull expectations back up. They resolved to do so, using the First Nations dialogues as a tool to garner a united Indigenous position and build political momentum. They vowed to fight on, as they always had.

Their perseverance and strength, in the face of bipartisan opposition to substantive recognition, was staggering. I had never seen such determination. They demonstrated radical hope. Those Indigenous leaders are my heroes.

News of the government's 'done deal' for minimalism trickled out. When they heard about it, Indigenous people made it even clearer they would not support feel-good fluff. It was a stand-off. Nolan Hunter confronted the Labor caucus directly, asking them straight: 'Do you have a predetermined position on constitutional recognition?' Burney in particular passionately denied it. The Indigenous MPs then each publicly denied any pre-done deal for minimalism. They said they'd wait for the Referendum Council's report with open minds.[1]

Meanwhile, the force of Turnbull's secret instructions was threatening to unravel the pockets of support we had built in Parliament.

On 23 February 2017, while the First Nations regional dialogues were underway and Indigenous support for a First Nations voice in the Constitution was consistently being declared, we held our book launch of *The Forgotten People* in Perth. We'd waited all these months to secure a date that worked for Christian Porter.

In the lead-up, Porter told us he no longer wanted to be the key launcher. Instead, he would join the panel discussion. He had been elevated by Turnbull to the Social Services ministry, and that new position was constraining, he said. We accepted the explanation. If we had misunderstood his support for the proposals, as expressed by him in our previous meetings, this was his chance to correct the record, to tell Damien and me he had changed his mind, or at least to politely withdraw from the event. He didn't. Instead, Porter turned up at our book launch and publicly opposed the Indigenous body proposal he'd previously described as 'elegant'. He denigrated it in front of the audience, at the launch of the book he had endorsed. He expressed a preference instead for a purely symbolic model, which was Turnbull's preference too. 'There are more mentions of lighthouses in the Constitution than our First People,' he said, as his defence for supporting minimalism—that word again, 'mention'. The lighthouses line was another that Recognise often used.

Previously, as a constitutional conservative, Porter had indicated he was opposed to the insertion of symbolic statements into what is fundamentally a rulebook. He had agreed with Julian and Damien. Now, his whole attitude had changed. It seemed he'd abandoned his constitutionally conservative principles and his support for the Indigenous advisory body proposal in favour of advancing his career.

I went head to head with him in defence of the proposal. He raised readily answerable technical concerns that he'd never raised with us before. That evening I said, 'Let's work together to refine it, Minister. Don't just reject it. Let's work together to make it work.' The audience were good-willed and applauded the suggestion, but Porter didn't budge.

Noel subsequently asked me to draft a letter for him to send to Porter, which was delivered in March 2017. The letter pulled Porter up on his change of mind, which he had not alerted us to, and his dishonourable behaviour at the Perth launch. 'Our people do not seek a mere "mention" in the Constitution, in the same way inanimate objects like lighthouses are mentioned,' Noel wrote. 'We seek fairer constitutional rules in relation to our people, to improve the way the nation does business in Indigenous affairs. This is not an ambitious objective, but a completely sensible one. Any constitutional reform should improve the systems governing our nation—otherwise why contemplate constitutional reform at all?' Noel urged Porter to work constructively with us to refine the technical concerns he had raised. Porter never replied.

After Turnbull's rejection of the Uluru Statement, I called out Porter's unprincipled shifting of views on Indigenous recognition, as well as the fickleness of other politicians including Turnbull and Abbott, in an article for *The Guardian*.[2] A month later, Porter wrote me an extraordinary personal letter that tried to rewrite history: he said he had never supported an Indigenous constitutional body and even tried to suggest he had never been aware of the proposal—a ludicrous claim. On 7 December 2017, I replied with a comprehensive recounting of the facts that exposed his claims as untrue.[3] In the letter I explained that I had written *The Guardian* piece because 'Australians needed to know about the duplicity of their elected leaders in this matter. The fickleness and lies needed to be called out.' My letter was pointed:

> Minister, it was open to you to stand by your principles as a constitutional conservative, to stand up for Indigenous people, and to stand by your support for an Indigenous body in the Constitution as an 'elegant solution' and 'the least worst option'. You chose to toe Turnbull's minimalist line instead. You hedged your bets, moving from support to opposition according to your calculations concerning your political advancement.
>
> One cannot claim to have the convictions of a constitutional conservative, or even a conservative, without demonstrating a principled willingness to stand by one's convictions. Whatever your long-term ambition to lead this country, your leadership was exposed to a basic moral shortcoming in this sorry episode.

Later that same month, Porter was elevated by Turnbull to the position of attorney-general. Turnbull's opposition was strangling the political support we had built.

Tim Wilson, at the Parliament House event with Rachel Perkins and Chris Kenny, had commented that he had his own ideas about how to achieve constitutional recognition of Indigenous voices. Damien followed up, and Wilson subsequently worked with him on a paper to be published by Uphold & Recognise that argued for a constitutional amendment recognising local First Nations bodies rather than a national Indigenous body. We welcomed Wilson's input—it was a way of broadening the debate and building wider consensus on the right. That Wilson was ex-IPA and a self-described constitutional liberal was significant. We had Julian Leeser's support, a young constitutional conservative. Now we were working constructively with Wilson, a young constitutional liberal, to incorporate his ideas. Uphold & Recognise was preparing to publish Wilson's essay to coincide with the final Indigenous constitutional convention at Uluru.

Wilson did not end up publishing that paper. My guess is that Turnbull's opposition to our approach was probably a factor.

As it happened, Damien and Nolan ran into Warren Mundine on one of their Parliament House lobbying trips. Mundine previously had opposed our proposal for an Indigenous constitutional body, just like he opposed a racial non-discrimination clause. In 2015 he declared to Chris Kenny on Sky News that an Indigenous advisory body was unnecessary—even though Mundine himself was then chair of the government's Indigenous Advisory Council. 'I have a legislative body already,' Mundine had said, though no legislative body was proposed—the proposal was for an advisory body. 'It's called the NSW Parliament, it's called the Commonwealth Parliament. I get the chance to vote in elections for those parliaments that make decisions. We've had more Aborigines going into state and federal parliament than ever before.'[4] Right-wing commentator Greg Sheridan at *The Australian*, in an opinion piece heaving with hyperbole (and multiple uses of the word 'magnificent'), profusely commended Mundine's opposition. 'I agree with Mundine that Pearson's proposals are dangerous, unpredictable in their consequences and offend basic liberal principles,' he wrote.[5] Sheridan was a self-proclaimed 'old-fashioned liberal on race', ostensibly a champion of equality but, like the IPA, he would quote Martin Luther King Jnr's equality rhetoric while hypocritically opposing any equality guarantee in the Constitution.[6]

I met with Sheridan in 2016, on Kenny's advice, and we had a long and exhausting conversation. Sheridan commended Noel and me for our 'shrewd' and clever approach with conservatives, but I was totally unable to move him.

Mundine, however, after running into Damien and Nolan at Parliament House while the dialogues were underway, seemed to slowly find more affinity with the Uphold & Recognise approach. He was also inspired by Wilson's work on the idea of constitutionalising First Nations local bodies. Mundine then worked with Damien to publish an essay building on these ideas and spoke to the proposals at an Uphold & Recognise event in Melbourne in May 2017. He said he was coming around to our approach, and his essay advocated recognising First Nations local voices in the Constitution. Wilson was on the panel too, and spoke positively about the need for the First Nations to have their voices heard, endorsing Mundine's paper, an excerpt of which was published in *The Australian*.[7] Noel also spoke. I sat in the audience, pleased that Mundine had given serious thought to the issue, and was coming round.

Though his growing support for a constitutional voice or voices wavered after the final Uluru convention, Mundine agreed to publish his essay advocating for constitutional recognition of First Nations bodies in another collection I was editing called *A Rightful Place*.

I didn't blame Mundine for wavering. Who wouldn't waver in their support for a First Nations voice in the Constitution, faced with Turnbull's decree for it to die? Mundine's enthusiasm for the proposal grew, however. Like so many others, he slowly came around to the logic of what was a modest and sensible idea.

As the dialogues were unfolding, Rachel Perkins, Damien and I met with Tony Abbott. Noting the strong support being expressed by Indigenous people through the dialogues for an Indigenous constitutional voice, Abbott told us he didn't have a problem with the advisory body proposal. He verbally took us through the arguments for and against, as if thinking out loud, then (yet again) suggested how the constitutional drafting could be improved. This was his strongest support yet. He had shifted a lot.

After the final Uluru convention, Abbott had breakfast with Noel and me in Canberra. 'Well done,' he said earnestly, referring to the Uluru consensus for an Indigenous voice, looking us both in the eyes as we ate our poached eggs. He said again that he had no issue with the Indigenous body proposal, and again suggested some more modest drafting, to which we nodded amenably. We asked him to come out publicly and support the proposal, to give Turnbull the cover he needed to lead on this reform. Abbott said he'd think about it. We never heard back.

A few months later, when Turnbull rejected the Uluru Statement from the Heart and the proposed Indigenous voice to Parliament, Abbott backed him—probably the only time he ever has.

As prime minister, Abbott had urged the 'con cons', and Noel and me, to help him build the necessary support on the political right for the proposals—an Indigenous body within the Constitution, a Declaration outside it. We tried our best to do so, and with hard work and perseverance that support had slowly grown. Abbott never helped us one bit.

Then after the spill, Turnbull used his power not to help build support for substantive change, but to ensure his 'snowflake's chance in hell' prediction played out as reality. His secret instructions tried to squash the support we had been trying to build.

The Indigenous advisory body in the Constitution was a good reform proposal that would improve the system and empower the First Nations, and so government wanted it destroyed, preferring instead to back a bad proposal that would maintain the failing status quo of the Indigenous affairs system and keep Indigenous people in their place. They backed minimalism.

Noel and I co-authored a legal article for the *Australian Law Journal* in 2017 in the lead-up to Uluru that set out what a minimalist approach means:

> Under this approach, symbolic words would be inserted and out-dated references to 'race' might be removed from the Constitution,

but its processes, rules and power dynamics would remain the same. In a sense, the aim is the insertion of a 'plaque': an emblematic statement that can be viewed with pride, but which contains no moving parts—or no intended moving parts. In essence: *words* of recognition, but 'business as usual' in the legal and political *systems* governing Indigenous affairs under the Constitution.

The distinction between words and systems is critical. It is the difference between surface and substance, between painting a squeaky bicycle to improve its appearance, and fixing its wheels so that it runs more smoothly.[8]

A minimalist model meant flowery words and cosmetic tinkering with the 'race' clauses. A mere 'mention' that Indigenous people were here first, perhaps symbolic recognition of their land, culture, language, which changes nothing of substance but probably appeases some white guilt. The constitutional status quo, stamped with some feel-good fluff. Boomerangs and bullshit, in other words. Brolgas in the wetlands, blah blah blah.

It wasn't what Indigenous people wanted, and they were going to fight back. They would have their voices heard, whether government liked it or not.

12

The Uluru Statement from the Heart

How likely would it be for snow to fall at Uluru? Or not even a snowfall: just a single, delicate snowflake, crystallising in an intricate symmetry of icy patterns and woven webs? Could those frozen particles come together, stick together and solidify, despite the oppressive heat at our nation's baking rock? One would expect a snowflake to melt in that hellish desert. Evaporate into hot air and return to the sky, a forgotten dream.

A snowflake surviving at Uluru would be about as likely, say, as 250-odd First Nations representatives—chosen by their own people in their regions around Australia, hailing from different language groups and clans, bringing different traditions and ways of life, different politics and ideologies, spanning urban, regional and remote, north and south, carrying different allegiances and objectives, and harbouring a decent spattering of anti-Noel prejudice on top of it all—coming together and rising above their differences to form a united, national consensus on how they want to change Australia's Constitution to guarantee their people a fairer go than in the past.

I previously thought that Indigenous people ever forming such a consensus had a snowflake's chance in fiery, devil-poking hell of happening. The petitions, letters and advocacy of the past always tended to emanate from a particular region or First Nation. Never before had there been a national Indigenous position on constitutional recognition. Yet in May 2017 they achieved just that. The First Nations of Australia got organised, stood together and asked for a single constitutional reform: a voice in their affairs.

They formed a precious snowflake at the nation's great red rock, our country's spiritual heart and cultural hearth.

They sent the snowflake to Canberra, where it was rejected and directed to die. Not in the desert, but in a cold-hearted hell of Turnbull's creation.

I can't tell the full story of the First Nations regional dialogues and their historic culmination at Uluru in May 2017. The tireless Indigenous leaders who ran them and participated, not least the courageous Megan Davis and Pat Anderson, who organised and led the unprecedented discussions in the toughest of circumstances and with little support—they are better placed than me to tell that detail. I offer here only my own reflections on what I saw and heard from the outside looking in, and how I felt watching the seminal discussions unfold.

I travelled around as an observer to most of the regional dialogues on Noel's instructions. They were extraordinary and detailed, passionate and groundbreaking.

The First Nations in the 1800s were wrongfully excluded from the constitutional negotiations that created the Commonwealth. Now they were getting the belated opportunity to have their say on how they thought the Constitution should be reformed to recognise, include and empower them. It was history in the making. I felt privileged to see it unfold.

The trial dialogue in Melbourne, held in November 2016, saw Indigenous leaders from around the nation gather to prepare for the dialogues in their local regions. For most of that weekend at the Melbourne University Law School, I listened to Indigenous advocates from all corners of the country rally and rouse each other. It was inspiring—the start of several arduous months of endless travel and lost weekends undertaken by Anderson, Davis, and Davis's team of dedicated lawyers and helpers.

Even in the trial dialogue, passions began to flow. Rachel Perkins stood and eloquently explained how the Constitution provides the sole means to achieve enduring reform—reform that cannot be struck down on a government whim. An old man from the Torres Strait orated like a preacher: *We need to put our voice in the Constitution! We gotta lock it in and throw away the key!*

Terry O'Shane, a hardworking unionist from Queensland, urged the mob to get it done, to go for it, to make change happen. He wanted to see recognition happen while he was alive. Young up-and-coming black lawyers sat and listened, not missing a trick; they piped up at various points in the conversation. One of them, Teela Reid from the University of NSW, who would powerfully challenge Turnbull's rejection of the Uluru Statement on *Q&A* the following year, seemed to absorb the ambition of the elders as they spoke. She was an intelligent future leader. The formidable Davis stood regularly to provide insights on constitutional law: I could see she was the pride of her people. During the dialogues, I watched her come into her own as one of Australia's most impressive Indigenous leaders. Anderson provided calm moral guidance, bringing wisdom and experience that settled the room and offered direction.

I watched them all in quiet awe, and thought of Tudge's quip that there were no impressive Indigenous leaders who could sit on an effective advisory body. How wrong he was.

The discussion allowed for healthy scepticism and caution to meld with enthusiasm and ambition. These were smart and hardworking people who knew about politics and the difficulties and risks, but who were willing to do the work to change Australia for the better.

It was the impressive young Maritime Union of Australia branch secretary Thomas Mayor from Darwin, drawing on his experience as a union battler, who gave the advice that galvanised the room. 'We need to organise to win,' he said. The older advocates stood and reiterated his sentiment. They would not passively concede defeat, nor would they quietly accept whatever minimalist crumbs government was offering. They resolved to organise to win, despite Turnbull's secret instructions.

The dialogues were a vehicle for unity. As these leaders knew: in unity, there is power.

The dialogues proper kicked off in Hobart in December 2016. It was apt. The conversation began in earnest where Aboriginal people had suffered the worst and where the destruction wrought by colonisation had perhaps been the most unrelenting. Noel writes of this harrowing chapter of Australia's colonial history in *A Rightful Place*. I'd read his words, but had never been to the island.

The quaint colonial seafront, the harbour with its fish shops and sleepy streets created a strange environment from within which to think about the task at hand. I could see no obvious traces of the 'war of the worlds' that, as Noel described, had played out centuries prior. The past seemed covered over by a picturesque calm—the memory of slaughter disguised by architecture reminiscent of England by the sea. Not for the survivors of that violence, I suppose, who I'm sure could never forget.

'Was this what thousands of Aboriginal lives made way for?' Noel wondered out loud as we crossed the street from the hotel to the water. I knew what he meant. There was no churning metropolis to show for the bloodshed. No tall city standing above the buried bodies of the last 'full-blood' Tasmanian Aborigines. Instead, Truganini and her ancestors had been almost wiped out for a seaside village and a handful of boats, for producers of great wine and seafood. The prettiness of Hobart made comprehending the bloody history difficult.

I reflected that this tiny island is today guaranteed twelve senators—an equal voice—under the Australian Constitution. The prize for the almost-annihilation of the Tasmanian Aborigines was successful negotiation by Tasmanian colonial representatives securing equal representation for the former colony in the Australian Senate. The constitutional compact guarantees Tasmanian Australians, Tasmania being the least populated state, a proportionately greater say in the government of the nation than citizens anywhere else on the continent. Nothing spoke more to the purpose and challenge of Indigenous constitutional recognition than the unjust incongruence of this bizarre fact: the Tasmanian colony that had overseen the most effective attempted Aboriginal genocide in the country had also won for its residents the strongest proportional voice in the federation. To say it seemed unjust feels like an understatement.

If it is fair that Tasmania has special representation in the constitutional compact in recognition of its distinct historical and political status, its identity as a former colony and its ongoing political identity as a state—which Australians accept without question—then surely it is fair, too, that the original peoples of this land should also be recognised and represented in their affairs. Having survived the impacts of colonisation and continued as distinct identities within the Commonwealth, the First Nations also should have a voice within the Constitution, at least in relation to the political decisions made by the parliamentary majority in respect of their distinct Indigenous rights and interests. 'We live in a country that gives 500,000 Tasmanians 12 senators inside the Commonwealth parliament according to a Federation deal struck in the Australian Constitution in 1901,' Noel, Davis and Anderson told *The Australian* in February 2018, challenging the prime minister's continued rejection of the call for a voice. 'And yet 117 years later do we seriously think the Australian people would reject the proposition that 600,000 indigenous Australians should not have a constitutionally recognised body outside of the Commonwealth parliament? If they did then the country would not be serious about recognition.'[1]

Such insights were not lost on the contemporary Tasmanian Aborigines, who, under the leadership of Aboriginal activist and lawyer Michael Mansell, had for years been grappling with various possible mechanisms for First Nations representation within Australia's constitutional system. Mansell often suggests a separate Aboriginal state and reserved seats in Parliament. There are multiple other ways representation in their affairs could be guaranteed.

The broad message from Hobart was clear: they, like the people at all the following dialogues, wanted substantive constitutional reform. They would not accept symbolism alone, no matter what the politicians were pushing. Some delegates expressed regret at the recent achievement of Indigenous recognition in the Tasmanian Constitution: it was a symbolic mention in the preamble (like in other state constitutions) and gave them nothing of practical benefit. Some said they had voiced concerns about the proposal at the time but had been ignored by government, which pushed ahead regardless, flanked by those Indigenous people who were happy to endorse symbolism. 'How do we know the same thing won't happen at the Commonwealth level?' the delegates wisely asked.

I thought about the question: there is no easy answer. I think the only possible answer is unity, solidarity and a smart strategy, to force government to a better position. Division gives governments an easy way out—they can find the weaknesses and take the path of least resistance. And when I say solidarity, I don't only mean Indigenous solidarity. Non-Indigenous Australians will also need to show solidarity with their Indigenous fellow citizens. Then, perhaps, government might be forced to listen.

Noel made his position clear to those Tasmanian delegates: constitutional recognition needs to be for the Tasmanians as much as for his own people in Cape York. 'If it doesn't work for the Tasmanians, then it won't work for the rest of us,' he said. His words built a sense of unity in struggle.

Noel knew how to rally consensus. He was in this for all his people.

As time went on, I began assisting the co-convenors of each meeting to write opinion pieces expressing the key messages from their dialogue. I would listen to the discussion and debate and make notes, then construct a draft reflecting their words. Then I'd seek input from the co-convenors and other leaders, make appropriate changes as requested, and get their final sign-off so the piece could get published. I was accustomed to supporting Indigenous leaders other than Noel with writing work: it was an integral part of my job, a way of using my writing skills to support Indigenous voices, and I enjoyed doing it. It also helped me absorb and understand the messages I was hearing.

The dialogues provided delegates with civics and constitutional education so they were able to discern which models were strong and which were weak. This was an incredible strength of the dialogue process. It allowed Indigenous people to make informed, educated, empowered decisions. Noel, Davis and Anderson didn't hide the fact that the politicians seemed set on minimalism. The delegates were also aware of the role Recognise had played in pushing a minimalist model.

Things ramped up at the Melbourne dialogue, with some radical-left delegates arguing for a 'sovereign treaty' or nothing, and other delegates eager for substantive constitutional reform as well as treaties.

After the Melbourne dialogue in March 2017, co-convenors Jill Gallagher and Jeremy Clark threw down the gauntlet in the *Sydney Morning Herald*. 'If the politicians have cooked up a "done deal" for mere minimalism on constitutional recognition, Aboriginal people will say no,' they declared. 'Substantive reform, or nothing at all. That was the clear message relayed at the Victorian dialogue in Melbourne this weekend.' Their opinion piece concluded with ferocity: 'Any done deal on minimalism is a deal-breaker. It is a deal-breaker that will kill this referendum.'[2]

The message sent shockwaves out to Parliament. Two days later, the politicians denied it. There was no 'done deal' and no 'politicians' model', the Indigenous MPs maintained. 'There is not, and never has been, any such thing as a politicians' model for constitutional recognition,' said Dodson. Wyatt also denied any deal but expressed personal opposition to the Indigenous constitutional body proposal, claiming it would not be supported by Australians (in the same way he had claimed it would not be supported by Indigenous people in years prior—now he was being proven wrong).[3]

Indigenous people fought on, rejecting minimalism and calling for a constitutional body.

Drawing on their experience of the Northern Territory Intervention, the co-convenors of the Ross River dialogue in April rejected a minimalist approach in *The Guardian*, demonstrating their civics education. 'The intervention was an exercise of the territories power, not the race power,' they wrote, which is why 'we Territorians understand that a minimalist model—removing references to "race", tinkering with the race power and inserting some symbolic words—would be pointless. Without a substantive constitutional guarantee like a racial non-discrimination clause or a constitutionally mandated First Peoples body, it's just pretend change.' So much for Tudge's claim that Indigenous people wouldn't know what's in the Constitution—they could learn.

The delegates accordingly rejected the 'Recognise "racism out, recognition in" slogan' because, they explained, 'removing section 25 and amending the race power is a superficial, cosmetic change ... not real reform. The proposed section 51A power might contain some nice words which tell a good story, but it is basically just the race power dressed up in fancy clothes and wearing a frilly symbolic hat. Our people see past the disguise. We are not fooled.'[4]

This was Indigenous empowerment in action. Delegates had successfully dissected Recognise's 'racism out, recognition in' catchphrase and were rejecting the minimalist model it represented. I knew the genesis of the catchphrase: it had come from Liberal Party pollster Mark Textor, who had used it at a Recognise conference I attended—the same event where I'd heard him subtly disparaging the Indigenous body proposal being pushed by Noel and Marcia. I previously mentioned Textor's comment that 'there are more than just two Indigenous leaders in this country'. It was now clear to me that this classic divide-and-conquer remark was his subtle attempt at undermining the leaders who were pushing against minimalism.

Yet the dialogues were proving that Textor had been dead right, in fact: there weren't just two. There were hundreds, indeed thousands, of influential Indigenous leaders—they'd all caught on to what the pollsters were up to and were now making their voices heard. As Gallagher and Nolan pointed out, the 'racism out, recognition in' slogan 'sounds substantive, but it isn't ... Removing the word "race" doesn't prevent racism. Nor does it prevent Parliament being able to make racist laws.'[5] They were fully clued in.

After the Adelaide dialogue, co-convenors Cheryl Axleby and Klynton Wanganeen wrote in *The Guardian* to join in on the rejection of minimalism, 'like our counterparts across the country', they said. 'We all want a bit of blackness in this country's white document—but not just for symbolic effect. We want this reform to make black lives better. Otherwise what's the point?' They offered sound strategic justification for their position: 'If we go for a weak option, we will never have another go in this lifetime.'[6]

At each dialogue, the proposed Indigenous voice in the Constitution was identified as the preferred reform. Perth delegates spoke of feeling invisible to bureaucracies and politicians and of lacking a political voice and power. The proposed Indigenous body should be representative of First Nations lands and waters across Australia, underpinned by First Nations cultural authority, they suggested.

Through the dialogue process, stories of history, bloodshed and injustice affected everyone involved. Cairns delegates in particular spoke powerfully about past discrimination at the hands of government in Far North Queensland. Their stories were harrowing. I listened, and helped them draft an article to reflect their shared pain. Co-convenor Terry O'Shane unexpectedly read the resulting draft to the entire room, to obtain their endorsement. He choked up as he read it, and Megan told me later many people were crying. The draft was resoundingly endorsed for the story it shared, and was published by Kaylene Malthouse and Terry in *The Australian*.

I repeat its words here, because this story should be read by all Australians. 'On 15 November 1963, the Queensland Police forcibly removed Aboriginal residents of the Cape York community of Mapoon and relocated them to Bamaga, 200 kilometres north,' Terry read. 'They were taken away on a barge and their homes burnt down. The people of Mapoon had said they didn't want to move. The government didn't listen. They thought they knew what was best for our people and made decisions accordingly. Force prevailed over what was fair. First Peoples voices were not heard ... Similar memories are etched across Queensland and across each corner of our continent ... It is this shared history that drives our people's resolve for real change, as well as the common struggles of our present which unite us with common purpose.' With tears in his eyes Terry concluded: 'Constitutional recognition can begin a new chapter in the shared story of this country. It is an opportunity to put in place substantive constitutional reform, to help ensure that past wrongs don't happen again.'[7]

Their passion and empathy were overwhelming. These people had endured immense suffering, had survived, and were responding with deep and resilient hope. They wanted to heal themselves, but also heal the country. Given this history, was a voice in decisions made about them really too much to ask? I fought back my own tears and wished hard that they might win their modest desired reform. I also wished the Indigenous politicians, and Turnbull and Shorten, had been there to hear it. I understand they were invited to the dialogues, but never came.

Listening to Terry, I recalled Twiggy Forrest, who had sat next to Christian Porter, Nolan Hunter, Ben Wyatt, Indigenous Labor member in the West Australian assembly, and me on the Perth launch panel back in February. Twiggy listened to Porter's negative comments about the proposed constitutional body and, to my great relief, did not agree. He backed the modest reform Indigenous people were rallying behind in the unfolding dialogues. 'It doesn't seem like much to ask, to consult with Indigenous people,' he told the room, contradicting Porter. Sorting the wheat from the chaff.

Twiggy was a direct descendant of one of the original founders of Australia's Constitution. He was a conservative with a personal and historical stake in upholding the Constitution.

If Twiggy could be persuaded, then surely many decent Australians could be too. And if decent Australians could be persuaded, what right did these politicians have to claim the people would reject a just proposal, and to deny them their fair say?

On 26 May 2017, the day before the fiftieth anniversary of the 1967 referendum, First Nations aspirations from across the country coalesced at a historic gathering in the spiritual heart of Australia, at Uluru. Under the rock's majestic shadow, the opening ceremony took place: the Gumatj of Arnhem Land danced, the Kaurareg of the Torres Strait sang homage to their shark constellation, and the Anangu people of Uluru wished the delegations full strength in their pursuit of a fair place in this ancient country.

The three days of deliberations, the culmination of the regional dialogues held all across the country, were ambitious yet pragmatic. These people had dealt with structural powerlessness for the past 200-plus years and carried the strategic tenacity of those accustomed to dealing with the unilateral exercise of government power over their affairs. The 250-odd gathering achieved a powerful majority consensus.

All regions rejected minimalism or mere symbolism in favour of substantive reform. All wanted to take responsibility and exercise increased authority in their affairs. All wanted a 'First Nations voice in the Constitution', a representative institution constitutionally empowered to have a say in political decision-making affecting their communities. A First Nations voice to Parliament. All wanted a just settlement—a Makarrata Commission, set up in legislation, to undertake treaty-making and truth-telling about history. (*Makarrata* is a Yolngu word meaning 'coming together after a struggle'.) This was the culmination of decades of Indigenous advocacy calling for political representation and empowerment.

There were of course dissenters—seven people walked out of Uluru (citing concerns about giving up their sovereignty), which is to be expected, because no group can reach agreement without first sorting out their disagreements. Dissent is a logical and necessary part of human beings finding a majority consensus position. And frankly, I find it ridiculous when people expect Indigenous Australians to always agree—as if a minority ethnic group can't have a diversity of views like everybody else. Come to my Indian family Christmas if you want to see some proper intra-ethnic disagreement, then mull over the enormity of what Indigenous people achieved at Uluru.

The Uluru Statement from the Heart offered Australia a way to resolve the fundamental moral problem that has troubled our country since 1788. In forming this consensus, Indigenous people did what everybody said they couldn't. They did what the politicians had asked for: they spoke with one voice. They did the work, canvassed the views, mediated the dissent and achieved their consensus position.

It was a historic moment.

The Uluru Statement wisely moved away from a racial non-discrimination clause, which had been proposed by the Expert Panel in 2012 but was rejected by politicians as a 'one-clause bill of rights' and did not win the bipartisan support necessary for a referendum. As noted, a similar clause hadn't won political consensus prior to 1967, when it was proposed by Liberal MP Billy Wentworth. Back then, the government did not want to give up its power to the High Court, and exactly the same arguments hold sway today. One only needs look at constitutional history to see how smart Indigenous delegates were in adopting this approach. No attempts at inserting new rights clauses into the Constitution have ever succeeded at referendum, and Australia can't even manage to implement a legislated federal bill of rights, let alone a new constitutional rights clause.

Moving away from a rights clause, from a judicial, High Court solution, to a proactive political, participatory solution, was an intelligent move on the part of Indigenous leaders. It is also deeply in keeping with the decades of Indigenous advocacy for increased self-determination, representation and authority in their affairs.

The other smart thing the Uluru Statement achieved was to step away from uncertain symbolism in the Constitution, which constitutional conservatives warn would yield unintended consequences—but which, more importantly, Indigenous people themselves realised would make no practical difference to their lives, so why bother? It stepped away from simply cleaning up the race clauses, which on its own would fix nothing of substance. Because without a proper racial non-discrimination clause, simply removing the word 'race' from the Constitution would not prevent Parliament from being able to enact racist laws. The delegates at the dialogues understood this fact. They also understood the political blockages to a racial non-discrimination clause, and accordingly chose to make only one substantive recommendation for constitutional reform: a First Nations voice, which might hopefully prevent discriminatory laws.

The Uluru Statement is full of passion. It is written in inspiring and emotional prose. I urge every Australian to read it. But it is also pragmatic and politically hard-headed. It proposes a practical and modest reform. It asks not for a veto, but a voice. It is a generous and constitutionally conservative proposal. The First Nations achieved this.

Yet after Uluru, Mark Textor sent an angry text to some Indigenous leaders, suggesting that Noel had killed the recognition referendum by advocating an Indigenous constitutional body. Though we tried to prevent it, the text ended up with journalists at *The Australian* who later reported that Textor was furious with the Uluru outcome. They also reported the quiet demise of Recognise, which could not withstand the criticism emanating from the dialogues.[8]

No doubt Textor was imparting his negative view on Uluru to his Liberal Party colleagues.

The Referendum Council report, delivered in June 2017, backed up the Uluru Statement. It called for a constitutionally guaranteed Indigenous advisory body and added the idea of a Declaration, outside the Constitution, to recognise the three parts of our national story. Practical reform to establish a voice within the Constitution. Symbolic language outside the Constitution.

This report was remarkable and unprecedented: it was the first report on Indigenous recognition that intelligently melded constitutional imagination with constitutional conservatism.

It is truly a 'radical centre' report.

For if it takes progressives to imagine how the future can be better than the past, it takes conservatives to discern how to make things better while upholding tradition and respecting our evolved democratic institutions. The Referendum Council did both. This was constitutional imagination firmly grounded in constitutional tradition. The proposal for a First Nations voice in the Constitution was the result of years of searching for the common ground. The Referendum Council found it: a way to achieve Indigenous aspirations for substantive, empowering reform, while upholding the Constitution.

There is a reason arch constitutional conservative Julian Leeser—that Constitution-clutching, rulebook-defending, unelected-judge-judging nerdus maximus who ran so many 'No' cases in the past, against the republic referendum (defeating Turnbull, Keating and other republicans), against a bill of rights (defeating Frank Brennan and the human rights lawyers) and against the push for local government recognition (defeating Gillard and the Local Government Association)—is an ally and not a foe on this issue. Julian supported the Uluru Statement and its call for an Indigenous voice in the Constitution because he says it is 'the kind of clause Griffith, Barton and their colleagues might have drafted, had they turned their minds to it'.[9]

Imagine, for a moment, that Julian's alternative founding story had played out. Imagine if Indigenous heroes like Pemulwuy, Windradyne or Jandamarra had sat down with Griffith and Barton at the Windsor Hotel, or aboard the *Lucinda* on the Hawkesbury River, to draft the Constitution. And imagine if these Indigenous representatives had been viewed by their colonial counterparts not as subhuman or inferior or as members of a 'dying race', but as equal, empowered and worthy of fair and negotiated inclusion in this nation's founding agreement.

It is likely they would have negotiated themselves a voice.

Consider our Constitution: it's a unity compact. It is the deal the colonies struck to form one nation. The rulebook set out how the disparate colonies would coexist in peace and shared prosperity. It was a compromise between separateness and togetherness, unity and independence. And Australia's Constitution already recognises pre-existing political communities—the former colonies, now the states. It ensures their representation and guarantees them a say, a voice, in the government of the Commonwealth.

Our Constitution is unique, because it protects our human rights not through a bill of rights or an equality guarantee, like so many other countries, but by giving the constituent parts of the federation a fair say. That is the genius of our check-and-balance federal system. Even the minority states like Tasmania are guaranteed an equal voice in the Senate.

As noted, there are more Indigenous Australians than Tasmanians.

The First Nations too are a distinct and pre-existing political community in our country. They were not at the negotiating table with the founding fathers when the original deal was done, when power was distributed and this Commonwealth was created. But they should have been.

The Uluru Statement, and the Referendum Council's report, for the first time in Australia's history, offered a sensible, achievable and constitutionally conservative way of rectifying this original omission. The reform proposed was, as eminent constitutional professor Greg Craven described, 'modest yet profound'. It was a radical centre solution.

After the Uluru Statement, the position of the Labor Party began to correct itself, dragged up by Indigenous ambitions. Bill Shorten backed the statement's proposals, and Labor began to reassert its pressure. By this stage, however, it evidently wasn't enough.

As soon as the Uluru Statement was released, incorrect interpretations of its meaning arose. The ABC erroneously reported that it was a rejection of constitutional recognition in favour of a treaty. It wasn't: it was a rejection of minimalism and a resounding endorsement of substantive recognition through a First Nations voice in the Constitution, as well as a Makarrata process.

Then Deputy Prime Minister Barnaby Joyce called the proposal a third chamber of Parliament. This too was incorrect: the proposal was for a First Nations voice *to* Parliament, not *in* Parliament—an advisory body with no veto powers. I suspected Turnbull had sent Joyce out with the 'third chamber' line. Joyce also said the proposal was 'overreach' and would not be supported by Australians.

The Uluru Statement initially did not win clear enough solidarity from the Indigenous MPs. Though Shorten strongly endorsed it in his notable speech at Garma in Arnhem Land, his party members did not immediately fall into line.

Patrick Dodson on TV called the proposal 'a bolt in the dark', suggesting that the idea of a constitutional body had come too late and was a new or unknown concept. He also suggested that previous reports, like those of the Expert Panel and the joint select committee, which had proposed a racial non-discrimination clause, should not be dismissed—minimising the significance of the Uluru Statement. Linda Burney expressed disappointment at the 'limited' nature of the Referendum Council's recommendations, suggesting they should have recommended fixing up the race clauses. 'I think we are on a path that it is further away than what I anticipated,' she said pessimistically.[10] And in the Coalition, Ken Wyatt seemed to suggest the Indigenous body should just be legislated, not constitutionalised, taking a similar negative tone to Barnaby Joyce.

It was Marcia Langton who, with characteristic strength and accuracy, said what everybody was thinking. 'The noise coming from our federal parliamentary representatives seems to dismiss the 250 delegates at the Uluru convention and their thoughtful approach to the technical difficulties, the threads and strings of constitutional change propositions,' she stated. 'Their resolution of these issues is intelligent and in the national interest, as well as serving the Indigenous sector and polity. Are the Indigenous parliamentary representatives serving party interests rather than the national interest?'[11]

Although the Indigenous MPs would adopt supportive positions down the track, at this stage it was clear that the government had successfully deployed a divide-and-conquer strategy, pitting the Indigenous MPs against the Indigenous consensus forged at Uluru. This strategy had been playing out since the 'snowflake's chance in hell' meeting of November 2016, at which the Indigenous MPs indicated agreement with Turnbull's minimalist position. The early negativity towards the Uluru Statement from the black MPs on both sides sent a strong signal: lack of internal pushback on Turnbull. Lack of political tension. It initially suggested they were letting Turnbull get away with dismissing the proposal for an Indigenous voice in the Constitution.

It wasn't all negative voices, of course. There were strong supporters. In June 2017, Julian Leeser explained to Parliament that Indigenous people were providing them 'an important direction. They are telling us that they want to be consulted and have a voice in the way in which policy is developed, and consultation is good.'[12] Former

Aboriginal affairs minister Fred Chaney, who launched our edited collection at Garma, also spoke in support of the Uluru Statement, and Jeff Kennett wrote an enthusiastic piece advocating its merits. There were many others who slowly galvanised.

But faced with government opposition and the initial ambivalence of the Indigenous MPs, supporters were largely powerless. From the moment Dodson, Burney and Wyatt expressed disappointment at the Uluru result, I feared the proposal may be doomed. People change their minds, however. Often, leaders who change their minds can become the most passionate advocates for the cause.

13

The Rejection

IN 2011, Malcolm Turnbull wrote in *The Monthly* a review of James Boyce's book on John Batman's historic attempted treaty in the colonial founding of Melbourne in the 1800s. As a resident of Melbourne, Turnbull's words moved me. Reflecting on our historical relationship with Indigenous peoples, he wrote:

> When governments say doing the right thing is 'too hard', what they are really saying is that it is more lucrative, or expedient, to do the wrong thing. Our forebears preached protection of native people and the blessings of Christ while they largely destroyed a people and a way of life.
>
> So if you ever walk quietly along Robert Hoddle's wide boulevards or along the banks of the Yarra, tamed to look like an English river, listen carefully. You may hear the weeping of the Kulin—betrayed, dispossessed, but not yet quite forgotten.[1]

In October 2017, Prime Minister Malcolm Turnbull rejected the Uluru Statement from the Heart. He said the proposal for an Indigenous body in the Constitution was neither 'desirable nor capable of winning acceptance at referendum'. Doing the right thing was too hard. It was more expedient to do the wrong thing.

The government's rejection was based on six lies that need to be corrected.

The first was that an Indigenous voice in the Constitution would undermine Australia's equal citizenship and would be contrary to the principle of equality. This assertion is false.

There is no equal citizenship under Australia's Constitution. We are not the United States of America. We have no constitutional equality guarantee: the political right opposed such a reform when Noel and I pushed a racial non-discrimination clause. And I have already explained how Tasmanians are disproportionately represented in the Senate—a fact we all accept as part of our unequal constitutional system, which gives a fair voice to our pre-existing political communities, even the very small ones. Not to mention the fact that our Constitution contains racially discriminatory clauses, or that many of the privileges of Australians' citizenship have historically been shared supremely unequally, especially with respect to the dark-skinned among us. Despite these basic underlying errors in the prime minister's assertion that some kind of equal constitutional citizenship operates in Australia (it does not), an Indigenous voice in Indigenous affairs is in no way contrary to principles of equality.

It was Turnbull who vowed to 'to do things *with* rather than *to*' Indigenous people: was that concept, the just idea of consultation, contrary to principles of equality? The proposition that Indigenous people should have a better say in laws made specifically about them—native title, indigenous heritage, closing the gap and so on—is no more contrary to principles of equality than Turnbull's own hand-picked Indigenous advisory body, which already exists and operates, albeit largely ineffectively. Because let's face it—what good is a government-appointed body? Government will obviously choose individuals who are likely to tell it what it wants to hear. That is why any Indigenous body should be chosen by the First Nations themselves, to be a strong, independent voice to Parliament—as Indigenous people insist.

How can Turnbull claim that an Indigenous body to advise on Indigenous affairs is contrary to the mythical concept of equal Australian citizenship when his own collaborative slogan and his appointment of Indigenous advisers to have input into Indigenous affairs demonstrate not only that an Indigenous voice is sensible, but that it is crucial to making good Indigenous affairs policy? Remember: in 2015 Turnbull told Noel and me the proposed Indigenous advisory body was sensible. That in 2017 he asserted otherwise, on the basis of false equality rhetoric, in my view shows a man who lacks principles.

An Indigenous voice in Indigenous affairs is not contrary to equality. That was the first lie.

The second lie was that the proposal for an Indigenous body was too short on detail. In fact, the proposal was deliberately designed to leave Parliament to design and enact the detail of the body through legislation—this is how it respects parliamentary supremacy, and why it's a constitutionally conservative proposal. If Turnbull wants to complain there is a lack of detail, he needs to blame himself and his Parliament for not being prepared to do the work—for it would be his Parliament's job to work with Indigenous people to create that detail. (Not to mention the fact that Cape York Institute delivered to the PM a report of 78 or so pages, which he read and notated, and discussed with Noel Pearson.) The proposal is not short on detail. It sensibly leaves detail design to Parliament and appropriately defers construction of the detail to legislation, like many existing constitutional clauses. There is a plethora of policy detail upon which Parliament could draw—if it wanted to and if it could be bothered.

'Lack of detail' was Turnbull's second lie.

The third was that this proposal would create a third chamber of Parliament. This is incorrect, and in direct contradiction to what Turnbull said in his meeting with Noel, Richard Windeyer and me in June 2015, back when he was communications minister. His claim that an Indigenous advisory body would 'come to be seen as a third chamber of Parliament' is a dog whistle to the far right.

The proposal is no third chamber. As explained in the Referendum Council report, it is a voice *to* Parliament, not *in* Parliament. An external advisory body, with no voting powers, no veto over legislation and no power to make laws—whose make-up, functions and operation are ultimately for Parliament to decide. The proposal involves no change to the make-up of the Houses of Parliament.

That was the third lie.

The fourth lie was that the proposal for an Indigenous voice in the Constitution came too late in the day. Indigenous people have been asking for a stronger political voice in their affairs since at least the 1920s, if not long before that—since William Cooper's letter to King George in 1937 asking for reserved seats in Parliament, since the Yolngu bark petitions in 1963 calling for fairer consultation in decisions made about them, and since the Barunga Statement in 1988, which called for an Indigenous body to oversee Indigenous affairs, and a treaty. A First Nations voice is about self-determination and empowerment. It is a very old idea, not a new one.

In terms of the current proposed constitutional voice, Cape York Institute first proposed it in 2014 and it was put forward in numerous submissions after that. The contemporary iteration of the idea was at least three years old, and the excuse that the proposal comes too late is disingenuous. Australia has been waiting over 200 years for proper Indigenous recognition. We should take time to get this right and do it properly.

The proposal was not too late. That was the fourth lie.

The fifth lie was that the Indigenous MPs are a voice for First Nations people and so no independent voice is needed. Nothing disproved this claim better than the fact that, when the Uluru consensus was first formed, the Indigenous MPs did not seem supportive. Indigenous MPs, like Greek, Indian or white MPs, must represent their electorates—the people who voted for them—but primarily their political parties. They necessarily carry allegiances that often override their Indigenous allegiances, and this is as it should be. They are politicians after all, elected by all Australians and representing their parties.

In December 2017, Teela Reid asked a question on Q&A challenging the prime minister's claim that the Indigenous MPs provided the necessary First Nations voice. Turnbull suggested she was calling the Indigenous MPs 'tokens'—his word, not hers. With impressive strength in the face of his attempted manipulation, Reid rejected his implication. 'Absolutely not what I'm saying, at all,' she said. Turnbull's attempt to drive a wedge between the Indigenous MPs and Indigenous citizens was obvious, undignified and un-prime-ministerial. And as Reid correctly pointed out, to observe the reality of an Indigenous politician's political role was not to show disrespect. Everybody should be happy there are Indigenous MPs in Parliament—indeed, there should be more. But they do not represent the First Nations, because they are not chosen by them. That is why an independent Indigenous voice to Parliament is needed, to better inform all politicians—Indigenous and non-Indigenous—in their decision-making on Indigenous affairs.

The claim that the Indigenous MPs are a First Nations voice was part of Turnbull's divide-and-conquer strategy, and it was incorrect.

The sixth lie was worst of all. The prime minister claimed that Australians would not support a First Nations voice in the Constitution and predicted that such a proposal would fail at referendum. Government did no polling, by the way. Indigenous Affairs Minister Nigel Scullion said he didn't need to—he was following his gut.

This verballing of the Australian people underestimates their intelligence and goodwill. Independent research conducted by Omnipoll in August 2017 showed that 61 per cent of Australians would in a referendum vote yes to an Indigenous constitutional voice. Does that number sound familiar? It is exactly the same percentage of Australians who voted yes to same-sex marriage in the postal survey, which has now become law. Then, in February 2018, Newspoll research indicated 57 per cent support for an Indigenous constitutional advisory body—and that is in the face of sustained government opposition and fearmongering.[2] By this time the Indigenous Labor MPs had well and truly abandoned their previous equivocation, and were advocating passionately in favour of the Uluru Statement's call for a voice to Parliament, rallying behind Shorten.[3]

The polling confirmed what Noel and I already knew: it is not the people blocking progress on Indigenous recognition, it's the Coalition politicians.

Noel was heartbroken. So was I.

'Malcolm Turnbull has broken the First Nations' hearts,' Noel said on ABC radio. I could hear the emotion in his voice as he spoke.

This was his life's work and his people's hopes—destroyed. I sat at home in Melbourne, listening on my phone. Turnbull had accused John Howard of breaking the nation's heart after the 1999 referendum and now Turnbull had 'done the same thing in relation to recognition of Indigenous Australians'.[4] Noel sounded out of breath in anger. I was out of breath just listening.

Bill Shorten wrote to the prime minister to tell him 'a unilateral decision of this kind' was contrary to his 'repeated promise to do things with Indigenous Australians, and not to them'.[5] Patrick Dodson told the media it was 'a real kick in the guts for the Referendum Council and certainly a slap in the face of those proponents'.[6]

The outpouring from Indigenous leaders was visceral in its grief.

Joe Morrison, an Indigenous leader from the Northern Territory, said the prime minister had 'failed the nation'.[7] Rod Little, of the National Congress of Australia's First Peoples, lamented that 'Aboriginal and Torres Strait Islander people have been let down once again'.[8]

The furious Pat Anderson nailed Turnbull's know-it-all pomposity. 'The prime minister has turned himself into the latest mission manager,' she seethed. 'He knows what's best for us and also he's omniscient because he knows what the Australian public are going to—how they're going to vote at a referendum.'[9] All of her and Megan Davis's tireless work, cruelly dismissed. Jill Gallagher fiercely refuted Turnbull's unfair verballing of the Australian people. 'I believe fully in my heart of hearts that the Australian population would have supported a referendum' on the voice proposal, she said. 'And I don't think anyone should pre-empt what the Australian population would do.'[10] Turnbull was doing the old 'blame the constituency trick', this time about the Australian people, and it wasn't fair.

Constitutional expert Dylan Lino tweeted to declare Turnbull's rejection 'a despicable act of mean-spirited bastardry'—a phrase that made headlines. The law fraternity quickly stepped up, reiterating their support and affirming that the proposal was no third chamber of Parliament. Supportive statements from the NSW Bar Association and the Law Council of Australia, ironically, had been released a few days before the government's rejection. They offered to work with government to salvage the proposed reform. But it came too late.[11]

Despite Turnbull's criticism of the proposed Indigenous constitutional body, Australians across the political spectrum immediately began to prove the prime minister wrong by expressing their solidarity with Indigenous people and their call for a voice. On Sky News, Labor-aligned Kristina Keneally marvelled at the oddity of being in passionate concurrence with right-wing commentator Chris Kenny, who slammed the government's rejection. The 'Indigenous voice option was a neat model created by constitutional conservatives in concert with Indigenous activists … It's hardly a radical idea,' Kenny said.[12]

Former Labor prime minister Kevin Rudd noted on *Q&A* his unexpected 'unity ticket' with Alan Jones in support of the Indigenous advisory proposal. Though Rudd and Jones were on opposite ends of the political spectrum and usually disagreed on most things, they found themselves in passionate agreement on the merits of an Indigenous voice to Parliament and the foolishness of Turnbull's rejection. 'The body would be outside the Parliament, and on Indigenous matters the Parliament would be able to consult those people. How hard is that?' Jones told the *Q&A* audience, explaining the proposal perfectly. My heart swelled with pride to hear him. Our constant explanation and refuting of Turnbull's errors were evidently filtering through. Rudd agreed and called the Uluru proposals 'unremarkable', expressing disappointment in Turnbull's lack of sensitivity and leadership. The proposal was unifying left and right as well as Indigenous and non-Indigenous Australians, despite government's rejection.

Indeed, one of the positive side effects of Turnbull's rejection was that it helped propel the Indigenous Labor members to a more strongly supportive position. And by February 2018, Labor Shadow Treasurer Chris Bowen on *Q&A* also passionately backed the Uluru Statement's call for an Indigenous constitutional voice and even saw fit to commend constitutional conservatives (particularly Greg Craven) for their support of the proposed reform. Bowen also unexpectedly praised our book, *The Forgotten People*.[13] Labor had come a long way from Shayne Neumann's antagonism towards the 'con cons' and the body proposal in 2015—now there was a sense of Labor solidarity with the 'con cons' in support of the Uluru Statement.

Turnbull's rejection made it easier for the left to step up and advocate—because now it was about opposing the Liberal Party, not conceding to constitutional conservatives. It was the natural partisan dynamic. Still, our radical centre logic was now coming to fruition: this truly was a proposal on which both progressives and conservatives, and Indigenous and non-Indigenous Australians, could find common ground.

The Indigenous recognition movement was, as Noel described, 'gazumped' by the same-sex marriage plebiscite, which overtook the national agenda.[14]

For all its inefficiency, the same-sex marriage postal survey delivered a just result. But it also lay bare the disconnect between politicians and the Australian people. As noted, in Tony Abbott's electorate of Warringah, 75 per cent supported same-sex marriage, and Abbott's claim that his oppositional view represented a 'silent majority' was disproven. There was also less support for same-sex marriage in Labor electorates than Liberal electorates. This too was telling, since Labor politicians were more passionately in favour, whereas more Liberal politicians were against.

Politicians don't always represent their constituents. When they claim to represent a 'silent majority' or 'ordinary Australians', their claims must be interrogated. As the same-sex marriage result showed, Australians can be ahead of politicians on social justice. Turnbull's rejection of the Uluru Statement, and his unsupported claim that the Australian people would reject the proposal, must be equally interrogated.

The double standard demonstrated by the prime minister with regard to the two issues is clear.

When the religious freedom detractors asked for more legislative detail on same-sex marriage, Turnbull's response was happy-go-lucky. We'll see Parliament 'at its best' in developing such detail, he assured

Australians. On same-sex marriage, he indicated it was acceptable for Parliament to provide necessary detail after the vote—such detail has now been developed and legislated. But on the Indigenous voice proposal, he used 'lack of detail' as an excuse not to have a vote. No assurances that his parliament would be 'at its best' to flesh out such detail in due course. On same-sex marriage, Turnbull promised to do the necessary parliamentary work. On Indigenous recognition, he makes the 'No' case and shirks responsibility.

On same-sex marriage, Australians voted around 60 per cent in favour—*with* the prime minister advocating for it. Yet on Indigenous recognition, polls have found that around 60 per cent of Australians would vote yes in a referendum for an Indigenous voice[15]—with the prime minister pushing *against* the proposal: in the face of his government's sustained negative spin.

Turnbull says the Australian people would not support an Indigenous voice in the Constitution, but the evidence says the opposite. His rejection not only dismissed the Indigenous voice, it denied the voice of the Australian people.

The Coalition rejected the Uluru Statement while Labor and the Greens ultimately backed the reforms. Shorten's advocacy in defence of the statement was powerful and impressive.

The progressive left are not without blame, however. Progressives were for too long missing in action.

Earlier in 2017, I was asked to do a short talk at the Wheeler Centre's 'Festival of Questions' at the Melbourne Town Hall. I decided to address their question: Is a treaty more important than constitutional recognition of Indigenous peoples? It was a leading question that demonstrated the regular leftist bias. I argued the radical centre position: trying to rank the importance of a treaty against constitutional recognition is the wrong question. It's a false dichotomy. Both are equally important.

When I walked into the green room before my speech, two influential progressive lawyers who were also speaking (on different topics) promptly came up and advised me they thought a treaty was more important than constitutional recognition. Both men let me know they didn't particularly like Noel's proposed advisory body: they felt it was too weak, and a treaty would be much better. I was baffled—this was after the Uluru Statement. Indeed, it was in October 2017, not long before the prime minister's rejection. I could understand good-willed Australians *before* Uluru taking different positions and cherry-picking the views of whichever Indigenous leader was their favourite. But now there was a national First Nations consensus position calling for a voice in the Constitution—it wasn't just Noel Pearson.

The two lawyers seemed to imply that the Uluru Statement had got it wrong and that they knew better. Though one eventually signed prominent professor Fiona Stanley's petition in support of the statement and began advocating for its reforms, and the other, after my talk, said he'd think more about the arguments, which he said I'd argued clearly, Turnbull's rejection came soon after. The time for thinking was gone.

I raise the absence, or tardiness, of support from progressive advocates not to single them out, but because it saddens and frustrates me. I regret that influential progressives did not help sooner. I hope next time, if there is a next time, those people will offer more prompt and passionate backing of their Indigenous compatriots. Progressive lawyers should have made it their business to understand the Uluru Statement from the Heart and support it as an act of Indigenous self-determination.

Yet the ambivalent or confused position of progressives on Indigenous constitutional recognition has a long history, which was further complicated by the influence of Recognise—an organisation that was led by a Labor man.

For a long time, people viewed a treaty as automatically strong and cool, and constitutional recognition as weak and uncool. You were either in the treaty camp and you were a groovy lefty, or you were in the constitutional recognition camp and seen as selling out to the feel-good fluff Recognise was flogging. Or you at least ranked one as more important than the other. These two camps for too long divided good-willed Australians. And when Australians of goodwill are divided on the right way to proceed, it lets government off the hook more easily. The division was detrimental to both causes, and helped lead to October's rejection. It meant there was a lack of political tension and made it easier for Turnbull to do what he did.

The reality is that a treaty and constitutional recognition are complementary goals. Both are about power. Both are about reforming an unfair power relationship—the relationship between the First Nations of this country and the colonising state, the Australian government.

The Constitution—whether we like it or not, whether we philosophically agree with its existence or not, whether we think it is an illegal document or not—is Australia's highest legal and political rulebook. It is the document that distributes power across the Commonwealth, and shares power out between the constituent parts of our federation. But as noted it creates for Indigenous peoples a position of perpetual powerlessness. That is the problem constitutional recognition seeks to fix. It's not a problem that, as the Uluru Statement correctly identified, can be fixed with mere symbolism. It can only be fixed with substantive constitutional reform, which is what Indigenous people asked for and what good-willed Australians should back.

What is the purpose of a treaty, then? A treaty has that same fundamental goal. Treaties too are about empowering the First Nations and creating a fairer relationship. The dichotomy dissolves once you think seriously about the objectives of these reforms, which are complementary.

The Uluru Statement undeniably exploded the false dichotomy once and for all. It said: we want both—we want meaningful, substantive constitutional recognition through a First Nations voice guaranteed in the Constitution, *and* we want a Makarrata Commission, or treaty-making process, to be set up in legislation. It shows decisively that these two goals are not mutually exclusive.

And the practical reality is that the one supports the other. The First Nations are going to need a representative structure in order to negotiate and sign off any treaty with government. Having representation of First Nations is a necessary first step. There needs to be a structure to engage with government and assent to the treaty.

When I observed some early treaty discussions in Melbourne, the need for a representative structure for the First Nations of Victoria was immediately recognised by delegates. From what I understand, such a structure has been designed—because people see that you need representation before any negotiation with government can proceed.

Well, the white progressive lawyer typically says, just legislate the structure! Why do we need to tinker around with the Constitution, which is so hard to change? Government should just legislate the First Nations body. To that I say: look how easily ATSIC, implemented by Labor then abolished when Howard was in power, was struck down with the flick of a white politician's pen. The Constitution is much harder to change than legislation. A constitutional guarantee provides permanence.

Indigenous Australians have now said what they want.

There is no longer any excuse for progressive supporters to be missing in action. A better question to ask now is: now that Australians of goodwill know what reforms Indigenous people want, how are we going stand in solidarity with the First Nations to ensure these reforms are achieved?

That the attorney-general took the reform to Cabinet arguably shows how close the Indigenous constitutional body got to being accepted. Brandis's department had advised us that the proposal was legally sound and constitutionally modest, and thus their preferred option. It was backed by serious constitutional conservatives, and now it had unprecedented Indigenous consensus. All this was achieved despite concerted undermining of the model by government, pollsters and Recognise over the years.

Turnbull could have just said no. Instead he made the dishonest 'No' case. Why? My best explanation is that he got scared by the Indigenous consensus. Scared by the growing, widespread public support. A constitutionally enshrined First Nations voice, modest as it is, would empower Indigenous peoples and hold Parliament to greater account in Indigenous affairs. Government wants to keep all its power. It doesn't want to share. The status quo works well for its purposes— so why change it? That's why the government wants minimalism.

Recently I chatted to a Liberal Party backbencher who explained the underlying concern. They knew there was no veto, and they knew no 'third chamber' was proposed. Some Coalition members were simply scared to give Indigenous people a guaranteed say in their own affairs, because they were worried such a voice might have political influence, and that it might disagree with government policy. It was ironic: the party championing liberal values, freedom and a robust democracy, was afraid of Indigenous free speech. Afraid of Indigenous dissent. Paul Kelly conveyed a similar fear in a phone conversation with Noel, which Noel later described in *The Monthly*: 'Kelly said something startling. He understood the voice proposal was not a third chamber, and Turnbull was wrong to describe it as such. The startling thing he said was that the voice, even though only having an advisory function, would operate virtually as a veto on parliament. A body without the legal power to direct parliament would hold some sort of non-legal veto over the parliament. *Really*? This late in our history and here is a great old white man conjuring a great old white fear about Indigenous voices. A stalwart defender of free speech, now saying he opposes the mere expression of an Indigenous opinion, for fear it might influence Indigenous policy.'[16]

Such fears were unwarranted. The only risk in giving Indigenous people a voice, and allowing better debate and discussion in Indigenous affairs, is that Indigenous policy and outcomes might be improved. This would be good for Indigenous people, and good for the nation.

Turnbull must also have calculated (wrongly, in my view) that the rejection was a vote winner. Yet he is paying a political cost for his heartlessness. This is another example of his inability to provide the kind of progressive leadership he promised Australians, another example of a politician selling out his principles in exchange for political ascendancy.

It is also a foolish decision on his part.

A minimalist model would be opposed by the majority of Indigenous people, who have now made clear they seek substantive reform over mere symbolism. And constitutional conservatives will galvanise against the insertion of flowery statements, to uphold the Constitution and prevent the transfer of power to the High Court. Indigenous advocates in favour of substantive reform over empty symbolism will find unexpected allies in constitutional conservatives. Together they will form a powerful coalition that would defeat a minimalist referendum.

There is an important analogy here with the failed republic referendum. During that campaign, the direct-electionists joined forces with the monarchists to successfully oppose constitutional reform for Australia to become a republic. The alliance demonstrated the way in which people who might ordinarily disagree can unite against a common enemy in a referendum fight. In the recognition debate, constitutional symbolism would become the common enemy of Indigenous advocates and constitutional conservatives. It would animate an alliance between Indigenous people seeking substantive reform over decorative words, and constitutional conservatives seeking to uphold the Constitution and protect it from uncertainty. But with the right model, these two groups can unite as passionate advocates for sensible yet substantive reform.

Such an alliance may yet play out as reality. A new Joint Select Committee has now been appointed to further Indigenous constitutional recognition. The Uluru Statement and the Referendum Council's report are part of its terms of reference, indicating that Turnbull's rejection is far from the last word. The Committee's co-chairs have been named as Patrick Dodson, the father of reconciliation, and constitutional conservative, Julian Leeser, co-designer of the constitutional voice and an integral part of our 'con con' alliance. The opportunity to realise a historic radical-centre solution on Indigenous constitutional recognition now looms in the federal parliament. Leeser and Dodson can forge the pathway. Indeed, if they unite in commitment to the dual sensible imperatives of meaningfully recognising Indigenous peoples, and upholding the Australian Constitution, Leeser and Dodson together may be able forge the path to justice. Both will need resolve and courage. Both will need to back the Uluru Statement from the Heart.

The productive political tension is now back, and this bodes well. The Indigenous MPs have risen to the challenge posed by the Uluru Statement. Ken Wyatt contradicts Turnbull and seems increasingly in favour of an Indigenous voice to parliament. 'Noel Pearson made the comment that it was not about vetoing parliament, it was not about a third chamber, it was about a voice that governments would listen to that represented a reflection of what came at a community level,' Wyatt said. 'If you build the model on empowered communities right around Australia then you would have very powerful local grassroots level voices percolating to the top and informing ... Governments make the mistake of hand selecting people that they will listen to.'[17]

Linda Burney calls out Turnbull's misleading 'straw man' arguments against the voice proposal, and Patrick Dodson, with impressive courage and honesty, characterised Turnbull's rejection as a return to the 'dog-whistle' politics of the Howard era.[18] These impressive leaders are no longer letting Turnbull off the hook.

And public support continues to grow, despite the rejection.

It grows despite the lies, and despite the fears. It grows because this is a just and modest proposal. It grows because this is a noble compromise, radical-centre reform, capable of bringing all Australians together.

Conclusion:
Towards a Fairer Australia

PART OF THE lesson of this story is that the Australian people must ask more of our political leaders. We must demand that they stick to their principles and behave with honour. We must demand that they speak the truth, treat the First Nations with respect, and act in the national interest—rather than just their own interests. Otherwise, how will Australia ever move forward?

There remains an extraordinary political opportunity to achieve the vision set out in the Uluru Statement from the Heart, if only we have the moral courage to demand it. I urge Australians not to be missing in action. Do not cherry-pick the Indigenous dissenters. Do not second-guess the Uluru Statement. Do not play divide and conquer. Stand in solidarity with Indigenous people.

We must not squander this historic opportunity because of our own complacency. We must not sit back and watch as the politicians kick this can down the road in favour of constitutional reform for a republic, constitutional reform to give themselves longer terms in power, or constitutional reform to water down their accountabilities under section 44 citizenship requirements.

Non-Indigenous Australians must now insist the government act to guarantee the First Nations of Australia a voice in their affairs. Indigenous people have done the hard work to achieve a consensus.

Now the rest of us must back them. This is what I have learned as an Indian-Australian woman striving to work in solidarity with Indigenous people to help achieve the justice they seek, and that we all seek.

It is not up to Indigenous people to achieve this alone. We all bear a responsibility. We cannot be shy or lethargic in our advocacy, or be stymied by the political correctness that says only Indigenous people can advocate for Indigenous justice. That is a cop-out. Non-Indigenous Australians owe it to our Indigenous compatriots to advocate alongside them for change. All Australians carry a duty to create a better country.

I do not believe this reform is beyond us as a nation. Until we resolve it, we will never know peace.

———

Every year, as 26 January approaches, the pressure for national justice grows greater—2018 was no different.

I think about the Crown's unfulfilled instructions when Australia Day rolls around. 26 January commemorates an unrealised good intention—a broken promise. Weirdly, we expect all Australians to celebrate what was in many ways the opening of a national wound, rather the healing of it. No wonder there is division: our nation has not yet done the necessary work to make right the wrongs of the past.

Turnbull, with his head in the sand, pretends the day unites Australians—though it clearly doesn't.[1] Alan Tudge inanely recites the three parts of Australia—the Indigenous, the British and the multicultural—and pretends each is already equally celebrated: they're not. 'On Australia Day we increasingly recognise Indigenous people through the awarding of the Australian of the Year award to Indigenous people,' he says, bizarrely.[2] In other words: let's appease our national guilt by handing out awards to Indigenous people while also denying them a voice—an argument for tokenism: dumb and disrespectful, even for Tudge.

I am not yet persuaded that changing the date fixes the problem. My concern is that changing the date is largely symbolic and lets us off the hook too easily. I agree with Indigenous activist Tony Birch, who argues that changing the date:

> ... suggests that the offence being caused by current Australia Day celebrations can be reduced to the narrowness of the date in question—January 26. The logic of such an argument would suggest that if we were to return to July 15, or March 29 even (my birthday), the history of violence towards Indigenous people would become less offensive? Or forgotten perhaps? ...
>
> Such is the rhetoric of symbolic gestures in settler-colonial societies incapable of countenancing either the relinquishment of power, or the contemplation of genuine remorse ...
>
> If the young are our future, and I sincerely hope that they are, their pathway will be forged in action and a call for self-determination rather than hollow symbolism and a patronising call to display patience.[3]

Birch calls for substantive justice over symbolic date changes. I tend to agree.

I have come to the view that Australia Day tensions will persist, and should persist, until our nation comes to terms with the wrongs of the past and resolves them through formal reconciliation—and by that I mean substantive reform, not mere symbolism.

Rather than changing the date, why not transform and redeem it? Reform the Constitution. Sign the Makarrata. Unify the nation.

With a bit of vision, 26 January could be the date we belatedly include a First Nations voice in the Constitution and establish the Makarrata Commission, as the Uluru Statement from the Heart requests. And bring together the three parts of our nation through a legislated Declaration enacted by all Australian parliaments, as the Referendum Council recommends.

If we did these things on 26 January, the date would become a solemn day of historical reconciliation. A day of healing, resolution and inclusion. This to me seems the radical centre solution. It would not repudiate our British heritage, which is the only thing currently commemorated by 26 January. Rather, it would formally embrace our ancient Indigenous heritage and right the wrongs of the past.

Of course, achieving such reforms, whether on 26 January or any other date, requires morally courageous political leadership. It requires political leaders willing to lead for the national good, rather than dog-whistling to try to win votes. We will need a new government, a new prime minister, and a younger, brighter, better generation to rise to the fore.

In the meantime, why not keep the productive tension 26 January creates, and use this to propel change? Change to redeem the date and make good, finally, on the Crown's secret instructions. Let us do that which should have been done in 1788 and in 1901: declare our shared country, guarantee the First Nations voice in our constitutional compact, and sign the treaty that will unite us as one Australia.

It was December 2017, post Uluru Statement rejection. A few days before New Year's Eve.

We had arrived in the picturesque Sunshine Coast hinterland to deliver talks at the Woodford Folk Festival. It was my third or so stint at Woodford with Noel, organised by Jimi Bostock, who has longstanding rock music and hippy festival roots—one of his many quirks. On these trips, I'd listen to him and Noel rant about rock bands, old country stars and the best pop artists (weirdly, Noel is a Taylor Swift fan). Though I'd been a singer in funk and soul bands, jazz duos and original outfits, my repertoire was impoverished, and Noel's music knowledge was an education. Our jamming—him on acoustic guitar, both of us on vocals, and Jimi on bongos or whatever he could find—was a way to unwind from political combat. We'd sit around on the grass near our tents, watching the fading Queensland light, churning out tunes and laughing.

I was grateful for these moments of fun and friendship: like spirits, enjoying simple pleasures. 'The three amigos—I should take a photo!' joked Tracey, Noel's partner, flanked by their three spirited children when she saw us coming up the dusty Woodford track.

The music breaks were short and our minds would quickly turn back to the problem: the Constitution and how we might change it.

The politics. The players. The correct policy. We were obsessed. It didn't matter if it was 7 a.m. on Saturday or 10 p.m. on Friday, if it was Boxing Day or New Year's Eve—the last three we'd spent at Woodford, talking, planning and advocating constitutional recognition, counting down to midnight on the vast hill overlooking the biggest stage, Noel's kids in tow. We'd sit under the tree commemorating Lew Griffiths, whose steadfast friendship Noel, Tracey and Jimi have never forgotten.

I both begrudged and loved the 24-hour nature of it. It was professional and personal and had become my life, as it had Noel's. I begrudged and loved Woodford too, which was smack bang in the middle of the Christmas break, when the office was closed and everyone else was relaxing—but I had to hang out with these blokes, thinking about politics and strategy.

Brain-addled and exhausted, we'd trawl the fried-food stands, laugh at our failures and concoct future wins. I'd sweat out the year's stresses in the steamy green room, crammed with perspiring musos and hipsters, their dreadlocks splayed out like tentacles on cushions. I'd sprawl under a fan, wishing for winter, the persistent waft of marijuana attacking my faculties from every direction—Woodford's staple aroma, discernible 500 metres outside the front gate. Then we'd give our talks on constitutional reform, Noel always to a standing ovation. That progressive Woodford crowd could never get enough of him—he'd be stuck for hours chatting. Thinking back, he was probably more progressive than me, at least on some things. The Woodford audience knew it: deep down he was one of them.

This festival, I was to give a keynote speech—my first hour-long proper lecture. I was vaguely nervous, but confident: I'd been doing this for seven years now. As I climbed on stage at the Songlines tent, the sparse audience was immediately depressing. I'd flown all the way up from Melbourne that morning, plus a two-hour bus ride. Sweaty and frizzy, I must have looked tragic in the largely empty marquee with just some old white hippies, a smattering of politically engaged music lovers, and some nonchalant Indigenous Australians in the elders' tent to the side. Outside the marquee, the festival rolled on. People cavorted, danced and drank; gigantic puppets roamed like ghoulish revellers from an ethereal realm; and scantily clad face-sparkled women chatted about free love, making haloes of smoke around their beaming smiles—much to Jimi's frustrated, middle-aged delight. It was Woodford at Christmastime. People were there to party, pick up and see cool bands. No one wanted to listen to a sweaty Indian chick talk about the Australian Constitution. Especially not after Noel had already stolen the show two days prior.

I spotted Noel and Jimi up the back in the audience and immediately pepped up. As I spoke, more people milled in, sat and started nodding. I fired up, and there were several bursts of spontaneous applause. I was making the case for a First Nations voice in the Constitution and exposing Turnbull's dishonest rejection of the Uluru Statement from the Heart. Occasionally I looked up the back to see Noel's reactions, half-expecting him to be poking out his eye in boredom like in the old days. But his face was alert and engaged. It was the look not just of a proud mentor: he was interested in what I was going to say, and how I was going to say it. The look of a colleague and ally, not just a boss.

The speech was well received. I gave it splashes of poetic prose together with chatty asides of simple explanation. People laughed at my few jokes. This was how I liked to persuade: with energy and variety, eye contact and direct connection. And over-gesticulation, my friends complained. I couldn't help it—I was too fundamentally theatrical. Plus, I wanted to be different from the usual dry media appearances and lectures, so why not spice it up with some energetic body language, as was my style? (That Woodford, Jimi got a picture of me doing what looked like a 'Heil Hitler'—so I decided to watch out for that particular pose.) Some Aboriginal women gave me a small painting afterwards and said a heartfelt thank-you. Some police liaison officers wanted a picture. Australian singer Lior commended my passion, and I got starstruck. Others told me to keep doing what I was doing. I was humbled by the feedback, which made the diversion from holidays seem worthwhile.

Afterwards, Noel and I were driving down the Sunshine Coast, discussing what job I should do next. He argued that I should use my persuasive skills for the public good and go into politics. 'That speech today: no one can do that. You're a better persuader than me,

Shireen,' he said overgenerously. It wasn't true, but I was flattered. 'And that's saying something, because I'm fucking good!' We laughed, but I noted the seriousness of his challenge. If I had this skill, how was I going to use it?

Noel was the greatest orator I'd heard, and a true leader—courageous to his own detriment. The kind of principled, passionate, audacious thinker I hoped I could be: a leader unafraid to stand up to those in power. I thought back on our work together and felt proud of our persistence and teamwork. Despite our many losses, we'd had remarkable wins.

I have learned many things over these seven years.

I've learned that performance and persuasion are powerful tools: a combination of rational argument, empathy and theatrical finesse. Forging common ground to bridge that which divides us—this is where my heart lies. I've learned that progressives and conservatives don't always behave as you'd expect. I've learned that people change their minds over time, and this is to be respected. I've learned that Australians are fair-minded and intelligent and can be persuaded to come on board with just reform.

And I've learned that I am as Australian as anyone. If there was a time when I felt like an outsider in my own country, I don't feel it anymore. Australia has a black history and a multicultural present and future. I, like all Australians, must take responsibility for that shared future to help make our great country even greater, for all Australians.

I didn't respond to Noel's question, but it rattles in my brain.

I quietly resolved to use my skills for the national good and in defence of our nation's most vulnerable and disempowered. Noel and so many other advocates, friends and allies will continue the fight for meaningful reconciliation and recognition, and I will fight beside them.

We won't give up. We will keep fighting for a fairer Australia.

Acknowledgements

I'm grateful to Louise Adler, Sally Heath, Louise Stirling and the wonderful team of editors, copy editors and publicists at Melbourne University Press who supported me in writing this book. Your enthusiasm for this cause and your faith in my work are hugely appreciated. Thanks to Shelley Kenigsberg for her editing assistance on early chapters.

I thank my parents, Drs Shastra and Naren Morris, my brother Nishant, and my cousin, Shamma Clarke, for reading drafts and helping me fact-check. Mum and dad—thanks for chasing up that missing 1%—your pushing has paid off. Thanks, too, to Bud (my aunty Sarita Naidu) for coming to my passionate defence when the family politics got too hard—you are awesome. Family—you are always so supportive and excited about my endeavours—nobody could ask for more.

Thanks to friends Dariush Etemad, Michael Drake, Jason Cheng, Natalie Mandel and Andrew Ball, and all your partners, for always being interested in my work. Thanks Zoe Ellerman for encouraging, Dani Toon for listening, and Jimi Bostock for reading and re-reading drafts—Cape York Institute has been a wonderful place to work and learn.

Thank you to the many Indigenous leaders and young people who won't ever stop fighting for justice: Rachel Perkins, Marcia Langton,

Megan Davis, Pat Anderson, Jill Gallagher, Thomas Mayor, Stan Grant, June Oscar, Sean Gordon, Nolan Hunter, Fiona Jose, Harold Ludwick, Geoff Scott, Teela Reid, Geoffrey Winters, Adam Bray, Nigel Craig … and so many others (too many to list!).

Thanks to Damien Freeman for your camaraderie, creativity and dedicated collaboration. You and the team at Uphold & Recognise continue to do excellent work for this cause.

And most of all thank you, Noel—for your leadership, guidance, encouragement, your wisdom and friendship. Like with so many things, it was your idea for me to write this book.

Notes

Introduction: Seven Years
1   Simon Benson, 'Bill Shorten raising Voice a winner with voters: Newspoll', *The Australian*, 20 February 2018.

Chapter 1: Where I Come From
1   Jason Burke, '"Racist" Gandhi statue banished from Ghana university campus', *The Guardian Australia*, 7 October 2016.
2   Graham Davis, 'Despot for diversity', news.com.au, 6 October 2009.
3   Statement by Commodore Josaia Voreqe Bainimarama, Prime Minister of the Republic of the Fiji Islands, 62nd Session of the UN General Assembly, 28 September 2007.
4   Graham Davis, op. cit.
5   Johann Gottfried Herder, 'Shakespeare', 1773.

Chapter 2: Discovering Cape York
1   Kenny Bedford and Josephine Bourne, 'Constitutional recognition must do more for Torres Strait Islanders', *The Australian*, 8 May 2017.
2   Noel Pearson, 'Mabo legacy is still misunderstood', *The Australian*, 2 June 2007.
3   Fiona Jose, 'Smallbone Report: past wrongs to blame for Aurukun crisis', *The Courier-Mail*, 18 March 2016.
4   *Director of Aboriginal and Islander Advancement v Peinkinna* (1978) 17 ALR 129, 52 ALJR 286 (PC): 183.
5   *R v KU; Ex Parte Attorney-General* [2008] QCA 154.
6   Tony Koch and Padraic Murphy, 'Child rape sentence "pathetic"', *The Australian*, 10 December 2007.

7 Marcia Langton, 'Trapped in the Aboriginal reality show', *Griffith Review* 19, 2008.
8 Ibid.
9 'Pearson discusses alleged Cape York abuse cover-up', *AM*, ABC, 14 December 2007.
10 'Alcohol bans discriminatory: Newman', *Brisbane Times*, 6 February 2013.
11 Geoff Chambers, 'Police failure to halt Aurukun brawl shows "cultural sensitivity"', *The Australian*, 18 May 2016.

Chapter 3: The Expert Panel
1 Shireen Morris, 'No Australian should feel like a stranger in their own country', *Sydney Morning Herald*, 26 January 2016.
2 Galarrwuy Yunupingu, 'Tradition, truth & tomorrow', *The Monthly*, December 2008 – January 2009.
3 *Miller v Jackson* [1977] 3 All ER 338.
4 Patricia Karvelas, 'Most want race discrimination removed from Constitution', *The Australian*, 11 November 2011.

Chapter 4: The 'One-Clause Bill of Rights'
1 Stuart Rintoul, 'Lawyer warns of hidden dangers in changes to Constitution', *The Australian*, 10 December 2011.
2 Patricia Karvelas, 'Historic Constitution vote over Indigenous recognition facing hurdles', *The Australian*, 20 January 2012.
3 Greg Craven, 'Keep the constitutional change simple', *Australian Financial Review*, 6 February 2012.
4 Patricia Karvelas, 'Warren Mundine and Tony Abbott unite over race', *The Australian*, 22 December 2011.
5 Patricia Karvelas and Lanai Vasek, 'A new proposal would see the Constitution amended to encourage respect for Indigenous Australians', *The Australian*, 19 January 2012.
6 Natasha Robinson, 'Warren Mundine ready to assume position of power under Tony Abbott', *The Australian*, 18 May 2013.
7 Latika Bourke, 'Attorney-General George Brandis busted reading poetry books during estimates hearing', *Sydney Morning Herald*, 5 June 2015.

Chapter 5: To the Right and Up
1 Damien Freeman and Shireen Morris (eds), *The Forgotten People* (Melbourne University Press, 2016), p. xii.
2 Commonwealth, *Parliamentary Debates*, House of Representatives, 13 February 2013, p. 1123 (Tony Abbott, Leader of the Opposition).
3 Joint Committee on Constitutional Recognition of Aboriginal and Torres Strait Islander Peoples: Roundtable Discussion, Parliament of Australia, 30 April 2013.
4 John Gardiner-Garden, 'The origin of Commonwealth involvement in Indigenous affairs and the 1967 referendum', Department of the Parliamentary Library Background Paper 11, 1996–97.

Chapter 6: In Search of the Radical Centre
1. 'The full transcript of Julian Leeser's maiden speech to Parliament', *Sydney Morning Herald*, 14 September 2016.
2. Ibid.
3. Gary Johns, 'Recognition: history yes, culture no', in *Upholding the Australian Constitution: Proceedings*, vol. 25, 2013.

Chapter 7: Forging The 'Con Con' Alliance
1. Noel Pearson, 'The start of serious national reportage on original Australians and our affairs', *The Australian*, 16 July 2014.
2. Anne Twomey, 'Putting words to the tune of Indigenous constitutional recognition', *The Conversation*, 20 May 2015.
3. Noel Pearson, 'Debate the substance, not the inconvenience', *The Australian*, 18 April 2015.
4. Ibid.
5. Noel Pearson, 'Betrayal', *The Monthly*, December 2017 – January 2018.
6. Amos Aikman, 'We need to be heard by Abbott, say Arnhem Land elders', *The Australian*, 13 September 2014.
7. Liz Burke, 'Tony Abbott blames "toxic egos" for Parliament's problems', news.com.au, 22 November 2017.

Chapter 8: Low Expectations
1. Joint Select Committee on Constitutional Recognition of Aboriginal and Torres Strait Islander Peoples: Public Consultation for Constitutional Recognition, Parliament of Australia, 6 November 2014.
2. All these quoted conversations are taken from *Constitutional Recognition of Aboriginal and Torres Strait Islander Peoples: Roundtable Discussion (private)*, Parliament of Australia, Friday 19 December 2014 (Proof Committee Hansard).
3. Patricia Karvelas, 'The long march to constitutional recognition', *RN Drive*, ABC, 17 April 2015.
4. Ibid.
5. Noel Pearson, 'Debate the substance, not the inconvenience', *The Australian*, 18 April 2015.

Chapter 9: Black Robe
1. Frank Brennan, *No Small Change* (UQP, 2015), p. 275.
2. Paul Kelly, *The March of Patriots: The Struggle for Modern Australia* (Melbourne University Publishing, 2009), p. 391.
3. Speech at the Launch of 'Acting on Conscience': Frank Brennan's Response to Kevin Rudd, Parliament House, Canberra, Parliament of Australia, 31 October 2006.
4. Noel Pearson, 'Betrayal', *The Monthly*, December 2017 – January 2018.
5. Michael Gordon, 'Noel Pearson slams advocate for "modest" Indigenous recognition', *Sydney Morning Herald*, 3 July 2015.

6 Michael Gordon, 'Academic Marcia Langton blasts Frank Brennan's recognition plan', *Sydney Morning Herald*, 3 June 2015.
7 Victoria Laurie and Natasha Robinson, 'Time to get a move on with recognition: Ken Wyatt', *The Australian*, 10 July 2015.
8 Ibid.
9 Ibid.
10 Noel Pearson, 'Betrayal', *The Monthly*, December 2017 – January 2018.

Chapter 10: The Art of Persuasion
1 Governor Phillip's Instructions, 25 April 1787 (UK). <www.foundingdocs.gov.au/resources/transcripts/nsw2_doc_1787.rtf>
2 Edward Wilson, 'The Aborigines', *The Argus*, 16 March 1856.
3 John Stone, 'Constitutional recognition? Tell 'em they're dreamin'', *The Spectator Australia*, 19 October 2016.
4 Shaina Rother, 'Bob Hawke's advice for Malcolm Turnbull: "resign"', *Sydney Morning Herald*, 30 December 2017.
5 Emma Griffiths, 'Indigenous advisers slam Tony Abbott's "lifestyle choice" comments as "hopeless, disrespectful"', ABC News, 11 March 2015.
6 *Q&A: Incarceration, Islam and Innovation*, ABC, 25 July 2016. <http://www.abc.net.au/tv/qanda/txt/s4485530.htm>
7 Ibid.
8 Brad Norington, 'Australia Day 2018: Gillian Triggs supports Aboriginal treaty', *The Australian*, 26 January 2018.
9 Patrick Dodson and Noel Pearson, 'Recognition referendum needs Indigenous input', *The Australian*, 18 July 2015.
10 Natasha Robinson, 'Recognise campaign: Tony Abbott sparks fury among Aboriginal leaders', *The Australian*, 3 August 2015.
11 'PM agrees to Indigenous consultation on referendum', *PM*, ABC, 20 August 2015.
12 Amos Aikman and Sarah Martin, 'Patrick Dodson's shift on racial discrimination ban in referendum', *The Australian*, 12 December 2015.
13 Caitlyn Gribbin, 'Q&A: Bill Shorten indicates Indigenous treaty possibility, will wind back border protection secrecy', ABC News, 14 June 2016.

Chapter 11: A Snowflake's Chance in Hell
1 Michael Gordon, '"No such thing": Aboriginal MPs deny settling on "politicians' model" for recognition', *Sydney Morning Herald*, 22 March 2017.
2 Shireen Morris, 'Turnbull's rejection of an Indigenous voice to parliament is immoral and foolish', *The Guardian Australia*, 30 October 2017.
3 Stephen Fitzpatrick, 'Christian Porter lashes out at lawyer Shireen Morris in recognition row', *The Australian*, 8 December 2017.
4 Greg Sheridan, 'Mundine's persuasive blow knocks out Pearson's case', *The Australian*, 11 June 2015.
5 Ibid.

6   Greg Sheridan, 'Constitutional change will divide not unite the nation', *The Australian*, 20 September 2014.
7   Warren Mundine, 'Constitutional recognition profoundly important for all of us', *Sydney Morning Herald*, 19 May 2017.
8   Shireen Morris and Noel Pearson, 'Indigenous Constitutional recognition: paths to failure and possible paths to success', *Australian Law Journal* 91, 2017, p. 350.

Chapter 12: The Uluru Statement from the Heart
1   Stephen Fitzpatrick, 'Uluru Statement voice must be in Constitution', *The Australian*, 12 February 2018.
2   Jeremy Clark and Jill Gallagher, 'Why Indigenous Australia will reject a minimalist referendum question', *Sydney Morning Herald*, 20 March 2017.
3   Michael Gordon, '"No such thing": Aboriginal MPs deny settling on "politicians' model" for recognition', *Sydney Morning Herald*, 22 March 2017.
4   David Ross and Barbara Shaw, 'Indigenous Australians know removing race from constitution is pretend change', *The Guardian Australia*, 10 April 2017.
5   Jill Gallagher and Nolan Hunter, 'What constitutes real Indigenous policy reform? Here are some clues', *The Guardian Australia*, 4 May 2017.
6   Cheryl Axleby and Klynton Wanganeen, 'Constitutional recognition must make Indigenous lives better. Otherwise what's the point?', *The Guardian Australia*, 20 April 2017.
7   Kayleen Malthouse and Terry O'Shane, 'Remembering Mapoon: shared history drives resolve for real change', *The Australian*, 26 March 2017.
8   Stephen Fitzpatrick, 'Indigenous Recognise campaign ditched', *The Australian*, 10 August 2017.
9   Damien Freeman and Shireen Morris (eds), *The Forgotten People* (Melbourne University Press, 2016), p. 87.
10 'Parliament Indigenous voice a challenge: MP', *The West Australian*, 18 July 2017.
11 Stephen Fitzpatrick, 'Put nation first, Marcia Langton tells Indigenous MPs', *The Australian*, 25 July 2017.
12 Calla Wahlquist, 'Turnbull's Uluru rejection is "mean-spirited bastardry": legal expert', *The Guardian Australia*, 26 October 2017.

Chapter 13: The Rejection
1   Malcolm Turnbull, 'Beneath the boulevards', *The Monthly*, July 2011.
2   Simon Benson, *The Australian*.
3   Calla Wahlquist, 'Pat Dodson accuses Turnbull of ditching bipartisan constitutional recognition', *The Guardian Australia*, 21 February 2018.
4   Dan Conifer et al., 'Indigenous advisory body rejected by PM in "kick in the guts" for advocates', ABC News, 26 October 2017.
5   Bridget Brennan, 'Indigenous leaders enraged as advisory board referendum is rejected by Malcolm Turnbull', ABC News, 27 October 2017.
6   Dan Conifer et al., op. cit.

7   Shahni Wellington, 'Indigenous leader says Parliament has "failed nation", months on from Uluru summit', ABC News, 26 October 2017.
8   Dan Conifer et al., op. cit.
9   Bridget Brennan, op. cit.
10 Ibid.
11 Calla Wahlquist, 'Turnbull's Uluru rejection is "mean-spirited bastardry": legal expert', *The Guardian Australia*, 26 October 2017.
12 Chris Kenny, 'Mundane end to historic reform to recognise Indigenous Australians', *The Australian*, 25 October 2017.
13 'Q&A Highlight: "We want to be the author of our own destinies"', 19 February 2018 <https://youtu.be/ikPa3pi1leY>.
14 Helen Davidson, 'Constitutional reform "gazumped" by same sex marriage postal survey, says Noel Pearson', *The Guardian Australia*, 24 October 2017.
15 'Government "underestimates public support for Indigenous recognition"', UNSW Newsroom, 30 October 2017.
16 Noel Pearson, 'Betrayal', *The Monthly*, December 2017.
17 Greg Brown, 'Wyatt contradicts PM on "voice"', *The Australian*, 28 February 2018.
18 Stephen Fitzpatrick, 'Dodson lashes Turnbull's "dog whistle politics"', *The Australian*, 21 February 2018.

Conclusion: Towards a Fairer Australia
1   Adam Gartrell, 'Turnbull government hits back at Greens push to change Australia Day date', *Sydney Morning Herald*, 15 January 2018.
2   Greg Brown, 'Australia Day date problematic, says Linda Burney', *The Australian*, 16 January 2018.
3   Tony Birch, 'A change of date will do nothing to shake Australia from its colonial-settler triumphalism', *@IndigenousX*, 21 January 2018.

Index

Abbott, Tony 44, 64
  affinity with New Zealand 107
  agreement to Indigenous
    consultation process 174
  at Kirribilli meeting with
    Indigenous leaders 146, 148
  on Indigenous advisory body 124,
    189–90
  on Indigenous seats in parliament
    122–3, 124
  lack of leadership on Indigenous
    recognition 124, 125
  loss of prime ministership 152
  meeting with Yolngu elders 123
  opposition to guarantee of equality
    62, 65–6
  relationship with Mundine 66–7
  relationship with Pearson 6–7, 163
  on same-sex marriage 216
  support for constitutional
    recognition 72, 73, 190
  undermining of Turnbull 125,
    153–4
  view of Howard 162

Aboriginal Land Act 30
Aboriginal and Torres Strait Islander
  Commission (ATSIC) 92, 220
*Aboriginal and Torres Strait Islander
  Recognition Act 2013* 72–3
acting career 14–17, 44
Ahmat, Richie 151
Alcohol Management Plans (AMPs)
  33, 35, 37
Allan, James 76–7
Allinson, David 156, 168
Aly, Waleed 76
Anderson, Pat 174, 184, 193, 194,
  214
Archer River station 34
Assange, Julian 159
Attorney-General's Department 220
Aurukun 32, 33–8
Australia
  creation of 40–1
  as triune nation 19–21, 114–15
Australia Day 40–1, 107, 225–7
Australian Christian Lobby (ACL)
  conference 170–1

Australian Constitution
  1967 referendum 43, 81–2
  adverse impact on Indigenous
    people 40–4
  creation of Australia 40–1
  head of power clauses 78
  Indigenous advocacy for reform
    43–4
  as power-sharing compact 41–2
  preamble 43–4, 59, 95, 143, 162
  race power 42, 58
  racially discriminatory clauses 42–3
Australians for Constitutional
  Monarchy 160, 169
Axleby, Cheryl 199–200

Barunga Statement 43, 212
Bashir, Marie 160
Batman, John 209
Bayles, Tiga 170
Bedford, Kenny 23
Bennelong Society 86
Berg, Chris 178
bigotry 36–8, 67
bill of rights issues 61, 132
Birch, Tony 226
Bjelke-Petersen, Joh 34
Bolt, Andrew 156, 177–82
Bostock, Jimi 111, 178, 180, 227
Bourne, Josephine 23
Bowen, Chris 215
Bradley, Sarah 35
Brandis, George 64, 65, 67–8, 78
Bray, Adam 155
Breheny, Simon 178
Brennan, Frank 122, 139–44, 145,
  146–7, 151–2, 164–5, 175
Brennan, Sean 49–50
Broadbent, Russell 159
Brough, Mal 152
Burmester, Henry 47, 58
Burney, Linda 176, 177, 178, 179,
  184, 185, 207, 223

Cairns 25–8, 71
Callinan, Ian 86
Cape York Institute (CYI)
  constitutional reform policy
    development 39, 44–51
  employment at 31–2
  funding 74, 98
  internship 24–31
  proposals presented to Select
    Committee 128, 146, 147
  research trip to New Zealand
    101–7
  submission to Expert Panel 50–8
Cape York Welfare Reform
  communities, Welfare Reform
    programs 32–3
Castan, Melissa 28, 50, 71, 72, 75, 93
Castan, Ron 28, 72
Chaney, Fred 47, 54, 75, 145, 208
Christensen, George 159
citizenship, and equality 210–11
Clark, Jeremy 198
Coen 32
colonialism 1–3
conservatives, objection to equality
  guarantee 61–3, 65–6, 76–8,
  80–1
constitutional conservatism 87–8, 91,
  93, 99
constitutional conservatives, workshops with 111–14, 116–21
constitutional forums, in Cairns 74,
  75
Cooper, William 43, 212
Costello, Tim 158, 171
Coxhead, Craig 105
Craig, Nigel 155
Craven, Greg 157
  on Act or Declaration of
    Recognition 80–1, 90
  advice regarding referendum 93–4
  on Indigenous advisory body 94,
    113, 142

on racial non-discrimination clause
   61–2, 73–4, 79–80
suggested approach to
   constitutional recognition 80–1,
   90, 111
Credlin, Peta 65, 123
Crossin, Trish 78

Davis, Megan 47, 50, 58, 75, 120,
   155–6, 173, 174, 184, 193, 194
Dean, Rowan 150, 169, 170
Declaration of Recognition
   letter to Abbott re 107–10
   notion of 80, 90, 92, 95, 105
Diamond, Jared 23
Direct Instruction schools 33, 37
Dodson, Patrick 47, 112, 115, 146,
   175, 176, 184, 198
   as co-chair of Joint Select
      Committee 222
   on CYI submission to Expert
      Panel 51–2
   election as senator 175
   on Expert Panel proposals 147
   on Indigenous advisory body 176
   push for Indigenous consultation
      process 173–4
   on racial non-discrimination clause
      175, 207
   response to Uluru Statement
      206–7
   on Turnbull's rejection of Uluru
      Statement 214, 223
Don Dale 168
Doyle, Robert 171
Durie, Edward 104, 106

education 12–14, 17
Ellerman, Zoe 76
Emerton, Patrick 71
equality
   and citizenship 210–11
   passion for 29

Expert Panel on Constitutional
      Recognition of Indigenous
      Australians 39, 44
   influence of CYI reforms 58
   CYI submission 50–8
   Indigenous solidarity 52–3
   meetings 47–50
   proposed reforms 58–60, 78
   response to report 61–4, 72

family background
   father's family 10–12
   mother's family 3–5
   parent's marriage 11–12
   siblings 11, 75
Fiji, political instability following
      independence 6–8
Finlayson, Chris 103–4
First Nations regional dialogues 174,
      183, 185, 189
   Adelaide meeting 199
   Cairns meeting 200–1
   Hobart meeting 195–7
   Melbourne meeting 198
   Perth meeting 200
   process 197–8
   Ross River meeting 198–9
   trial dialogue in Melbourne 193–5
   Uluru constitutional convention
      201–4
Flavell, Te Uruoa 105
Flint, David 150, 160
The Forgotten People (Freeman &
      Morris) 157–8, 171, 185, 215
Forrest, Andrew 'Twiggy' 53–4, 201
Forrest, John 53
Fraser, Malcolm 62
free speech 115, 158–9, 221
Freeman, Damien
   advocacy through Uphold &
      Recognise 135, 137, 188
   appreciation of Indigenous
      perspective 96–7

on Declaration of Recognition 135
on Indigenous advisory body 99, 106, 110
on instilling national pride 105
as mentor 99
research trip to New Zealand 102, 104, 105
on settlement of historical grievances 106
support for Indigenous constitutional body 135
support for Indigenous constitutional recognition 95, 99
on symbolic Declaration 95
voluntary work on constitutional recognition 137

Gallagher, Jill 198, 199, 214
Gandhi, Mohandas 2, 3, 18, 90
Gartrell, Tim 54, 74, 75, 82, 83, 97–8, 136, 138, 182
Gilbert, Danny 49
Gillard, Julia 72
Gillard Labor Government 39, 44
Gleeson, Murray 174
Golsby-Smith, Tony 65
Gooda, Mick 47, 50, 54, 115
Gordon, Sean 102, 105, 155
Grant, Stan 174
Greens 159, 217
Griffiths, Lew 57, 65, 69, 75, 228

Hall, Donna 104, 106
Hanson, Pauline 159–60
Harradine, Brian 141
Hastie, Andrew 158
Hawke, Alex 158
Hawke, Bob 162–3, 175
Henderson, Anne 167
Henderson, Gerard 167
Hindmarsh Island bridge case 47
Hopevale 32, 33

Hosch, Tanya 82, 174
Houston, Angus 172
Howard, John 43–4, 95, 141, 143, 162, 164
Hunter, Nolan 101, 104, 105, 155, 185, 188, 199, 201

I Can Change Your Mind on Recognition (ABC documentary) 177–80
immigrants 18–19
Indigenous advisory body
    Brennan's criticism of proposal 140, 142
    conservative support for 135
    discussed at Select Committee hearing 128–9
    ideas for 90, 92, 94, 99–100, 106, 113, 118–19
    Kenny's support for 156
    Langton's advocacy for 128–9
    legal workshop to critique and refine proposal 145
    as proactive approach 131
    proposed Chapter 1A to establish 119–20
    role 150–1
    Turnbull's rejection of 182–4, 190
    Twomey's defence of proposal 144
    as voice to Parliament 211
Indigenous Advisory Council 188
Indigenous affairs culture 98–9
Indigenous constitutional recognition
    complexity of challenge 8–10
    goals 68
    moral challenge of 21
    national Indigenous position on 192–3
    versus a treaty 217–20
Indigenous consultation process 174
Indigenous offenders, judicial treatment of 35–6
Indigenous property rights 30–1, 53, 59, 115

Institute of Public Affairs (IPA) 86,
    115, 178

Jackson, David 64–5, 66
Jeffrey, Michael 157, 160
Johns, Gary 86–7, 88–9
Joint Select Committee on
    Constitutional Recognition of
    Aboriginal and Torres Strait
    Islander Peoples (2015) 122,
    127–38, 146
Jones, Alan 215
Jones, Kerry 160, 161
Jones, Stephen 129–30, 132–3
Jose, Fiona 71, 76, 101, 105, 128
'Journey to Recognition' campaign
    75
Joyce, Barnaby 159, 206

Keating, Paul 140, 141
Kelly, Paul 141, 181, 221
Keneally, Kristina 174, 215
Keneally, Thomas 172
Kennett, Jeff 171–2, 208
Kenny, Chris 156, 157, 161, 167, 189,
    215
Kirribilli Statement 147
Koowarta, John 34
Kurti, Peter 166

Labor Party 173, 175–6, 184, 185,
    206, 215–16, 217
Laming, Andrew 158
Langton, Marcia 120, 133, 155
    at Expert Panel meetings 47–8
    at Select Committee hearings
        128–9
    on Aurukun rape sentencing 35, 36
    on 'black men in the black hats'
        52–3
    first meeting with 36
    on Indigenous advisory body
        128–9

    on politicians response to Uluru
        statement 207
    support and protection in meetings
        55–6
languages recognition 46, 50, 59
Laundy, Craig 158
Law Council of Australia 214
Leeser, Julian 157
    advocacy for proposals 167, 168,
        172, 205
    advocacy through Uphold &
        Recognise 135, 172
    as co-chair of Joint Select
        Committee (2018) 222
    constitutional conservatism 87–8,
        91
    on Declaration of Recognition
        135
    on Indigenous advisory body 97,
        110, 113
    lobbying of John Howard 162
    maiden speech as parliamentarian
        168
    support for Indigenous
        constitutional body 135
    support for Indigenous
        constitutional recognition 114,
        121
    on symbolic Declaration 95
    on Uluru Statement 207
Leibler, Mark 47, 48, 72, 174
Liberal Party 158–9
Lino, Dylan 214
Little, Rod 214
Ludwick, Harold 152, 155

Mabo decision 30–1
McCarthy, Malarndirri 176, 184
McKenzie, Bridget 132, 133, 157,
    159
Makarrata Commission 202, 219, 226
Malthouse, Kaylene 200
Mansell, Michael 196

Maori Council 103, 104
Maori Language Act 103
Mapoon 200
Mayor, Thomas 194
Merkel, Ron 72
Merritt, Chris 157, 181
Mitchell, Chris 181
monarchists 160–1
Morrison, Joe 214
Mossman Gorge 32
Mundine, Warren 62, 63, 64, 65, 66–7, 69, 188–9

National Party 159
Native Title Act 30
Nelson, Brendan 172
Neumann, Shayne 128, 137, 215
New Zealand
    Maori recognition and reconciliation 102–4
    research trip 101–7
    Treaty of Waitangi 102, 103, 104
Newman, Campbell 37
Ng, Bennie 123
Nick Xenophon Team 159
'no legal effect' clause 117–18, 121
'non-justiciability' clause 117, 119–20
Northern Territory Intervention 29, 33, 65
NSW Bar Association 214
NSW Law Reform Commission, internship 31

Orange, Claudia 105
O'Shane, Terry 194, 200–1

Parker, Kirstie 173
Parkin, Dean 65
Paterson, James 158
Pearson, Noel
    attempts to undermine his intellectual authority and credibility 149–51
    on Australia as triune nation 19–21, 114–15
    cancer diagnosis and treatment 64, 69, 71, 72
    criticism of Brennan's interference 143
    essay in *A Rightful Place* 121–2
    eulogy speech at Whitlam's funeral 127
    on Indigenous advisory body 129, 131–2
    intellect 48, 52
    on Kirribilli meeting 148
    letters to John Howard 45
    performance strengths 48–9
    radical centre political stance 28, 52, 85, 93
    regret at not entering politics 178
    relationship with Abbott 57, 163
    on Joint Select Committee (2015) 137
    speech at dinner for 50th anniversary of *The Australian* 114–15, 126
    strategic thinking and tactics 55, 72, 84–5, 114, 121
    Woodford Folk Festival speech (2017) 162
Pell, George 157
Peris, Nova 127, 132
Perkins, Rachel 116, 155, 172, 189, 194
Phillip, Arthur 160
Porter, Christian 146, 157–8, 185–7, 201
post-recognition settlements process 175
protection policy 33–4
public law 39–40

Q&A (ABC) 165–6, 212–13, 215
Queensland, frontier violence 33–4

Racial Discrimination Act (RDA) 29, 34, 66, 115, 158
racial non-discrimination clause
  and 1967 referendum 81–2
  CYI proposal for 51, 54, 58
  and empowerment of High Court 76–7, 112
  Expert Panel recommendation for 58–9
  opposition to 61–3, 65–6, 83, 84, 147–8
racial vilification law 115
racism 17, 88–90, 91
radical centre stance 28, 52, 85, 93, 112, 134, 159, 171, 217
radical hope 177, 185
Recognise 82, 99, 138, 175
  conflict with 75, 76, 97–9, 182
  demise 204
  funding for CYI 74, 75, 98
  funding for Uphold & Recognise 136, 182
  'racism out; recognition in' catchcry 199
  support for minimalist model 137, 199, 218
Reconciliation Australia 68
Referendum Council
  appointment 174
  brief 182
  report 204–6, 222
  seeks clarification re brief 185
  Turnbull's coercion for minimalist outcome 182–4
Reid, Teela 194, 212–13
republic referendum 222
A Rightful Place (Morris) 189, 195
Robb, Andrew 172
Rose, Michael 174
Rudd, Kevin 44, 215

same-sex marriage plebiscite 216–17
Samuel Griffith Society

  Conference, August 2015 167
  Conference, November 2013 86–92
Shanahan, Dennis 122–3
Shelton, Lyle 157, 170, 181
Sheridan, Greg 156, 188–9
Shorten, Bill 146, 148, 174, 175, 176, 184, 206, 214, 217
Siewert, Rachel 78, 132, 133
soft bigotry 36–8, 67
Spigelman, Jim 72
Stacey, Brian 146
Stanley, Fiona 218
Stanner, W.E. 42
Stone, John 161
Stott Despoja, Natasha 174
Sutton, Peter 28

Tasmania 195–7
Tent Embassy 21
Textor, Mark 54, 75, 82–3, 135–6, 138, 199, 204
treaties
  plans of state governments 175, 220
  versus constitutional recognition 217–20
Treaty of Waitangi 102, 103, 104, 105
Triggs, Gillian 165–7
Tudge, Alan 54–5, 167–8, 194, 199
Tuheitia, Kiingi 105
Turnbull, Malcolm 44, 62, 135
  unsuccessful coercion of Referendum Council 182–4, 185
  concessions to secure prime ministership 162–3
  rumoured deal with Howard 162
  on historical relationship of government and Indigenous people 209

Howard's support for 162
inability to provide progressive
    leadership 221
mocking of Pearson 150, 151
offer of support for CYI proposal
    145, 162, 183
opposition to Indigenous advisory
    body 182–4, 185, 190
rejection of Uluru Statement 137,
    209–16, 217
on same-sex marriage 216–17
Scullion, Nigel 213
undermining by Abbott 125,
    153–4
withdrawal of support 162, 164,
    173
Twomey, Anne 91, 92, 111, 113,
    119–20, 121, 144, 157

Uluru Statement from the Heart
    9–10, 222
achievements 202–4
as act of self-determination 218
incorrect interpretations of its
    meaning 206
Indigenous MPs' response to
    206–7
Turnbull's rejection of 137, 150,
    209–16, 217
UN Declaration on the Rights of
    Indigenous Peoples 120
Uphold & Recognise 135, 136–7,
    156, 172, 182, 188

Vanstone, Amanda 174
verballing, tactic of 117–18, 213, 214
voting rights 18–19, 33

Waddy, Lloyd 160
Waitangi Day 102
Waitangi Tribunal 106
Wanganeen, Klynton 199–200
wedge politics 82
Welfare Reform programs 32–3
Wentworth, Billy 81–2, 203
Whitlam, Gough 127
Wik controversy 72, 140–1
Wik and Wik Way peoples 33–8
Wild Rivers controversy 29–30
Williams, George 49, 57–8, 132, 145
Wilson, Edward 160–1
Wilson, Tim 115–16, 145, 157, 158,
    161, 168, 169, 172, 187–9, 189
Windeyer, Richard 144, 211
Windschuttle, Keith 167, 169
Winer, Mike 29–30
Woodford Folk Festival 162, 227–9
Wyatt, Ben 201
Wyatt, Ken 82, 122, 127, 128, 135,
    145, 147–9, 173, 176, 184, 198,
    207, 223

Yarrow, David 50
Yolngu bark petitions 43, 212
Yolngu elders, plea to be heard 123
Yorkston, Dalassa 174, 184
Yunupingu, Galarrwuy 43, 112, 174